Praise for *A Burning Desire*

"In this wise, compassionate, ɑ  *has*
swung wide the doors between tɩ *ɩall.*
His gentle voice speaks, with clɩ *ɩcts*
seeking freedom and awakeniɩ *?*
seminal text for the recovɩ

— **William Alexander**, st
Alcoholism, Mindfɩ ......y Recovery

"A truly helpful bridge between the power of 12-Step
work and the power of the Dharma."

— **Jack Kornfield**, author of *The Wise Heart*

*"**A Burning Desire** is a much needed addition to the growing field of*
Buddhism and recovery. Kevin is a master at building bridges between the 12
Steps and Buddhism. I highly recommend this book to anyone in recovery!"

— **Noah Levine**, author of *Dharma Punx* and *Against the Stream*

"There are many parallels between 12-Step programs and Buddhist
approaches to addiction recovery. Kevin Griffin gives a personal and
powerful account of how these concepts have helped him. I highly
recommend it as a landmark book in the path of recovery."

— **G. Alan Marlatt, Ph.D.**, University of Washington,
author of *Relapse Prevention* and *Assessment of Addictive Behaviors*

"Kevin Griffin's original burning desire was for alcohol, but it is now to
share his hard won wisdom with the world. This book is a gift to us all."

— **Roger Walsh M.D., Ph.D.**, University of California Medical School,
author of *Essential Spirituality: The Seven Central Practices*

*"Kevin Griffin's new book **A Burning Desire: Dharma God &***
***the Path of Recovery** is a beautiful interweaving of two vital paths*
of healing, ancient Buddhist teachings and the modern 12-Step tradition.
He unfolds the concepts of God and a Higher Power, so central to the
12-Step tradition, so that they become not just accessible, but deeply
meaningful to those who may have found the image of a grandfather
God difficult or confusing. It's a book to be read and re-read, to be owned
and loaned, and to be given as a welcome gift to anyone in recovery."

— **Jan Chozen Bays**, abbott, Great Vow Zen Monastery;
author of *Mindful Eating* and *Jizo Bodhisattva*

A Burning Desire

Also by Kevin Griffin

ONE BREATH AT A TIME:
Buddhism and the Twelve Steps

A Burning Desire

DHARMA GOD &
THE PATH OF RECOVERY

KEVIN GRIFFIN

HAY HOUSE, INC.
Carlsbad, California • New York City
London • Sydney • Johannesburg
Vancouver • Hong Kong • New Delhi

Published and distributed in the United States by: Hay House, Inc.: www .hayhouse.com • *Published and distributed in Australia by:* Hay House Australia Pty. Ltd.: www.hayhouse.com.au • *Published and distributed in the United Kingdom by:* Hay House UK, Ltd.: www.hayhouse.co.uk • *Published and distributed in the Republic of South Africa by:* Hay House SA (Pty), Ltd.: www.hayhouse.co.za • *Distributed in Canada by:* Raincoast: www.raincoast.com • *Published in India by:* Hay House Publishers India: www.hayhouse.co.in

Design: Riann Bender

Library of Congress Cataloging-in-Publication Data

Griffin, Kevin Edward.
  A burning desire : dharma, God and the path of recovery / Kevin Griffin.
-- 1st ed.
     p. cm.
  ISBN 978-1-4019-2321-1 (tradepaper : alk. paper) 1. Twelve-step programs
--Religious aspects--Buddhism. 2. Self-help techniques--Religious aspects--
Buddhism. 3. Spiritual life--Buddhism. I. Title.
  BQ4570.T85G73 2009
  294.3'4442--dc22
                                2009028626

ISBN: 978-1-4019-2321-1

15 14 13 12   6 5 4 3
1st edition, January 2010
3rd edition, September 2012

FSC
www.fsc.org
MIX
Paper from
responsible sources
FSC® C011935

Printed in the United States of America

For Dave, Jerry, Pat, and Michael,
the wolves who raised me

*"Before we close the meeting, does anyone
have a burning desire to share?"*
— Twelve Step meeting format

*"I believe, however, that this fervent thirst for wholeness, as well as the
discomfort with it, is the underlying impulse behind addictions."*
— *The Thirst for Wholeness,* Christina Grof

*"Is alcohol, then, a way of searching for God,
the ultimate source of wholeness and life?"*
— *Thirst: God and the Alcoholic Experience,* James B. Nelson

CONTENTS

PREFACE

As I was working on this book, I began to wonder if I was crazy taking on such a topic. What do I know about God? I'm not a theologian, and the religion that I subscribe to is considered by most people to be non-theistic. Besides, I tend to shy away from dogma and the trappings of ritual and devotion. In my circles, coastal, well-educated, politically progressive, God is pretty much a non-starter. Isn't that something for the fundamentalists and red-staters?

But I'm a recovering alcoholic and addict. For over 20 years I've been working the Twelve Steps, which have all kinds of references to God and Higher Power. I've had to deal with the incongruities of being a Buddhist practitioner who "turned his will and his life over to the care of God" for a long time. When I began writing and teaching about Buddhism and the Twelve Steps, it was largely because I'd seen so many people struggle with the God issue and I was hoping that I could ease that struggle a bit.

The Twelve Step tradition suggests we find a God of our own conception, a Higher Power we can understand for ourselves. In this way, we avoid affiliating with any religion or restricting people's spiritual options. This is one of the important ways that the Steps stay as welcoming as possible.

I'm not, in this book, suggesting that you adopt a God of *my* understanding. I honor and respect those who have a fulfilling sense of connection with the concept of God. Rather I am trying to help those people who struggle to find a reasonable, intellectually acceptable definition of God. Not everyone needs to understand God intellectually in order to feel comfortable in their Step work, but for those who do, I believe that the lens of Buddhism can give a vision of a Higher Power that makes sense.

I admit that I have another reason for talking about God from a Buddhist perspective. I want to address the neo-atheists and suggest that in throwing out the bathwater of magical, blind-faith-based religious beliefs, they may have also thrown out the baby of authentic spirituality, a spirituality that is in complete harmony with a rational, scientific viewpoint.

What I want to discourage—both in my readers and in myself—is the notion that my viewpoint is *right,* that it represents some absolute truth or is *the* way. Rather than seeking to create some new religious teaching, my interest is more in trying to correct what I think is an imbalance in our understanding of God—of that *word.*

You're not supposed to start a book by apologizing, but the scope of the question of what God is humbles me and shows me the limits of my knowledge. Writing this book has been fascinating for me as I've deeply explored ideas that have been banging around in my head for years, but I'm also afraid that some people will be disappointed that I don't address what they think is most important about God. I've written about what I felt I understood and could explain. I haven't tried to write a comprehensive study of God.

My knowledge of Buddhism comes primarily from the Southern tradition known as Theravada, the Way of the Elders. However, I am not an authority on any school of Buddhism, but only speak from my own experience, study, and personal understanding.

Not only do I not speak as an authority on Buddhism, I don't claim any special knowledge of the Twelve Steps, nor do I speak as a representative of any program.

With these admissions I don't mean to say that I have no authority. The scientific orientation of our culture seeks "objective" information and makes the claim that this is more accurate than that gained from personal experience. Both the Buddhist teachings and Twelve Step programs take the opposite viewpoint. This view says that if we haven't experienced something for ourselves, how can we know its truth? The Buddha was a scientist of the human condition and of reality. His subject of study was himself. And in Twelve Step meetings, it's through telling our own stories, sharing our "experience, strength, and hope," that we heal ourselves. In the same way, my search for God hasn't been in books or in academic studies. It's been an exploration of my own heart and mind, a study of my own life. In the end, this is what I have to offer you, a life lived in search of meaning and happiness. I can only hope that sharing my journey will help others on their own path.

One note about reading this book: the order in which I present my ideas isn't sacred. I wanted to separate my definitions of the aspects of "Dharma God" from my exploration of the "Path of Recovery," because I thought blending them could be confusing, but it also makes sense to move between the two. If you are reading about one of the Higher Powers and are wondering how it applies to one of the Steps, feel free to jump ahead and look at that.

Introduction

Taungpulu Kaba Aye Monastery, Boulder Creek, California, July 1992

I'm sitting on my black zafu, a hard, round pillow, in a small meditation cell on self-retreat. I came down the coast from Berkeley to this mountain monastery in the redwoods above Santa Cruz a few days ago. Less than a month after my seventh sobriety anniversary, I plan to practice intensive meditation for a week.

I've practiced Buddhist meditation for almost 12 years, and there have been a lot of ups and downs. At first I threw myself into the practice—this was before I got sober—and kind of burnt myself out. Then for the first few years of sobriety I was more focused on recovery and Step work than meditation, but now, having moved up here from Southern California to complete my B.A., I find myself drawn deeper into practice.

I've done a lot of self-retreat over the years, sometimes for convenience when I couldn't find a teacher-led retreat, sometimes because it was cheaper, and maybe sometimes to avoid other people. It's always been pretty easy and pleasant. But on the second day of this retreat I fall into a depression, not really about anything, just a swirling mass of negativity and self-hate.

1

Depression has been a theme in my life, even before addiction, but on retreat it's rarely reared its head.

I'm doing my best, now on day three, to just keep practicing, 45 minutes of sitting meditation, 45 minutes of walking meditation, alternating throughout the day with breaks for food and a bit of sleep. I mix my typical Twelve Step prayers with my meditation. In the late afternoon I sink to such a low point that I consider leaving. I've never left a retreat no matter how hard it got, but I'm not sure about this time. Finally, though, in the early evening, the mindfulness and concentration begin to nudge out the depression, and a sense of calm begins to come over me. I fall asleep relieved and ready to go deeper in the morning.

My window faces south, and as I sit first thing the next morning, the sunlight creeps up my chest. I feel at ease now—depression is so mysterious, so real when it's there, but so meaningless when it's gone. At the end of the sitting I begin to pray, try to speak to God, but something feels heavy and awkward. My mind is empty, my body still and grounded, and all of a sudden the word *God* sounds completely artificial. I ask myself what the word means.

I eat in my cell before going outside for walking meditation in the courtyard. The monastery, inhabited by Burmese monks, is usually quiet. Very quiet. But today a large Burmese family has arrived to serve a meal to the monks, a way of attaining good karma. Three generations of extended family bustle around the monastery setting things up. I go to the kitchen to make some tea and move silently around this group who largely ignore me.

My koan stays with me: "What is God?"

I do more sitting and walking meditation through the morning, then go to the courtyard and watch the meal offering. A long table has been set up outside the kitchen, and the family members are lined up behind it with serving spoons, tongs, and forks at the ready. The half-dozen brown-robed monks move silently down the line, their bowls getting more and more full. Mothers push sons forward to serve—it's important they receive the merit from this—and at the end of the line, a little nine-year-old girl tops off each monk's bowl with a Snickers bar.

Back in my cell, I continue to sit, my mind growing more spacious, my koan drifting through. I try out different words in my prayers: *Higher Power, All that is, Universe.* I try to feel my way into what I'm experiencing. This spaciousness, this stillness, this is what feels like God to me. I feel connected to something greater than my small self that's sitting on this cushion in this empty room.

Great Spirit.

The words pass through my mind and resonate. Even as I hear the words and feel their accuracy in describing what I'm touching, I feel silly: I'm not a Native American, and that's what I hear in those words, some old cowboy movie with white actors pretending to be Indians. But still . . .

I continue sitting for a few more days, and I start using this new name for God. For now it feels right. Soon I realize that what's important, though, isn't the words, but the experience. Instead of spending my time figuring out how to *name* God, I should spend my time figuring out how to *know* God.

Looking back, I know now that the week I spent at that monastery was a turning point in my recovery and in my spiritual life. In the early years of my sobriety, I hadn't thought much about the meaning of the word *God.* I actually had a fairly easy relationship with the word, just thinking of God as the power that I trusted to guide and take care of me as I discovered what being clean and sober meant and as I explored life from this bright new perspective. But at seven years sober, which happened to be the end of my first year as a full-time college student, my recovery began to encompass a more serious exploration of Buddhism, and also a more engaged and skeptical intellect. Playing with different names for God was just the beginning, it turned out, of a much more serious question: is God some mysterious power or entity, or is God something real, tangible, and comprehensible? When I began to teach on the topic of Buddhism and the Twelve Steps, I felt a responsibility to be clear about what God or Higher Power might mean and how Buddhism could inform the way we tried to do things like "turn our will and our lives over to the care of God." I wasn't satisfied with vague platitudes like "just let go" or "God is a mystery." The Dharma isn't a mystery; it's very clear what the Buddha taught—not that it's easy to fulfill his teachings or the insights he offers, but it is practical and down-to-earth. Suffering, impermanence, karma, and all the rest make perfect sense. I felt that if I was going to make the claim that Buddhism and the Twelve Steps could work together, then God, an idea that is at the center of the Steps, had to be understandable through the Dharma.

I've come to believe not only that we can use the Dharma as a Higher Power, but that, in fact, as Buddhadasa Bhikkhu, a towering figure of 20th-century Thai Buddhism, says, "the naturally self-existent Dharma, or the Power of Dharma," is the meaning of God "in the true sense of the word." This is a bold statement and, essentially, the basis for this book.

Bill Wilson, one of the founders of A.A., says in the book *Alcoholics Anonymous* (known as the Big Book) that his recovery depended upon a "belief in the power of God." His own efforts, his "self-will," hadn't kept him sober, but something—a "Higher Power," he thinks—allowed this transformation to take place. For those of us who struggled for years to control our drinking or drugging, our gambling or sex addiction, to control other people or untenable situations, this might make a certain amount of sense, whatever our attitude is about God: if *we* can't manage things, maybe some other power can.

The Twelve Steps tell us exactly what we need to do in relation to God in order to get and stay clean and sober, to heal: we must "turn our will and our lives over to the care of God," "humbly ask Him to remove our shortcomings," and "improve our conscious contact with God." In turning our lives over, we are trying to drop the ego-driven striving that characterizes addicts of all kinds; in asking to have our shortcomings removed, we are acknowledging our need to change; in improving our conscious contact, we are seeking to deepen our spirituality and bring serenity to our lives. This is all very well, in theory. But I've been sober long enough to have seen a lot of suffering around the six Steps that refer to God—people who are angry with God, people who are confused about God, people who rebel against the very idea of God, people who scoff at it, and, sadly, even people who drink and use in response to the demand that they believe. This, to me, is a tragedy.

According to Karen Armstrong in her book *A History of God,* "there is no one unchanging idea contained in the word 'God'; instead, the word contains a whole spectrum of meanings . . . Had the notion of

God not had this flexibility, it would not have survived to become one of the great human ideas." The Twelve Steps echo Armstrong's statement in the critical phrase "God, *as we understood Him,*" and I would argue that the Twelve Steps, too, would not have survived without this flexibility.

The spectrum of meanings creates the possibility that even people who identify as atheists might find a definition of God that satisfies them. Armstrong tells us that "atheism has often been a transitional state," that even Christians were considered atheists by pagans at a time when their vision of God was so new and radical. She asks, "Is modern atheism a similar denial of a 'God' which is no longer adequate to the problems of our time?" So, while the God of 1930s America might not be adequate to the needs of a 21st-century addict, the persistent problems of addiction may still require finding a "power greater than ourselves" to gain and sustain recovery. The Dharma can be that power.

People have asked me if I think it's really necessary to believe in God to get clean and sober or to get the benefits of the Twelve Steps. I'm not sure. What I do think is that some kind of spiritual path or connection tremendously improves the quality of life of a person in recovery, and that quality of life has a direct impact on the ability to maintain long-term sobriety. The Big Book says that when we get sober, we aren't exactly "cured" but instead have a "daily reprieve contingent on the maintenance of our spiritual condition." But what is our "spiritual condition"?

Like the word *God,* the word *spiritual* is difficult to define. And, just as many people are alienated by *God,* so too might they be turned off by *spiritual.* There can be the perception that if you are spiritual you are some kind of holy person, that you go around in orange robes reciting mantras all day long, or that you never get angry, or that you don't care about money. These superficial definitions distract us from the essence of the word *spiritual.*

The first aspect of spirituality is the understanding that happiness doesn't come primarily through the material world. This is in contrast to our culture's over-emphasis on money, power, and fame. While all these things may bring temporary gratification, they don't actually make you happy, which the authors of *How We Choose to Be Happy* define as "a profound, enduring feeling of contentment, capability, and centeredness." While feelings can be prompted by external things, "profound, enduring" feelings come through profound, enduring *inner* work. This inner work can take the form of a practice like meditation or a program like the Twelve Steps, it can be done with a counselor or therapist, or it can be done by one's own self-reflection and commitment. Though it can *involve* external things like yoga, ritual, creativity, service, or study, its focus isn't on the externals, but on how they relate to our internal experience. When we make this shift from the external to the internal, we start to emphasize integrity and a sense of wholeness that orients us toward finding what is really true, sometimes at the expense of our transient pleasure.

Addiction is, of course, an attempt to sustain happiness through continuous pleasure, and it's a perfect of example of the failure of this strategy.

A second aspect of spirituality is the recognition of our interconnectedness with other people, with nature, and ultimately with God. Our culture promotes the image of the "rugged individual," the cowboy who lives alone on the plains, the heroic single mother, the self-made man, the maverick. But, rather than self-actualization, what this orientation often brings is alienation, isolation, and a zero-sum competition between separate entities. The truth is we are so deeply dependent and related to each other that we can't take a step or have a thought without some aspect of this interconnectedness supporting us. Look around you right now. How many things in your sight were made by you? Even if you built your own house from wood you grew on your own property, did you make the wood grow? The sun shine? The rain fall? The book in your hands is the result of thousands of years of human technological development; the words go back even further to the miracle of language being developed from grunts and groans expressed by early humans. We live in a bubble of interdependence, from the food we eat to the water we drink, the clothes we wear, our jobs, our families, our teachers. When we think that we are separate, we put ourselves in constant conflict, trying to get ours, always in fear of losing what we have, alienating others whom we use for our selfish purposes, lying and cheating to make sure that we aren't left behind. This is the epitome of the addict, self-centered, fearful, isolated.

The sense of interconnectedness leads to another aspect of spirituality, living by moral or ethical principles. When we recognize that we are in relationship to everything and everyone, we realize that we have a responsibility to act in ways that don't harm others. Out of our exploration of our own internal lives, we come to understand pain, and because we see that others suffer in the same ways we do, compassion arises. Furthermore, as we look at our personal experience and our interconnection, we see the Law of Karma, of cause and effect, unfolding, and we see that certain types of actions do harm, while others do good. Addicts, disregarding interconnection, think they can ignore or bypass this truth with impunity.

Living a moral life is a vital part of the integrity and wholeness of happiness. When we live dishonestly, selfishly, or harmfully, we create an inner dissonance and conflict that never allows for real peace or self-respect. The Buddha praised the ethical life and said that it led to "the bliss of blamelessness."

Another aspect of spirituality is realizing the limits of our control over both our external and internal experience—and accepting those limits. Addicts desperately try to control how they feel through staying high; the addictive personality is one that seeks to hold everything and everyone around it under its sway. These efforts are inevitably doomed to failure, as life and the living rarely bend to our will in such ways. With spirituality we are oriented toward letting go, toward surrender. Rather than trying to maintain the tightly scripted life of the addict, we are open to what comes, to the ever-changing nature of life.

In order to live by these spiritual principles, we have to have a certain amount of faith, to trust that sacrificing immediate gratification for something more substantial is a worthy goal; that living with integrity and kindness is its own reward; that letting go and openness are ultimately freeing. It's important to distinguish this kind of faith, called *sadha* in Buddhism, from blind faith. Sadha is a tested faith, based on experience and wisdom. It gives us the courage to take the next right action. It helps us to overcome the fears that our minds throw up in front of us at every juncture. Without a certain amount of trust in the path, we can become immobilized, or worse, give up our inner work all together. Fear can undermine sobriety and recovery.

Maintaining our spiritual condition, then, is a daily challenge. It isn't easy to look inside for happiness—it can get pretty messy in there; interconnection puts some challenging demands on us as we suddenly have to start thinking about something other than our own self-interest; living morally can be inconvenient; letting go is rarely as pretty as it sounds; and fear often trumps faith in our stressful lives.

None of this spiritual work is in any way exotic or impractical. It doesn't require suspension of our intellectual faculties. It doesn't involve trekking the Himalayas to find a wise guru, walking on burning coals, or changing our wardrobe. What it does require is commitment and effort. "Being spiritual" can sound like some kind of airy New Age attitude, but I don't think it's that at all. I think that being spiritual is one of the biggest challenges we can take on in our lives, a kind of warrior's path. Neither passive nor impractical, a spiritual life is the foundation for happiness and success.

The logic of the Twelve Steps is that, if we are "powerless" over our addiction as Step One says, then we are going to need some other "Higher Power" or "God" to overcome the addiction. But what exactly does "powerless" mean in this context?

The easiest claim to make about powerlessness is that once we start drinking or drugging (or gambling, eating, acting out sexually, etc.) we can't control what happens. This was true of me. Sometimes I would have a few beers, smoke a joint, and go to bed. But many times I would start drinking and not stop until I'd blacked out or passed out. Any time I started drinking it was a crapshoot. I didn't know how I would react to alcohol, which is why I can say I was powerless over it.

My addiction to marijuana worked differently. Pot doesn't cause blackouts or the same kind of bingeing. Once you're high, there's not much point in smoking a lot more until it wears off, because you won't continue to get more high like you do with booze. The way pot worked for me is that I just wanted to be high all the time. I tried to control my use (and preserve my stash) by pacing my smoking through the day, so for nine years, I was, essentially, stoned all the time. When I eventually started to cut back, what I found was that if I went for a few days without smoking, the craving diminished. But, as soon as I got high again, the craving came back, and the next day I wanted to get high some more. This was addictive in the classic sense that once I took the drug I craved it over and over. I was powerless.

Both of these patterns point to the kind of classic powerlessness that takes over once we consume the substance. But I don't think that's the limit of powerlessness. The Big Book talks about "the phenomenon of craving." Many times powerlessness seems to start even before we get high, at the point when this phenomenon takes over. When I look at my own experience with addiction, this seems to be how it worked. There were times when I would start thinking about drinking or using and the idea would become more and more alluring until I felt that I had no choice, that I couldn't live without acting on that craving. What this pattern tells me is that powerlessness starts before I pick up the drink or drug. Once an obsession is in full swing, it's tough to turn it back. Somewhere in there, depending upon, I suppose, the individual and the strength of the craving, we cross the line into having no choice anymore, into being compelled to act, into powerlessness. I think it's easier to avoid actually taking a drug than it is to avoid this craving. Drinking and using are actions, and we have the most control over our actions, far more than we have over our thoughts and feelings.

Seeing this pattern, then, gives me some idea about how to approach the problem of addiction: I need to avoid obsession, find ways to keep it from arising, to counteract the power of addiction. If powerlessness represents our dark side, our destructive impulses, then Higher Power represents the healthy and sane part of us. The Steps are trying to help us to reconnect with our sanity—just as Step Two says. Admitting we are powerless and need a Higher Power is only acknowledging that these conflicting impulses live inside us. The spiritual tools of the Twelve Steps and of the Dharma can help us cultivate the power to turn toward sanity, toward the light.

Part I

Dharma God

A few years ago I was at Spirit Rock Meditation Center on their family retreat, a kind of Buddhist summer camp for kids and their parents. Here the young people learn about Buddhist values, get a taste of meditation, sing, dance, and explore the beautiful natural surroundings of this Northern California center. During certain parts of the day everyone comes together in the great meditation hall, then at other times the kids go off with counselors for their own activities and the adults spend time with the Dharma teachers.

One afternoon, a parents' group met with Ajahn Amaro, an Englishman who has been a Theravadan monk for over 30 years. Ordained by the great Thai master Ajahn Chah, Amaro is charming, lucid, and a great example of the wisdom and serenity these teachings promise. A grandmother who'd never been to a Buddhist center before asked him the fundamental question: "Is there a God in Buddhism?"

I felt a moment of anxiety. If a Theravadan monk, particularly Ajahn Amaro, who had been an important teacher for me, contradicted my thinking, it would create a lot of conflict for me. But he turned to her with his sly smile and said, "Buddhism is all about God."

I breathed out in relief.

Certainly this answer wasn't the conventional understanding of Buddhism's relationship to the God idea. More typical is Walpola Rahula, who in *What the Buddha Taught* says that the idea of God is a human construction, and that "according to Buddhism, our ideas of God and Soul are false and empty."

I find myself agreeing with both Amaro and Rahula. The distinction, I think, is between common ideas of what the word *God* means and a more mature viewpoint. Buddhadasa Bhikkhu talked about this distinction: "As long as people insist that God is a person in the conventional sense of people language, we can say that they will not know the real God . . ."

Buddhism isn't about a deity or Godhead that we worship. But it is about seeing the truth. And the truth is God.

The word for "truth" in Buddhism is *Dharma* (*Dhamma* in Pali, the language of the earliest Buddhist texts). Dharma is at the heart of what I'll talk about as God. But the word *truth* alone isn't specific enough to help us. There are many aspects of Dharma, of truth, that fulfill different aspects of our understanding of God. As I explore God, I'll look at each of these individually.

Buddhadasa talks about God being nature and the laws of nature: that which exists and the rules that govern that which exists. Step Two in the Twelve Step tradition calls God "a Power greater than ourselves." The laws of nature are clearly this—powers beyond our control.

Buddhadasa rejected the idea that some religions are theistic and others non-theistic. He said that some religions personify God and others don't, but that the essence of God was not to be found in the "outer shell and form of those religions," but in the universal truths that religions share.

When we think that God is a human or even superhuman being— or, in fact, any kind of "being"—we can't help but attribute human qualities to "him." First of these is gender. When God is a "him," it creates a certain bias. At one of my early workshops on Buddhism and the Twelve Steps, one of the women participants expressed the pain the idea of a male God caused her. "I was abused by my father as a kid. That made having a male God completely intolerable to me." For some time her solution was calling God "her," and there are many traditional sources for a female God. But while a female God might solve the problem for some people, it still leaves us with a human figure.

I enjoy following professional sports, and there seem to be a lot of religious athletes. When I hear them talking about God helping their teams or inspiring their performance, I have to wonder what they are thinking. If they mean that God has sided with them, then there's a problem. I cannot accept that the creator of the universe is a fan of certain sports teams and not of others. I read about one player, though, who said he prayed for both teams, that no one would be injured and that all the players would play to their potential. "Ah," I thought, "here is wisdom."

When I told one friend that I objected to the idea of "false gods," that I thought it was about "My God is better than your God," he told me that rather than taking the First Commandment literally—"Thou shalt have no other gods before me"—he found it to be a powerful image of his addiction. His false god was alcohol. He lived for that god, he "turned his will and his life over" to that god.

Here was more wisdom. His point helped me to see through the superficial concepts and language of religion to the more vital spiritual meaning.

For many of us, skepticism is a wholesome response to growing up in a culture rife with religious hypocrisies. And, as we confront the conflicts between our scientific understanding and the myths presented as facts in religion, God as "he" is offered to us becomes a less and less palatable idea. As Buddhadasa says, "The intellectuals will increasingly deny this ordinary kind of God and it will not be very long before people educated in the modern way will have eliminated God from their hearts altogether."

Clearly Buddhadasa sees the rejection of mythological religious beliefs as wise and appropriate. M. Scott Peck, in his book *The Different Drum*, says that the rejection of "formal, institutional" religion is a stage of spiritual development. He says that those in this stage of skepticism are actually more developed spiritually than those who, however devotedly, adhere blindly to religious beliefs. These skeptics are the people who Buddhadasa says "have eliminated God from their hearts altogether." And, while this stage may be more developed than blind faith, it can be a very difficult and painful place to be. When we've rejected our traditional faith without replacing it with anything, the world, and life, can be pretty dark. And this is a typical place for an addict/alcoholic to be. Such people often live in bitter cynicism about religion—and about a lot of other things. Their addiction has dulled their hearts. The density of their thoughts won't allow in the subtlety of the spiritual experience.

While it's true that the meditative experience is not intellectual, it's also not *anti*-intellectual. The spiritual life recognizes the limits of the intellect; we see its role in life, but we don't see it as the only way of understanding the world. If the true religious believer thinks that she knows all the answers, and the skeptic rejects all faith, then the spiritual seeker is somewhere in between: "don't know," open to possibilities. The spiritual experience isn't one of filling ourselves up—with either religious or intellectual beliefs—but of emptying ourselves so that we can experience what *is*, directly, unfiltered.

This is what the Buddha did—and what he taught. He, too, rejected the religious notions of his time. He dismissed the Brahmanic rituals as empty and missing the essence of spiritual truth, and he wasn't satisfied with the mystic teachings that could only offer temporary respite from *samsara,* the round of suffering. The Buddha applied a penetrating intellect to the problem, and he applied a penetrating practice. Only by combining the two could he uncover the basic problem that held back all spiritual seekers—the persistent craving behind our suffering. Seeing suffering and understanding its cause led him to the solution—simply put, letting go. The Eightfold Path that he taught, then, was a formula for learning to let go in all aspects of life. What we can see in the Buddha's journey, and in the journeys of all spiritually developed people, is that skepticism is an essential part of the path, one that can energize and inspire us. However, it can also hinder us if we see it not as a place from which to explore, but rather as a destination.

To return to the question "Does Buddhism have a God?", the answer is: it depends. It depends on what you call God. If you feel bound to the mythic version of the Abrahamic tradition of the dominant Western religions, Islam, Judaism, and Christianity, then, of course, Buddhism doesn't have that God, since it didn't grow out of that tradition. But if you are open to the possibility that all religions are essentially looking for truth, and that the ultimate truth is God, then Buddhism certainly does have God. Some people will object to this definition, like the skeptics who come to Buddhism to get away from God, but as Karen Armstrong points out, definitions change; that's the nature of language and the human mind. Isn't God the power behind everything? And isn't that what the Dharma is? It may take some rewiring of our cognitive processes—for instance, using the word "it" to refer to God—but soon we might be able to accept that God is not some bearded figure reaching out of the clouds to bring life to Adam, but something more subtle, complex, and real.

When Ajahn Amaro says, "Buddhism is all about God," and Ajahn Buddhadasa talks about a "Dhamma God," what do they mean? For the skeptic, there needs to be some explanation of this idea, and for the religious person who might feel that his beliefs are being taken away, there needs to be some replacement, some new way of holding the God concept.

Dharma is at the heart of this new understanding. Like many words coming out of the Buddhist tradition, its meaning is complex, layered, and even, at times, paradoxical. As I've said, it can, first of all, be understood as "truth." Ajahn Chah defines Dharma as "the truth of the way things are." This gets us a little closer. It's referring to the workings of the universe—not so much the physical laws, though these would be included, but what we could call "spiritual laws."

The reason these laws can be called "Higher Power" or even "God" is that, like the traditional concept of God, they are the unseen forces at work behind all of existence. They are truths that we are powerless over; they rule our lives whether we are aware of them or not. And perhaps more importantly, when we live in harmony with them, we reap the fruits of happiness and freedom.

Buddhadasa talks about four aspects of Dharma God. First is nature itself, which is clearly more powerful than us. From a Dharma perspective, besides what we typically call *nature*, this includes fundamental truths like impermanence and suffering. The second aspect is the laws of nature which we either work with or against, like the Law of Karma. Buddhadasa calls the third aspect of God "the duty of humans according to the law of nature." This is the kind of power that we can cultivate ourselves, like the powers of Mindfulness, of Lovingkindness, and the whole of the Noble Eightfold Path. These three types of power and our relationship to them are embodied in the Serenity Prayer, which asks for "the serenity to accept the things I cannot change, courage to change the things I can, and wisdom to know the difference." We accept things, trusting in God, but we also take responsibility for our role in things. Higher Power isn't all about God having power over us; it's also about us developing power in ourselves, wholesome power, the power for good.

Buddhadasa refers to the fourth aspect of God as "the fruits that human beings receive according to the law of nature." These fruits can be as significant as a full-blown spiritual awakening or enlightenment experience, or as simple as the ease that comes from a moment of letting go of fear, sadness, or anger. In another example, the power of the truth of Not-Self is in the fruits of seeing it: when we have a deep realization that ego is an illusion, our experience of life changes in powerful ways.

Dharma God is considered to be an impersonal power. There's no being behind this power. No one is watching over you. We talk about how there is nothing personal about suffering or impermanence or karma—they are powers that affect everyone equally. Dharma God doesn't like you or dislike you. And yet, in another way, Dharma God can be seen as intensely personal.

What is more personal than your karma? Mindfulness is right here with you—you can't get closer or more personal than the breath; lovingkindness touches and opens our hearts in the most intimate way; intention lives deep within us; suffering and impermanence touch us directly. There's nothing impersonal about any of these aspects of the Dharma. They are affecting our lives in every moment in a very real way. In fact, while the idea of a supreme being may sound personal, a distant, unknowable God seems more impersonal to me than a God I can experience here and now in all these ways.

Because the meaning of Dharma is layered, and its role as Higher Power is complex, it will be helpful if you keep all these perspectives in mind as we explore a variety of Buddhist teachings.

THE HIGHER POWER
OF KARMA

The Higher Power of Karma brings results from actions based on the moral fabric of the universe. It is the force behind addiction, recovery, and spiritual growth. We use this power to transform ourselves and our world through intentional thoughts, words, and actions.

When we say that the Laws of Nature are an aspect of God, the most obvious example of this is the Law of Karma, or cause and effect. When this Sanskrit word became popularized in the West, it was misunderstood to mean "fate." The actual translation of the word *karma* is "action." The results of actions are called "karmic resultants." Typically when we say "karma" we are referring to the resultants. The Law of Karma, then, refers to the relationship between actions and their results, to the idea that taking skillful or wise action will bring about positive results. In Twelve Step terms, this is a Higher Power. It is a force that permeates our lives; we see it in actions large and small. We can't escape it or avoid it, and we can't control it. We can only cooperate with it. That's why we can call karma "God": there's no point in fighting God. You'll always lose.

The core Buddhist teaching on the Four Noble Truths is a teaching on karma: the causes and results of suffering, and the causes and results of ending suffering. The Buddha talked extensively about

19

karma because it is only through this law, through cause and effect, through taming the mind and taking skillful action, that we can find freedom.

The Buddha refined the meaning of the word *karma,* saying that karma is really *intention.* He meant that the results of our actions are conditioned by the motivation we bring to them. For example, we can be openly generous or hesitantly generous. The results, especially our internal response, are significantly different. A doctor might be motivated by compassion or greed; the karmic results would be vastly different. The Buddha essentially traced cause and effect back to the energy informing the cause, not just the action itself. This, then, challenges us to be honest with ourselves about our intentions. Part of the path of mindfulness is to carefully watch and be aware of these motivations and try to act from our wisest and kindest purpose.

The Buddha's basic guidance on karma is embodied in the Five Precepts: not to kill, not to steal, not to harm others with our sexuality, not to lie, and not to use intoxicants. These provide the moral framework and foundation for all spiritual development. In the section on the Higher Power of Right Action I'll say more about the precepts.

In many ways, the decisions we make in life are based on our understanding—or misunderstanding—of the Law of Karma. Even political disagreements can be seen as disagreements about how karma works: one politician believes that the karmic results of cutting taxes will be an improved economy, another thinks the results will be harmful. Who's right? The answers aren't simple. That's all the more reason why the intention behind an action is so important. We might not know whether we're doing the right thing, but we can be pretty clear about why we are doing it.

Although the potential karmic results of our actions aren't always clear beforehand, in some cases, we can see that the results are fairly predictable. My own confusion about cause and effect had a profound influence on my early life.

My older brother Michael started to play guitar in the summer of 1962 when folk music was the rage. Michael is very resourceful and clever, and somehow he learned to play on his own, using books that illustrated chords and finger-picking patterns. I was 12, and anything Michael did, I was going to do. For Christmas I got my first guitar and Michael started teaching me to play. Every day after school we would rush home, get out our Pete Seeger songbook, and play "This Land

Is Your Land," "Where Have All the Flowers Gone?" and "If I Had a Hammer," as well as pop-folk tunes like the Kingston Trio's "Charlie on the MTA." Soon we were taking our guitars to parties and leading sing-alongs. It was a blast. In six months I could play the guitar well enough to get through most any folk song. This was a wonderful example of the law of cause and effect: practice the guitar every day and soon you will know how to play. In fact, whatever we do regularly with devoted attention we will get "good at," whether it's a thing we want to be good at or not.

I didn't appreciate my accomplishment very much, the fact that I learned a musical instrument quickly and well. I don't mean to say that I didn't enjoy it—I loved it—but I didn't give myself credit for having taken the necessary actions to bring about a desired result, or for what that said about the potential for my own musical development. I just took the whole thing for granted. When I joined my first rock 'n' roll band two years later, I saw what the lead guitar player, Brian, did and said to myself, "I could never do that." I don't know why. When I saw my brother play, I never had that thought, but when I saw Brian play, I had some limiting notions of who I was and the potential I had. What I was saying is, "The Law of Karma doesn't work." I thought that playing rhythm guitar, which I could already do, just required work—cause and effect—but playing lead guitar was magic, a magic I didn't have.

When people say, "We create our own reality," this is part of what they are saying: if I had believed I could learn to play lead guitar when I was 14, I could have. However, because I didn't believe I could, I never really tried. And because I never really tried, I delayed my musical development by quite a few years.

Over the years since then I've occasionally given guitar lessons, and one of the most common attitudes of people is "I could never play like you" or "I don't have the talent to play lead guitar." While I don't deny that a certain natural affinity for music is necessary to being a good musician, much more important is practicing. Most people could probably play an instrument very well if they devoted the time—if they trusted karma.

To a great extent, I think the same thing is true of recovery: if we have the motivation and take the necessary actions, most of us can attain freedom from addiction. Certainly taking those actions can be challenging as we come up against our deeply rooted destructive emotional states, the power of our habitual behaviors and beliefs, past traumas, and just the general mess we've made of our lives. But all of this can change, and it doesn't take magic or luck or a benevolent God smiling down upon us. Belief that "I can't do it, but you can" is essentially a cop-out—a refusal to take responsibility. There are those who think that their recovery had nothing to do with them, with their intentions and actions, but came about through the intervention of some external force that just happened to decide that they should get sober. If you don't believe that things happen as a result of cause and effect, you can accept such a notion, but otherwise, you have to be skeptical. Still, people cling to the belief that they are uniquely flawed or cursed—or blessed.

I find the same thing in the world of meditation as well. People often believe, when they start to practice, that they aren't good meditators or lack the ability to do it—"I think too much," they'll often say. (When I hear this, I wonder if they believe that I *don't* think much. It could be taken as an insult, implying that if they were dumb like me they could meditate, too.) But most people "think too much" in the sense that when they sit down to meditate, they discover a stream of thoughts or images passing through the mind and distracting them from the breath. Meditation, like playing music, isn't something that necessarily requires a special talent. It requires consistent effort, and effort activates the Law of Karma. Trust in this process is an expression of trust in a Higher Power, a trust in God. When we don't trust this process, we are denying God; we are believing in magic, in false gods. We are believing in fate—"I can't, you can, that's just the way it is." The Buddha made it very clear that things are not fated. He said that he would never have taught a path to freedom that requires consistent effort if that effort, through the power of cause and effect, wouldn't pay off.

Probably most people believe in the law of cause and effect, in karma. But look at the ways we don't act on this belief. When we limit our ideas of what career we could pursue, we deny karma. When we give up on our workout program, we deny karma. And, of course, it works the other way. Our prisons are filled with people who thought they could get away with something, that karma didn't apply to them. As addicts we try to get around karma all the time: "I can get high this once and it won't be a problem"; "I can eat just one cookie"; "I can play just one hand of blackjack"; "I can just glance at this porn Website." It's all the same; it's all denial of how our disease works. If we are really addicted to drugs, alcohol, food, gambling, pornography, or anything else, any slip is going to trigger our addiction.

In Buddhism, this denial is called *ignorance,* which doesn't mean you're stupid, but rather that you don't understand, or want to avoid, the reality of how things work.

As we grow in our understanding of karma, it becomes obvious how it is at the root of addiction. We use over and over, and the karmic result is more craving to use. When we always act on desire, we never learn to restrain ourselves or pull back from acting on it. People don't set out to be addicts. They think they can drink or use without it becoming a problem. And, of course, many people can. Those who can't seem to have those tendencies from the start. In Buddhist terms, this is seen as karmic as well, not in the sense that we created that tendency ourselves (at least not in this lifetime), but in the sense that there is always a cause for something. Oftentimes in the addict the cause is genetic and environmental—nature and nurture. But this isn't something we can go back and change, whatever its causes. We can only alter the existing karma, not change how we got it.

The Buddha talked about ignorance being at the beginning of the karmic chain that leads to suffering, and we can say the same thing about addiction, one of the most profound forms of suffering. Ignorance means not seeing the truth, not seeing what is right in front of you. It is the opposite of Right View, the intuitive understanding of the Four Noble Truths.

For the addict there are a few kinds of ignorance. First of all, there is the ignorance of the predilection for addiction. Most addicts don't realize before they start to drink and use that they are strong candidates for addiction. Then there is the ignorance, sometimes willful, of the true effects of the substance. I started smoking marijuana convinced that it was "non-addictive." And it certainly doesn't have the kind of withdrawal symptoms that something like heroin has. But addiction is caused by more than the physical pangs of stopping using. Addiction is a powerful craving that is usually more psychological than physical, and the message it gives us is "There is no choice but to use." We don't really think about it, once we are caught in that cycle. In our ignorance, we don't see any alternative. This is why mindfulness is so important in recovery. As Sandra Weinberg, a Dharma teacher in New York, says, "Desire narrows our awareness till we see only what we crave; mindfulness helps us see other possibilities." When I was smoking pot every day for nine years, I didn't think I had a choice. And, amazingly, I didn't think I was addicted, either. *That's* ignorance; it's also denial.

Another critical aspect of ignorance for the addict is the way we don't see what's happening to us and our lives. Marijuana has terribly crippling, though somewhat subtle, effects that held back my emotional, professional, and spiritual development for the years that I used. The first time I stopped using for any length of time, during a two-week period of abstinence required before learning Transcendental Meditation, I was shocked by the amount of energy I had. I was up early feeling clearheaded and going jogging. I knew it was because I'd stopped smoking pot, but somehow I didn't take that in as a good thing. I didn't recognize the implications, that for nine years my physical and mental energy had been severely curtailed. In fact, my main response was to drink more. The energy was unfamiliar and uncomfortable, so I stuffed it with beer.

Coming out of ignorance, out of denial, takes a willingness to be honest that is challenging. It's much easier to live in our bubble of delusion than to face and take responsibility for our failings. If, however, our true intention is to be happy and to grow, at some point we are going to pop that bubble. This intention, the root of our karma, is what will move us toward recovery and spiritual awakening. When the bubble pops, at first we'll struggle with the pain of bottoming out, but living in that place of clarity gives us the chance to move toward true happiness and freedom.

One of the hardest things to do is change the course of our karma. Zen teacher, Byakuren Judith Ragir, calls it "interrupting the karmic flow." Getting sober is one of these actions, one of these interruptions. It took me years of dancing around the issue to get sober. I tried every way I could to control my drug and alcohol use. I battled the criticism others had of me, resisted real change, always trying to find some other way out of my problems.

In fact, my early efforts at meditation were part
lack of understanding of karma. With a belief that er
going to fix all the problems in my life, I was immerseu ..
thinking. To think that sitting silently on a pillow will make you a roᴜ𝗄
star, get you lots of money, solve your drug and alcohol problem, and
cure you of depression is to be very confused about cause and effect.

This was also apparent in my beliefs about school. When I got
sober and woke up to how limited my career options were as a musician, I gradually got the idea I might go back to school. But when I
thought about getting a college education from scratch—I had only a
G.E.D.—it seemed insurmountable. Four years! I'd be over 40 by the
time I graduated!

When I said this to my sponsor, he looked at me and said, "You're
going to be over 40 in four years anyway. You can either have a degree
then or not."

Oh, right! I got it. Time was going to pass, and what I did over
that time was going to have results—or no results, if I did nothing.
As daunting as four years of school sounded at the outset (I wound
up going for seven years, and would have gladly stayed longer), the
thought of being in the same place four years down the road was more
frightening. This was when I started to really understand the Twelve
Step emphasis on "showing up." Getting through school was all about
going to "one class at a time," just doing today's work and being where
I was supposed to be. Dropping out of high school as I'd done (three
times—just to make sure I got it right) was the opposite: not showing
up, running away. And the reason I ran away was because I found
school unpleasant—in Buddhist terms, I had "aversion" to school.
Showing up means living with aversion to some extent, not being so
reactive, trusting in a process rather than running from the immediate
discomfort.

Magical thinking expects instant results, but real change rarely
happens this way. It's more the steady drip, drip of accumulating acts.
My attitude had always been that if something didn't work out right
away it wasn't meant to be. But this goes directly against Buddhist
teaching, which is that *nothing is meant to be.* Nothing is fated or
inevitable in our lives, beyond, of course, sickness, old age, and death.
In terms of what happens to us as we live, none of it is pre-ordained.
Just because something is difficult doesn't mean it's not "meant" to
happen. That doesn't mean that you have to stick with every single

thing you try. It does mean that when we say "everything happens for a reason," we don't mean that there is some being up in the sky deciding how things should be, but rather that, everything happens as a result of intentional actions.

So, this is how we interrupt the karmic flow. Through actions. But before we make those actions, we need to see what should be done, and this takes the wisdom that comes out of mindfulness. When we pay attention with a clear mind, we begin to get an idea what needs to change in our lives. Once we see this clearly, we have to make a plan and act on it. One way to support this is making vows. Traditional vows are more religious in nature, but the Twelve Step tradition gives us another form: "Just for today . . ." When we make a vow about showing up and following through on our intentions "just for today," we make tasks that may seem unachievable, like getting a college degree, manageable, cutting them up into more reasonable pieces. "Just for today I will show up for class," we might say, or "Just for today I will go to work," or my meeting or do my meditation. Interrupting the karmic flow takes mindfulness, intention, and action. If we want to change and grow, if we want happiness and satisfaction in our lives, we must find ways to follow through on what's really important to us.

One vital point about karma: in the Buddhist teachings it is said that the enlightened being no longer creates karma. This means that enlightenment stands outside the Law of Karma—Nirvana is not conditioned by anything—although its realization is a result of karmic actions. I don't know how this works or exactly what it means, but if I'm going to be accurate in talking about how karma effects us all, that it is "everywhere and knows everything," it's important that I note this exception.

The problem with this idea is that some have used it to excuse actions that harm others. So-called enlightened teachers have claimed that their actions were above the Law of Karma, so that when they appeared to be harming, committing adultery, abusing substances, exploiting people, and accumulating wealth, none of it was really destructive. This same idea can be heard from those who claim to be "born again," that they are somehow saved and nothing they can do will reverse that. Perhaps. But we need to be very careful before making such claims or accepting the claims of others. After all, if you are enlightened, why are you going around doing these things in the first place?

It's quite apparent that, while the Buddha may have transcended karma, he continued to be impeccable in his behavior, in fact devoting his whole life to passing on the wisdom, peace, and joy that he himself had attained. Having solved his own problem, he turned his attention to helping others to the same experience of transcendence.

Prayer: I turn my will and my life over to the Higher Power of Karma. I vow to live in harmony with the moral laws of the universe and to use the power of Karma to support my spiritual and worldly growth.

Exercise: Limiting Beliefs

Our beliefs about who we are have a great effect on our lives. In this exercise you will look at those beliefs and see how accurate they are.

1. Gather pen and paper and find a quiet place to sit. Begin by taking five minutes to sit quietly and still with your eyes closed. Breathe consciously and relax.

2. Now, reflect on the major decisions you made early in your life. Write a few of them down.

3. Ask yourself what was behind those decisions. Did you make decisions based on negative beliefs such as *I can't do X so I'll settle for Y*, or *I'm no good at Z so I won't even try?*

4. Write some of these beliefs down.

5. Ask yourself what early conditioning created that limiting belief. Was it based on empirical evidence or something else? Is there any evidence to the contrary?

6. Write down the contrary evidence.

7. Now, sit quietly with this information. Are there changes you might consider trying to make in your life if you realize that you've made decisions based on inaccurate beliefs about yourself?

Exercise: Karmic Responsibility

Our moral choices in many ways set the direction of our lives. When we align ourselves with the moral fabric of the universe, we come into harmony with the Higher Power of Karma. In this exercise, you will work with the Five Precepts, the basic set of moral guidelines the Buddha laid out. They are common to almost all religions, although in Buddhism, rather than acting as commandments or strictures, they are seen as guidelines for living. You can do the exercise in one sitting or over a longer period, taking one precept at a time.

1. *I take the training precept to refrain from taking the life of any living being.*

2. *I take the training precept to refrain from taking that which is not offered.*

3. *I take the training precept to refrain from sexual misconduct.*

4. *I take the training precept to refrain from false or harmful speech.*

5. *I take the training precept to refrain from the use of alcohol or drugs that lead to intoxication and heedlessness.*

To "take" a precept, elaborate what it means for you and how you are willing to follow it. For instance, does the first precept mean you must be a vegetarian? What if there are rats in your house? Can you kill them? Once you have elaborated each precept for yourself, choose one precept to follow strictly for a certain period, such as a week or a month. See how making this commitment affects your mindfulness and your relations with others, as well as your feelings about yourself.

THE HIGHER POWER
OF MINDFULNESS

The Higher Power of Mindfulness is the power of attention and non-reactivity. It opens us to wisdom and insight through clear seeing. Mindfulness is the foundation of all spiritual growth as it reveals the truth of the way things are, internally and externally.

Several years ago, a woman approached me in the bookstore of a Buddhist center where I was teaching a class.

"I've never been able to get the Higher Power thing," she said, wiping tears from her eyes. "I could never work the third Step, and I kept drinking around that. But now I see that my Higher Power can be mindfulness. Thank you so much."

Her relief was palpable. Something very heavy had been lifted from her shoulders. And I was as grateful as she was that, apparently, something I'd said had helped her make this connection.

Mindfulness has the ability to transform our experience. The act of paying attention changes how we perceive what's happening to us. Instead of being driven by impulse, reactivity, habit, addiction, self-will, and all the rest of the semi-conscious and destructive energies that run us so much of the time, mindfulness puts us in a position to choose our destiny.

I remember the feeling as I built up to a drunk. It was as if some force over which I had no control was pushing me. I was going to drink—there was no choice involved, I couldn't imagine an alternative. To not drink would be to die, would be to resist some fundamental natural law. That's the feeling that addiction gives you. That's the *power* of addiction.

Mindfulness runs counter to that. The power of mindfulness is the power to see outside the blinkers, outside the tunnel, to see ourselves and our experience from a different perspective. We call this "higher" because it has a positive effect, as opposed to the destructive, "lower" power of addiction. Mindfulness actually shows the world to be simpler than our mind perceives it to be. Instead of the complex of problems, issues, doubts, hungers, and resentments that obsess and confuse an addict, mindfulness shows our experience to be simply that of six senses and those things the senses can perceive. (The Buddha calls the mind the sixth sense.) The practices associated with mindfulness ask us to be aware of what is coming in through these six sense doors, without judging those experiences or trying to figure them out; without trying to repeat or repel those experiences; without being overwhelmed or losing interest in them. Simply allowing them to be.

As mindfulness is cultivated by these practices, it grows in power. But the powers we cultivate aren't typical ones, like controlling others, gaining material possessions, or affecting events. The power of mindfulness is the power to be: the power to experience life fully without flinching; to feel our pain without running away; to feel our joy without clinging to it. The power of mindfulness is the power to see—as the Big Book puts it, to "intuitively know how to handle situations that used to baffle us." The power of mindfulness is the power to know—to know beauty, to know love, directly, unfiltered. The power of mindfulness is the power of life.

On my first retreat I fell in love with the beauty of the high desert. With no music to listen to, with no distractions of work or TV or shopping, the mind searched for stimulation, and it found it in the stark landscape of cactus and sand, of mountains and hard, bright skies. During walking meditation periods, I would stop and just look. I finally understood what it meant to see, to feel the wonder of the natural world's beauty. A few weeks later, on a trip to my hometown in Pennsylvania, I walked the streets amazed at what I'd never noticed in over 20 years of living there. The town was beautiful: the tall elms lining the streets, the gabled 19th-century mansions, the brick sidewalks and old churches. I realized that mindfulness had opened me to an experience of the world I'd never had. And it made me think that only now was I learning what life was. The Higher Power of Mindfulness was beginning to transform me.

It's a truism that life is the most precious thing there is, and that's what people will say when they've lost something material or come through some life-threatening experience. It's also true that life is only lived here and now. And yet, when we start to look closely at how we engage life, we find that much of our time is spent somewhere else—in the past, in the future, in fears, calculations, plans, regrets—in short, in our heads, thinking. So, although we claim that life is the most important thing on earth, ironically, much of the time we're not really experiencing it, at least not in the deepest way.

Now I want to be quick to say that thinking is not a bad thing. It tends to get a bad rap in meditation circles. But in fact, thinking may be the most powerful human force, maybe the most powerful *living* force, on earth. I'm writing this on a computer as the result of some pretty amazing thinking (by other people). You're reading this because of your ability to think. Thought is the reason humans have survived. Our bodies were not the strongest survival mechanisms—bigger, faster predators would have killed us off a long time ago if it weren't for our ability to think.

The problem isn't thought itself, but the fact that thought takes over like some invasive weed. Our survival instinct is so strong and relies so much on thought that if we don't learn to put it aside when we don't need it so much, it will just keep running. Thought doesn't care that you don't need to be reminded about your financial situation 700 times a day. All it knows is that you need money to survive and so you better think about it—a lot. Thought doesn't care that your vacation plans have been set for weeks, it just knows that there is going to be pleasure on vacation so it keeps thinking about it. Thought doesn't care that your mother's been dead for ten years, it just knows that you're angry with her, so it keeps thinking about her.

When we finally take a look at what's happening in our minds, it can be shocking and disturbing. I remember hearing someone share in a Twelve Step meeting that she once tried to kill herself by taking a full bottle of aspirin just because she couldn't stand listening to her thoughts anymore; she just wanted to shut them up. One of my teachers says, "If someone followed me around all day whispering the same things in my ear over and over, I'd go crazy. But that's what my mind *does*." It's a funny image, and an apt one.

All these thoughts get in the way of being mindful because they take us away from the present moment. With mindfulness, it's not so much that we try to stop thoughts—although that can happen at times—but more that we try to change our relationship to them. One way we change that relationship is to question them or to take them less seriously. A current bumper sticker says, "Don't believe everything you think." And that's it. But we do believe our thoughts, don't we? We're so used to these words and images passing through the mind like a CNN scroll bringing us facts, updates, comments, criticism, that we rarely step back and realize that these "objects of mind" have no authority. They're just spit out over and over based on past conditioning. They may contradict themselves, they may have no basis in reality, but they don't care. As Wes Nisker, the author of *Buddha's Nature*, says, "Your mind has a mind of its own." Once we actually start to look at the content of our thoughts, to question them, we start to change our whole way of being. Our basis for decision-making changes; our understanding of reality changes. What we had taken for facts are now called into question. In Twelve Step programs they say, "Feelings aren't facts," and they might add, "Thoughts aren't facts either."

Mindfulness has two components: the aspect of just being present and knowing clearly what is happening, and the aspect of intuitively responding to our experience in a skillful way. Before we do anything, we need to be aware of what is really going on, not just react to stimuli in an unconscious way. The tendency of addicts—and many other people—is to act without clarity, without carefully exploring what is happening. This, again, comes out of the survival instinct that tells us we have to protect ourselves—fight or flight. Most situations, though, don't demand this kind of instant reaction or decision. So, the first thing that mindfulness gives us is the ability to just be with our experience without running. This can be a huge challenge. Many thoughts and feelings are unpleasant and trigger our addictive or reactive patterns. We just want to *do* something. The power to be is the courage that the spiritual path cultivates, the warrior's ability to face our demons.

As my meditation practice developed after that first retreat in the desert, I struggled with knee pain whenever I sat for longer than 20 minutes. My teachers emphasized that I needed to just be mindful of the pain, a very challenging task. Instead of having any sense of relaxed mindfulness with the pain, as soon as it started I would get frustrated, then fearful, and finally I would give up and move my legs to relieve the pain. And moving had the effect of disturbing any concentration I was developing.

After practicing for several months and two short retreats, I went on a three-week retreat. After the first few restless days, I began to explore the knee pain. During a sitting one morning, I caught the first twinge of sensation about 20 minutes into the period. Instead of moving, I took a breath, exhaled, and relaxed. Like easing into a cold swimming pool, I gingerly took my mind into my knee. Immediately my body tensed, so again, I breathed and relaxed. Now I was able to get closer to the sensation. It was in my right knee, a burning feeling. As my teachers had suggested, I tried to locate the sensation, but it was hard to pin down exactly where it was. It wasn't just sitting there; it seemed to be migrating around the whole area of the knee. Where was its center? It didn't seem to have one. Where was its outer edge? That too kept shifting, along with its shape and the sensation itself. Sometimes it felt like a burning, other times like a pulling or a tightness. I kept breathing. I snuck a peek at my watch. Time was passing very slowly. The pain felt sharp again—I realized that when I looked at my watch I'd stopped being mindful of the pain and I'd tensed and pulled away from it. Aversion made the pain worse. Again I breathed, relaxed, and went back to exploring the sensation. I found myself interested. I'd never really felt pain in this way before. The resistance was falling away, and I felt a sense of brightness and presence. I saw how any time my attention faltered, the sensation became pain, but as long as I was clearly focused, it stayed in the realm of sensation; that is, I just felt something intense but not necessarily unpleasant. Finally I realized that the sensation was getting stronger, and I felt my energy flagging.

I couldn't sustain my concentration, so very slowly and intentionally, I moved my leg to a more comfortable position, following the sensations the whole way. As I came to rest in my new posture, I felt the burning dissipate and the relief of pain fading away. Again I breathed. For the first time in my life I'd seen pain not as a problem, but just as what is. Like the experience of seeing my hometown after my first retreat, I felt that I'd come alive in some new sense. A part of life that I'd always tried to avoid had opened up to me.

My relationship to pain changed that day. Not that I'm always able to rest and open to pain, but I know that such a thing is possible, and sometimes I manage it. The craving to get high or to fix myself is another pain that I've learned to explore with mindfulness, trying not to react or run away. I can't always manage to keep a balanced mind around this pain, either, but I try. Knowing that there is another way to relate to pain is an insight that we can carry with us, even when overwhelmed. This insight tells us that pain isn't a mistake, it's part of life; that our fear and resistance don't have to control us, that there's another way we can respond; that what might feel like an unmanageable, constant pain is really a flowing set of sensations that can be accepted and taken in as a part of our lives, something that, like everything, will pass.

This work with pain taught me to *be,* to just accept what was happening in my sense experience without trying to fix it or change it. But just to be isn't enough. We also need to act, and mindfulness helps us to decide what to do. When I learned to open to my knee pain, I was actually doing a lot more than that. I was dropping all the thoughts and emotions those sensations triggered. As I held the intense sensations in a more open, spacious awareness, those thoughts and emotions also were given space. I wasn't feeding those mind states, so they were weakened. All of this opened up the space for something deeper, an intuitive wisdom, to arise. When we aren't being pulled so hard by our impulses and reactivity, our thinking is much more clear, less conditioned. Unobscured by neurotic fears, judgments, and obsessions, our minds effortlessly bring forth the guidance or knowledge that we need. When, in Step Three, we "turn our will and our lives over," the faith needed for that surrender comes out of the understanding that this wisdom is, indeed, within us. We stop trying to control and begin to trust our own awareness, opening ourselves to a deeper level of thought and contemplation far wiser and more effective than our agitated, fearful surface mind.

A critical way our intuitive response is tested is in our relationships with others. Early in sobriety I learned a set of helpful, though generic, responses to people's drinking problems. "Go to meetings every day; get a sponsor; turn it over to God; write an inventory." This is some of the traditional guidance given newcomers and others, and it's a good template for recovery. But problems can't always be fixed with a stock answer. As I started to work with newcomers and "sponsees," I saw how my robotic answers to their issues were sometimes a turnoff.

Of course, those responses were at least attempts to help. And if they weren't the wisest of words, they were at least not angry or reactive, as I had been in my drinking days. When we're drunk or high, our ability to call on any wisdom, or be rational at all, is severely challenged. This was especially true for me in a relationship I had with a singer in my 20s. We worked as a duo at first, Jessica playing rhythm guitar and singing lead, while I played lead guitar and sang backup. In the summer of 1973 we got a gig on Cape Cod at a club called the Buccaneer on Route 6A, the old road that winds through the scenic villages on the bay side of the Cape. There we'd go through our repertoire of folk-rock and pop tunes to an appreciative audience, soaking up the beer and vodka tonics that the club owner gave us free. The two of us drank equally heavily, and after the gigs, we often got into drunken arguments. One night, after weaving home down 6A to our apartment, our conflict spilled out onto the lawn, as we screamed and yelled and kicked at each other. What were we fighting about? Who knows? Neither of us knew how to listen. I would insult her guitar playing and she'd react; she'd criticize the way I drove, and I'd lash out. In that drunken state there was no such thing as mindfulness, much less wisdom. Eventually, I jumped into the red Pinto—which belonged to her—and sped away. But I didn't get far. The police pulled me over before I got out of town, and Jessica was riding with them. When they got me out of the car, my reaction to seeing her there was to throw the car keys into the woods by the roadside. Insanity . . .

Unfortunately, in those days drunk-driving laws weren't enforced the way they are today. I belonged in a program, and it's too bad that a judge on Cape Cod didn't get the chance to send me to one. Instead, the cops simply let me go with a warning.

I'm not going to pretend that I don't still have a temper, or that I take criticism well from my wife, but obviously, without the booze and drugs to fog things up, things don't escalate to the level of needing law-enforcement officers to mediate things. And when it comes to listening to the problems of people in a meeting or a meditation group, mindfulness has given me a whole new way of relating.

A couple of years ago I was waiting to be interviewed at a radio station in Ohio with my brother Jerry. A staff member approached me and started to share with me about a relative's drinking problem, asking my advice. We talked for a little while, and when she walked away, Jerry told me what he'd noticed: that I had just listened at first, not saying anything, then when the woman was through I had shared a similar experience, and only then had I given some careful advice. I'd never noticed this pattern, but I realized that it was an accurate description of how I try to relate to someone who is sharing a struggle. The listening is the most important part, because if I don't listen carefully, I'll tend to make a quick judgment and fit the person into some category as I used to do early in sobriety, giving a stock response. Instead, listening involves dropping my own thoughts and opinions for a moment and trying to fully take in what's being said to me. Besides hearing the words, I also try to feel the emotions that are being communicated. Listening to someone means trying to hear between the lines, to try to get to the motivation behind what's being said. And I will often ask people a few questions before I even start to respond.

Sharing my own experience, we can call it "stage two" in this process, is a way to earn trust. When people know that you have a personal understanding of what they are going through, they are more likely to believe you. You're not just telling them your opinion. You've lived this.

Giving suggestions or advice is the riskiest stage, and the one that has to be done with the most care. If I'm really not sure, which isn't unusual, I will tell the person that I don't know, but that this is the best I can come up with. Oftentimes, though, after listening with mindfulness and an open heart, an intuitive response arises, not a boilerplate answer, but something that feels authentic, and when I share it, I often see that it has hit home, that I've touched the place in this person that needed to be touched.

Does all this help? I really don't know. Rarely does one conversation change someone. They usually need to go through a process, and talking to me or their sponsor or therapist or friend is just part of that process. When we are trying to help others, it's easy to fool ourselves into believing that our wisdom is all they need. But whatever results come from our attempts to help, the experience for *us* when we listen and respond mindfully to another is valuable. Any time I can draw on my heart's wisdom, any time I can listen with openness and compassion, I am enriched.

Prayer: I set my intention to be mindful today. I will try to stay in my body; I will try to let go of greedy and hateful thoughts; I will be present and open to my feelings; I will be awake to the needs of those around me.

Exercise: Mindfulness of Breath

Mindfulness of the breath is a core practice shared across many Buddhist and other meditative traditions. The breath is a simple thing to feel, and yet within it we find a vast array of experiences.

1. When you begin to follow the breath, it can be with an awareness that the entire body is involved: the air coming in the nose or mouth, flowing down the throat as the chest and belly and the whole trunk expand. Then you can notice where it's easiest to feel the breath—often it is the belly or the nostrils. Once you have found this particular point in your body, it becomes the anchor for your attention.

2. Now that you've found your anchor, you can begin to explore the breath at that point in the body with precise awareness. First, notice the difference between the sensations of an in-breath and the sensations of an out-breath. Notice if there's a moment between inhaling and exhaling, or between exhaling and inhaling, where nothing is happening. Notice how each breath is different in subtle ways, longer, shorter, more smooth or ragged, fast or slow, subtle or obvious, gentle or rough.

3. Then see if you can start to feel more sensations in each breath. As you become more able to discern all the elements of the breath, you can try to notice three sensations on each in-breath and three sensations on each out-breath. This nudges your attention closer as you try to distinguish the tiny variations.

Exercise: Mindfulness of Thoughts

The heart of mindfulness meditation is our relationship to thoughts. There are many ways to develop this quality. Here is one of the most basic and essential ones.

1. Sit comfortably in an alert posture and take a few moments to consciously relax the body, just settling into your sitting position. Then begin by spending several minutes focusing on the breath. You will use the breath as your anchor, the place where you return your attention any time it wanders.

2. Now, start to be aware when thought interrupts your awareness of breath. You might notice right away, or you might get lost in thought for some time before realizing that you're not on the breath. Don't worry about that.

3. When you do realize that you're thinking, just make a soft mental note to yourself, "Thinking, thinking," and then gently return to the breath. Try not to add a judgment about the fact that the mind is wandering. If you do, note that as "Judging, judging," or just more thinking. Analyzing what's happening or criticizing ourselves is just another way we get sidetracked. Try not to be seduced by the mind's desire to pick things apart.

4. Notice any tension in the body that arose while you were thinking, and try to relax again.

5. As you watch thoughts, see if you can change your relationship with them. Instead of seeing them as "your thoughts," just see them as words or images passing through the mind.

Over time you can make more varied notes on thinking, like "Planning, planning," "Wanting, wanting," "Anger, anger," and so on. As you watch the mind in this way, patterns may emerge, and you'll learn about the habits of your own thinking. Thoughts are how we create our self; as you watch the patterns of thought, you'll be seeing how that image comes to be.

Exercise: The Space of Mind

Using spatial awareness can be an easeful way to change our relationship to thought. Rather than working with a close attention to breath or thoughts, with this practice we open more to the space in which breath, thoughts, and all perceptions are happening. One of the ways to observe thought in meditation is to get a sense of where thought is happening in the "space of mind."

1. Begin your meditation by listening to sounds. Notice faraway sounds, notice close-up sounds, notice sounds in your own body. Then notice how all of these seem to be appearing in a spatial way; sounds are coming from different directions and different distances, and you can feel that. Notice how hearing has a kind of open, spacious, and light quality to it.

2. Bring your attention to your body sensations. You'll notice that those are happening in a different part of the space of mind, closer in, and that they have a different quality to them, more dense, and full of energy, almost electrical.

3   Bring your attention to the breath at the nostrils, and have a sense of this as the center of consciousness, as the center of the space of mind.

4. When thoughts come, experience them in this space of mind, as just another object, like sounds, sensations, and breath, just an energetic force moving through consciousness.

This shift of perspective, into a spatial sense of thought, can move us from an intellectual relationship with thought to a sensory relationship. No longer driven by the content of thought, now we just experience it as a "thing."

When we use the power of mindfulness and observe thought from different perspectives, our whole life can change. Instead of being driven by thoughts, we actually make choices about how we're going to respond to them.

Exercise: Daily Mindfulness

One of the biggest challenges in mindfulness practice is to bring this kind of attention into our daily lives. Here is a suggestion on how to begin to do this.

1. Choose one common daily activity to be aware of for the next week. It could be going to the bathroom, washing the dishes, starting the car, walking the dog, or anything else that doesn't involve reading, watching a screen, or interacting with someone else.

2. Each time you perform this action, take a breath, drop your thoughts, and bring your attention into your body, feeling what it feels like to do this action. Keep it simple. You don't have to do anything special or expect any special results. Just be there.

3. After one week, add another activity. Now you have two common activities you are doing mindfully. For one month, add another activity each week until you have four activities you are doing mindfully every day.

The Higher Power
of Wisdom

The Higher Power of Wisdom has three components that pervade and color all experience. Insight into these truths brings freedom from greed, hatred, and confusion and leads to liberation.

The wisdom we gain through practice gives us the power of insight, to see the truth and to respond to it. In the Buddhist teachings the insights that arise from awakening to the Three Characteristics of Existence—Suffering, Impermanence, and Not-self—are at the heart of this wisdom. The understanding of these truths guides us to freedom.

We can grasp these insights directly through mindful exploration of our hearts and minds, a silent knowing that appears in the stillness of meditation. We can also develop our understanding through contemplation. And one of the most direct ways to absorb these insights is to remind ourselves of them in each significant moment of our lives. Here their truth becomes obvious.

SUFFERING

*The Higher Power of Suffering is the energy of craving and resistance
that creates struggles in our world. Its power reveals the ways we
need to change and inspires our efforts to overcome internal
and external adversity. Insight into suffering evokes the powers
of acceptance, compassion, and forgiveness.*

It may seem odd to talk about suffering, called *dukkha* in Buddhism, as an aspect of God. Isn't suffering what we're trying to get away from? Isn't God supposed to help us get free from suffering? Or maybe we think of suffering as God's retribution for our sins. In any case, there's surely nothing holy about suffering. Is there?

In the months leading up to getting sober, I hit one miserable bottom after another. I was struggling, as I had for a dozen years, to make my living as a musician. I played one gig with an oldies band that represented for me the epitome of schlock and losing my identity, then moved on to a Top 40 band. After a month or so I realized that I hated that even more than the oldies band, which wanted me back. Their next engagement was an audition at a club in Chino, California, a prison town. While waiting for the other acts to finish before we went on, I drank the free beers and tequilas they were giving us. By the time we got to play, I was drunk. When the bandleader called "Johnny B. Goode," I jumped up on a table and blasted my guitar solo, totally uncharacteristic performing for me. The manager of the club loved it and booked us immediately, but when we came back to play for money a few weeks later, I couldn't duplicate the feat—I was in one of my "controlled drinking" periods—and the band was soon fired.

Like most alcoholics, I was regularly trying to make my drinking work. I was also a pothead, so one of my main tricks was to cut back on one and do more of the other. It was agonizing, these attempts to balance something that couldn't be balanced. That winter my girlfriend showed me the "20 Questions," a list of behaviors that are supposed to characterize alcoholics. If you answer yes to just a few of these, it's supposed to indicate that you have a problem. At the time I was only willing to admit to three, but apparently that was enough to brand me. I resented the whole thing and, like many people before me, set out to prove the questions, and my girlfriend, wrong. The first thing I did was say I was going to stop drinking. That night I went to the drummer and asked if I could get high with him on our break. From then on I smoked pot almost every day until the following summer, when I got sober.

But smoking pot wasn't going to be enough. Shortly after my resolution to quit drinking and prove that I didn't have a problem, I was back at it.

My girlfriend and I had a bungalow in Venice Beach, and our bedroom was on the second floor where it got a lot of light in the morning. My hangovers were becoming torturous, and waking up with the bright sunshine and crushing headaches started triggering suicidal thoughts. Margaret, a deeply committed feminist, was writing her Ph.D. dissertation on *Cosmopolitan* magazine, and stacks of the thick, glossy periodical were always underfoot as I stumbled to the bathroom.

In an effort to make more money, I invited a friend of mine who was an amateur songwriter to come visit me in California and record a demo tape. David's drinking and drugging habits were, if anything, more intense than mine. In the studio we added cocaine to the mix of pot and booze. By now it was probably March and my run was getting worse. The band was playing a pitiful gig where a dozen customers was a good crowd, but with David in town every night was a party.

When you're on a binge like that, there's a certain insane invulnerability when you're loaded, even as you swing back to deep despair each morning. At the gigs I was high and feeling good with my guitar, and soon I struck up a relationship with the beautiful waitress who worked at the club. Like me, she was involved with someone else. In her spandex and her blue Corvette, she epitomized everything that my intellectual college-professor girlfriend in Venice was not. Mostly we hung out in her car and smoked dope during the breaks, but there was enough physical contact that I would find it necessary to wash my face and hands when I got home at 3 A.M. so that I wouldn't smell of her perfume. It was the kind of sleazy life that I found disgusting in others, and I began to carry around a burden of shame and guilt along with my hangovers.

Finally in June—six months after taking the 20 Questions—it all came crashing down. The band got offered a road gig, and I turned it down, thinking I could throw my own band together to keep the job at the club in L.A. The musicians I hired were all top-notch players, some with impressive studio credentials. But we literally did not practice, the three of them actually meeting for the first time on the stage at the bar. The result was that we were sloppy and unfocused, obviously not a real band, and the club owner fired us. That brought it all home to me. I was miserable and I was broke. I'd just been fired from one of the worst gigs I'd ever had. I was strung out on booze and pot and cocaine. I was cheating on my girlfriend. My life was a wreck. I was desperate, and giving up drinking and drugs seemed like the only thing that might help.

Amazingly enough, I didn't think that drugs and booze were actually the problem. I had spent years trying to solve my problems, going so far as to take silent meditation retreats and follow a guru around the country; I had tried vegetarianism as a solution; as a teenager I'd had years of therapy; and I kept thinking that becoming a successful musician would fix me. Nothing had worked, and I didn't really believe that a Twelve Step program was actually the answer. I'd just run out of other options. I figured, "Why not?" I believed it was pointless to get sober, but I didn't know what else to do.

The Higher Power of Suffering had brought me to my knees. And that power began the process of healing.

In the Buddha's first discourse, the first truth that he defines is the Noble Truth of Suffering. He says that if we are going to solve the essential problems of being a human being, we're first going to have to see this truth clearly. And it's this truth that alcoholics and addicts don't want to face. Our goal is, in fact, the opposite of this, to avoid suffering. We certainly don't want to look at it or think about it. This avoidance is how addiction begins and what sustains it. But, as the Buddha points out, suffering is too powerful to avoid.

Typically, we wouldn't think of this power as "higher," as having a spiritual quality. We might acknowledge that suffering is powerful, more powerful than we are, but our instinct would probably not be to put it in the category of God. But when the Buddha shows how suffering can be the gateway into resolving our struggles, he reveals its transformative spiritual essence.

When I came face to face with the depth of my suffering in that first week of June in 1985, my transformation began. No longer trying to escape or deny my addiction, I began my recovery by facing my suffering. This is the first power that we can recognize in suffering, the power to wake us up to our condition, to our need to change. When our lives are comfortable and undisturbed, there's no reason to question anything, no reason to challenge ourselves or to grow. It's only when we are faced with failure, pain, or struggle—with suffering—that we are forced out of complacency to look more deeply at ourselves, at our lives, and at life itself.

Recovery—in fact, any spiritual path—demands that we keep growing, that we continue to look *within,* to go more deeply into our hearts and minds, and that we continue to look *without,* to live with more care and kindness. Step One, getting clean and sober or abstinent, is only the first of many stages of transformation that the path of recovery promises. In the chapter on Step Six, I will explore further how becoming more aware of suffering can prepare us for these transformations and make us "entirely ready" to change.

Suffering's role as Higher Power doesn't just involve forcing us to change. Recognizing the Higher Power of Suffering is also key to acceptance, one of the essential elements of recovery. When describing suffering, the Buddha first points to those inevitables, sickness, old age, and death. While some might think he's being morbid by focusing on these, in fact, it is in accepting them that peace comes. When we fight these things, we just create more problems for ourselves. When we learn to live with them without struggle, we let go of suffering.

When we take the first Step and admit our powerlessness, we are seeing the truth of our suffering. When we accept our addiction, we are ready to change. At first we might think that saying we are addicts or alcoholics is a defeat or failure, but it's actually the beginning of recovery. This acceptance can bring us the first peace we've experienced around our addiction.

This points to the critical relationship that we must take to all the forms of Higher Power: a relationship of living in harmony with God. When we struggle with the truth, with these powers, our lives are painful. When we live in harmony and acceptance with the suffering aspect of God, a great relief comes over us. This doesn't mean that there isn't still unpleasantness, but it means that there is no confusion over it. Things are as they are.

Suffering can also send us deeper into ourselves and our sense of connection and compassion. I once heard Stephen Levine tell a story about a mother whose surfer son was mangled and killed by a shark. When she went to identify his body and saw the horror of what was left of him, something cracked open in her, and she had an enlightenment experience, completely letting go—there was nothing to hold on to anymore.

While I've never had a moment so profound, when my father died a little more than a year after I got sober, I experienced something of that grace. I certainly was familiar with sadness, as someone who had struggled with depression for much of my life, but the grief over my father's death touched something that felt completely different. Whereas depression always seemed destructive and pointless, this grief felt healing. I knew that I was touching something universal, the shared sense of loss that all children feel when they lose a parent—the cycle of life. It wasn't self-indulgent or self-pitying, but natural and necessary. I knew it was important to give this grief the time it needed, so each night I would read a book about loss that allowed me to re-experience my grief, to give it the space to move through me and to heal itself.

This, too, is the Higher Power of Suffering, that which brings us in touch with the round of birth and death, and that cycle's primal, impersonal reality. When we let go into the Truth of Suffering, it stops being something to fear and becomes just another aspect of life. If we are opening ourselves to life, we must receive suffering; if we want to experience the fullness of life, we must be present for suffering as well. Eventually we find that, like a sad song or a tragic play, suffering enriches our lives with something heart-opening, bittersweet, and moving. It brings depth and meaning to life, awakens compassion, and inspires us to grow and change.

Prayer: I open myself to the Higher Power of Suffering, letting go of resistance and allowing its truth and power to guide me. I recognize that suffering is not personal, but shared by all beings, and I offer compassion and love to myself and all beings everywhere.

Exercise: Seeing Suffering

It's easy to think that cultivating an awareness of suffering will cause us to have a negative view of the world. However, if we don't see the Truth of Suffering, we are missing a big part of reality. Learning to hold suffering as a natural part of life helps us to find balance. With this exercise you will let yourself look at suffering to see how that recognition affects your experience of life.

1. Make a commitment for one day to see all the ways that the Truth of Suffering is evident in your life. This could include physical sensations like hunger, the need to go to the bathroom, or the desire for a shower. It could include creaking bones and sore muscles. Notice painful thoughts of wanting or regret, anger or anxiety. Be aware when difficult emotions appear.

2. Bringing mindfulness to this experience, stay attentive to your fear of seeing and feeling these things. Try to keep a broad, impersonal perspective, seeing suffering as a natural part of life, something that comes and goes. Maintain the point of view of an observer studying your own experience.

3. Notice too, the suffering around you. This could include the homeless person you see on the street, the sick relative who calls you, or the cat stuck in a tree. Observe, too, the suffering you see in the media, from typhoons in South Asia to war in the Middle East to anger over a political debate. Moving into this broader awareness of suffering can be overwhelming, so be careful how you hold this broader suffering.

4. Suffering, *dukkha,* has many forms, both gross and subtle. As you observe all this dukkha, notice what happens to your heart. Can you stay open and compassionate; are you overwhelmed; do you become numb?

5. The Higher Power of Suffering inspires us to change. As you do this exercise, see if you learn about anything in your life that needs attention. Are there ways that you are causing yourself or others suffering? Are there ways you are reacting or interacting with the world that harm you? Just because some degree of dukkha is inevitable, doesn't mean that we have to be passive in its face. How can you work skillfully with the Higher Power of Suffering?

IMPERMANENCE

*The Higher Power of Impermanence is the energy of change that
continuously transforms us and our world. Engaging this power
helps us see through the illusion of solidity, showing us the futility
of clinging and the frailty of life. Insight into impermanence inspires
us to let go and to deeply engage life as it is in each moment.*

The Higher Power of Suffering and the Higher Power of Impermanence are deeply intertwined. When the Buddha asks us to contemplate sickness, old age, death, and loss, he is not asking us to look
closely at suffering alone, but at impermanence as well. In the same
way that we want to avoid suffering, we also want to avoid impermanence. To consider our brief lives in the scope of history can seem
depressing, but, just as with suffering, the Buddha relentlessly guides
us to engaging and understanding the profound implications of the
Truth of Impermanence.

Addiction is a fight against this truth. Getting high for me was
always an attempt to hold on to something, whether the carelessness
of booze, the utter peace of downs, the wild thrill of ups, or the sense
of awe and wonder of psychedelics.

In my late teens and early 20s I went through runs on different
drugs and forms of alcohol. For a while I was into speed: Dexedrine,
Benzedrine, and Methedrine. The intense excitement of these stimu-
lants was thrilling, although the crash was awful, hours and hours
of agitated discomfort. I loved barbiturates and drugs like Quaaludes.
These gave the feeling of being drunk in about 20 minutes. However,
mixing them with alcohol, as I often did, can kill you, and I was fortunate to survive some harrowing blackouts. The worst was waking up
covered in scratches and scrapes after, apparently, crawling home from
the local bar. My drinking at that time usually involved combining
beer with shots of tequila, ouzo, or some other hard liquor. Getting
sick and blacking out were common occurrences. And the hangovers
and disruption to my digestive system were horrifying.

At some point in my early 20s I realized that I just didn't have the
constitution for this kind of excess—it didn't occur to me that I might
actually have a drinking and drugging problem. The only problem I
saw was that I needed to learn to handle things better. My solution,
which for me was "growing up," was a nice beer-and-pot regimen. I was

beginning to work steadily as a professional musician, and I needed to be functional enough to play until one or two in the morning. I couldn't drink to excess on the nights I was working.

What I tried to do, at this point, was create a steady, reliable routine by which I could be high all the time, but still function. I tried to make every day just like the one before: get up, have a cup of tea (the speed had ruined my ability to use coffee), eat breakfast, roll a joint, get high, practice my guitar, go to rehearsal, smoke more dope, go home (usually a motel room), get high, take a shower, eat dinner, go to the gig, play a set, get high, play another set, drink a beer, play another set, get high and drink another beer, play the last set, and go home and drink beer and smoke dope until I was ready to sleep—or until I passed out.

If you actually got through reading the last paragraph, you have some idea how ridiculous this was. Fundamentally, this routine was about stopping time, about creating a safe, unchanging life so that I could always be in control of my feelings, moods, and experiences.

And that's impossible.

That's impossible because of the Higher Power of Impermanence. Even with this routine, every day was different—of course! I was never under control of myself or what happened, not in any absolute sense. The band played well or the band played poorly; the audience liked us or the audience hated us; the beer wasn't enough, so I drank tequila till I blacked out; one bag of pot made me sleepy, another made me paranoid; and my emotions, naturally enough, waxed and waned from day to day.

Life is full of ups and down, but addicts only want the ups. We think we can make it into one long party. Some of us strive for one moment of excitement and fun after another, while others strive for an uninterrupted routine, no disturbances. Neither goal is realistic. Neither one accepts the reality of life's unpredictability and challenges.

Like the power of suffering, the idea of impermanence as an aspect of God can be confusing. Usually we are trying to fight change, not embrace it. But, as with suffering, the Buddha shows us how we can use our understanding of impermanence as the doorway into transformative insight.

The essence of this insight is founded in the logic of the Dharma. The Buddha shows that suffering is caused by clinging. When we see that everything is constantly changing, we realize that it's impossible to really hold on to anything; our clinging is bound to fail. In that realization there can be a profound letting go. And this letting go is the transforming moment.

One aspect of "turning our will and our life over to the care of God" is trusting in impermanence. If we are living in harmony with karma, then change is moving our life in a positive direction. As we sit in meditation, we experience the flow of life in a visceral way, right here and now, the sounds, sensations, thoughts, energies flowing through us all in flux, all in change. Watching how life moves moment to moment helps us to see that we can trust change. Not that everything is always going to be okay in our lives, but that if we can bring an open, engaged heart to each moment, then we can manage. It's the resistance to change that creates our biggest struggles.

For someone coming onto the path of recovery, there can be a huge fear of change. How are you going to live without your drug? What about your friends? Will you ever have fun again? If you're addicted, how are you going to handle withdrawal? We've been living this way for so long that it can be hard to imagine a life without our addiction. Perhaps it's only when our awareness of suffering gets stronger than our fear of change that we are actually able to take this step. We need to move slowly. Realize that we don't have to solve all these questions right away. Trust that when we lose the things we've come to depend on, there will be something there to replace them. The fact is that life in recovery is so much more rewarding that after a little while most people are just disappointed that they didn't get clean and sober sooner.

In the Theravada Buddhist teaching on the Progress of Insight, there is a stage called "rolling up the mat." At this point, some people have visions of death, everything dissolving and disappearing before their eyes. It's supposed to be terribly frightening, though I've never experienced it on such a level. It is, of course, a powerful vision into impermanence, and one can easily be tempted to give up the whole meditative enterprise. However, most people who reach that stage don't falter because they've built up a foundation of trust and calm with intensive meditation that allows them to sit through the visions.

Many of us want to roll up the mat of our recovery when we first arrive, but if we're lucky, the group, the other people in recovery around us, reminds us that what we're going through is impermanent, that if we stick with it things will get better. We are really being asked to trust in the Higher Power of Impermanence. Moments like this can actually happen at any time in our recovery. When things fall apart, as they almost inevitably will at some point, one of the things that can get us through is remembering that we haven't arrived at our destination, but that we are just passing through hard times. It's the nature of the Dharma that things rise and fall. When we understand this truth, the dark times are seen as a natural part of our life's journey, the trough before the next uplifting wave.

One friend and teaching colleague, Heather Sundberg, emphasizes paying careful attention during periods of transition, both in practice and in daily life. She talks about how easy it is to lose our focus during moments of change. I suspect there is a tendency in these moments to either stay stuck in what just happened, in the past, or to jump ahead to what's coming, the future.

Transitions are often triggers for addiction. One woman I met at a treatment center only began drinking alcoholically when her husband died in his 50s. She simply couldn't come to terms with the loss, with the change.

Aging is probably the most challenging transition. When I was 41, I was having my hair cut when the young man with the scissors commented on the small bald spot at the crown of my head. As I couldn't see that spot with my single mirror at home, I didn't know about it, and it shocked me. *I'm losing my hair?! Not me!* My hair had been a huge emblem of my identity from my teenage years when I'd first grown it to look like the Beatles. In my early 20s it had reached Grateful Dead length. The idea that it would fall out was a blow. Part of me didn't believe it, and part of me was mad at the kid for telling me—denial and anger, stages of grief. As I write this and try to sound spiritual, I realize I've never completely come to terms with losing my hair. Aging just keeps happening—one insult after another. My solution has been to buzz it, while others try to grow what they've got as long as possible, and of course there's always the artificial solution. The lengths men go to deal with this aspect of change and aging in their lives point to the difficulty of dealing with the Higher Power of Impermanence.

One of the most difficult transitions in life is from being a child to being a teenager. This is the point at which many people start their careers as addicts or alcoholics. Childhood, even a difficult childhood, has a quality of magic. As children we don't see the true nature of suffering in the world and we don't understand how hard it is to be a responsible person. I watch my ten-year-old daughter, how she sees the world, and I can tell that even when she hears about tragedies or when she has to fulfill some responsibility, she doesn't see those things as central to life, more as distractions from the essence of life, which is to have fun. I know this was true for me. When I reached my teenage years, the responsibilities became more real, and the truth about things like war, hypocrisy, sickness, and suffering started to sink in. But I wasn't ready to make the transition to adulthood; I still wanted to hold on to the magic of childhood. At the same time, I didn't want to *be* a child or have childish fun. That's when I discovered drugs and alcohol. Talk about magic! Here were things I could drink or smoke or pop to put myself right into euphoria, to make me relaxed, wild, playful.

Unfortunately, of course, the magic didn't really work in the way I thought it would. There were karmic results, debts to pay for this avoidance of life. What happened to me, and I think this is a common experience, is that I didn't grow up. I stayed emotionally immature. That immaturity infected my life so that in every area—relationships, work, spirituality—I was crippled, until I finally got clean and sober and started to live like an adult, to make the transition out of childhood and adolescence at last.

What I was doing for all those years was trying to fight the power of impermanence. Life kept changing around me, but I didn't cooperate with it; I was out of harmony with change. It's one thing to fight with the change of losing your hair and quite another when you fight with growing up. When I did finally learn to live like an adult, it was such a relief and so gratifying. Living in harmony with change, trying to adapt to life instead of fighting it, is exciting and inspiring. I'll probably never be fully grown up, having gotten such a late start, but at least I've learned to have an adult-like life.

Buddhist meditation practices are meant to help us touch impermanence in a profound way, not just to think about it, but to know it
on the visceral level.

Spirit Rock Meditation Center, March 2004

I'm sitting in the great hall on the hillside of this Buddhist
center in Marin County. I'm almost three weeks into a month-long
retreat, and over an hour into this period of sitting meditation.
The late afternoon sun warms my back through the west-facing
windows as I navigate a unique inner landscape. This past week
my concentration has gone to a level I've never experienced
before, and as a result some odd and fascinating altered states
have appeared. My teachers have been encouraging me to move
through these states, not to get too hung up in what they might
mean or how they feel. Just see them clearly and stay present to
the changing experience. I've just gone through an intense few
minutes when my body felt elongated, my mind crystalline.
With the passing of these feelings, my mind is now focused solely
on the sensations of my breath right at the tip of my nose. I've
paid attention to thousands of breaths in my decades of practice,
and yet, this time there is a sense of intimacy and absorption I've
never quite touched before. In . . . out . . . the delicate movement,
the softness of the touch at my nostrils . . . Suddenly I'm overwhelmed with the sense of frailty, my body, my very life, totally
dependent on this simple movement of air. It could stop at any
time. It is so fragile, so tenuous, this existence. Not only for me,
but for each of us, for every being. I'm still with my breath; it's
so light now, barely moving. I see that I really don't know what's
going to happen next. I think I'm going to keep breathing, but I
don't know that for sure.

This isn't just some meditation moment. The concentration
has allowed me to touch something very real, something that we
all know, that is embedded in our genes, in our survival instinct.
Every moment people are being born and dying. Only this thin
thread of breath is keeping me alive right now. Each of these
breaths has its own birth and death. Each one is unique.

When I have a meditation experience like this, I know I've
deepened my understanding of impermanence. This direct seeing

undermines my clinging. There's no substitute for this kind of practice. But I've also learned how helpful it is to contemplate impermanence in my daily life. The Buddha taught both approaches, the experiential, meditative approach and the intentional contemplative approach. This latter form of practice is embodied in the Five Daily Recollections, which suggest that we should remember the inevitability of our own aging, illness, death, and loss and recall that our fate is determined by our intentions and our actions.

When I first got the meditation instruction to watch the "arising and passing of all phenomena," I was fascinated by the idea of having an enlightenment experience. In my grasping way, I struggled to "get there," to have this breakthrough. What I didn't see right away was that even without such an epiphany, the persistent focus on impermanence is chipping away at the underlying tendency to think and feel as if things are going to stay the way they are right now. The Daily Recollections actually reinforce and support the meditative breakthrough, so that in the moment of engaging impermanence on a deep and profound level, we are prepared to see and accept this truth.

Seeing impermanence as central to our life's experience isn't just some spiritual exercise. It is a direct way to freedom from suffering. When we don't appreciate the pervasiveness of change, we are far more subject to the fear and distress that arises when the inevitable occurs. Without this kind of focus, we often wake up to change only when we reach a turning point or something extreme happens. Think how it feels when you lose a job, when a relationship ends, when your new car gets its first scratch, when your "baby" goes off to her first day at school: There's a kind of shock, coming out of the dream of solidity, and remembering, again, the fragile nature of reality.

The Buddha was once asked how long we could be sure to live. "Until your next out-breath," he said. That's it. Just this breath. So, he's implying, pay close attention because this might be all you get. When I hear a traffic report of a fatal accident, I often reflect that the person didn't expect to die today. And I remind myself that here in my car is a very common place to die, that I might not get home, that I may be dead in a few moments. This helps me to hold a little more loosely the plans I have, the fears and hopes, to see that they are only thoughts, often stressful ones, and that what's real is this moment, this sense experience, this feeling, this breath. This is one of the teachings of impermanence, to be fully engaged in this moment, because it's going to change; the flip side of this insight is not to cling to this moment, because it's going to change. How to engage fully without clinging is one of the skills that mindfulness meditation helps us to learn.

It's interesting that whether things are going well or going badly, there tends to be this delusion that they are going to continue the way they are. When we're on top of the world with a new job or a new relationship, it rarely occurs to us that this is just a passing situation. In the same way, when things are bad, when we're unemployed or lonely, there is this feeling that we're *stuck*. Many difficult emotions are exacerbated by this mistaken sense. Depression and anxiety are especially prone to this problem.

One of the reasons we can think of things as permanent is a trick of the way humans remember. When we are in a particular mind state, we tend to remember other times we were in that mind state. This is a result of the survival instinct: in any situation, the mind tries to find similar memories it can come up with that might help in dealing with the present moment. When we're fearful, the mind remembers moments of danger, trying to be helpful and give us tools for dealing with what's going on right now. Unfortunately, with negative emotions, this has the side effect of creating the illusion of solidity, the impression that these emotions are always there. So, when we're depressed, it's easy to think, *I'm always so depressed,* not remembering all the happy times. Then, when we're happy, we think, *I really don't have a problem with depression. I'm happy most of the time.*

Another byproduct of this process is the sense of self created by the repetitive memories. When we remember the same events and feelings over and over, it gives us the idea that there is something solid about who we are. And even if the memories and the feelings associated with them are painful, our craving for identity grasps at them. It seems odd, but our desire for stability, even if it's a stable state of misery, seems to be more powerful, in some ways, than our craving for happiness. And this craving is much like the way that desire itself functions in us: it keeps us on the treadmill of grasping after the ungraspable. It keeps telling us that *this* mind state, or *this* job, or relationship, or car, house, iPod, computer, this *whatever,* is going to last. Like Charlie Brown trying to kick the football Lucy holds or Wile E. Coyote trying to catch the Road Runner, we keep falling for the same old trick of the mind. This is *samsara,* the endless cycle of birth and death, of ignorance and suffering, that the Buddhist path seeks to escape.

So, what to do about this Higher Power, this "God" of Impermanence? We can see it, know it, be aware of it in all things. We can honor it, respect it, accept it, and learn to live in harmony with it. This God, so much more powerful than us, this God which has buried civilizations, transformed a lifeless rock into a home to myriad creatures, created galaxies and universes, this God is truly awe-inspiring, beyond comprehension, relentless, pervasive, touching everything, everywhere, from the tiniest atom to the greatest structures in our world. We can touch this God, become absorbed into this God, be devotees of this God.

When we open to change in this way, we see that impermanence isn't always bad news. There is the tendency to associate it with loss and death, but the Hindu God of Impermanence, Shiva, creates *and* destroys. Just imagine a world *without* impermanence: unchanging, static, repetitive, a true hell realm. When I've focused on impermanence in my own meditation practice, it's never felt quite the way the teachers were describing it, as some almost mechanical and separate arising and passing. It's always felt like a mass of roiling energies, all the senses taking in a stream of experiences, like a great bubbling soup with a thousand ingredients. When my mind is especially clear, I feel as if I can sense the body down to the cellular level, birth and death and birth and death. Ultimately impermanence is life. That great, beautiful, tragic, wild, and magical unfolding that keeps us ever wondering, never knowing. To engage impermanence is to engage life. To embrace impermanence is to embrace life.

Prayer: I turn my will and my life over to the Higher Power of Impermanence, embracing each moment and letting it go. I open myself to transformation and to the unknown. Recognizing that everything is in the process of perpetual change, I let go of my clinging to mind states, objects, and other beings.

Exercise: Remembering Death

The Buddha suggested that we should remember how fragile life is so that we will devote ourselves to liberation in the limited time we have. This exercise helps us to remember death.

1. The place where we are threatened with death the most is in our cars. Make a commitment that each time you get into an automobile or other vehicle you will remind yourself that you might not get to your destination. This becomes even more obvious when you are on a freeway driving 60 or 70 miles per hour. Occasionally glance at the other drivers. They too think they are going somewhere. Remind yourself that this ride, this day, might be the last of your life and theirs.

2. One more thing: when you hear a traffic report of a fatal accident, remind yourself that the person who died thought she was going somewhere.

3. You don't know where you are going or if you will get there. The only moment you have in your life is this one. Value it. Use it. Find freedom here and now.

NOT-SELF

The Higher Power of Not-Self gives fluidity and flexibility to identity, allowing for the possibility of transformation. Engaging this power helps us see through the illusion of separateness, the false identity of ego. Insight into not-self breaks our habit of self-centeredness and guides us toward generosity, service, and compassion.

The Buddhist teaching on corelessness, or not-self (*anatta* in Pali), is entwined with the Truth of Impermanence: Simply put, if everything is constantly changing, how can I say that there is something constant called "Kevin"? In this sense, identification of any kind is a convenience, not an absolute. One way to arrive at this understanding is by asking the question "Who am I?" and deconstructing each answer that comes: Am I my body? Certainly not, as my body keeps changing. Am I my name? I can change my name anytime I want, so that can't be me. Am I my job? There's nothing stable there. What about my emotions? They are changing all the time. Or my memories? How can the past be me? Where is the past, anyway? Or maybe I am my mind? What is that? Or perhaps I am consciousness itself . . . ah, well, perhaps . . .

In the meditative tradition, the realization of not-self is considered a profound breakthrough, just as are the realizations of suffering and impermanence. Given the challenges of attaining or touching this kind of ultimate wisdom, many of us may not have the highest awakening experience; however, that doesn't mean we can't have a significant and transformative understanding.

Who I think I am has a tremendous effect on my life. What I think I am capable of, how I think people perceive me, how much I believe in the roles I play, all of these can create happiness or pain in my life; can give me confidence or undermine all my efforts; can alienate or welcome others.

One of my early memories is of sitting on the living-room floor and putting a model airplane together. I wasn't having much success, and at some point my father lowered his newspaper and looked at my work and said, "You don't have much manual dexterity." I took that statement as an absolute truth. I stopped working on models. Instead I became my older brother's assistant, running upstairs for a hammer or a screwdriver when he needed one. I wouldn't do my own projects, because I "knew" that I wasn't good at that.

Some years later, as a teenager, I told this to someone who had been watching me play the guitar. "How can you say that?" he said. "Look at how you play the guitar. That takes great manual dexterity." Shocked, I looked at the guitar I was holding in my hands. How could I not have noticed? How could I have held this belief even when everyday I was disproving it? I *did* have manual dexterity. But all those years I had avoided doing things that I thought I couldn't do, so, of course, I couldn't do them.

As I observe myself now, when I try to put together a table from Ikea or repair my bike, I see that a lot of anxiety comes up, clearly rooted in old beliefs. The other thing I see is an impatience that makes it hard for me to stick with a manual task to completion. That impatience is a karmically formed personality trait, but it isn't solid and it isn't me. If I identify with the impatience and anxiety, if I believe the messages they're giving me, I quit. But if I can see through that identification and realize that it's just a feeling, then I can overcome it simply by sticking with the task.

The Higher Power of Not-Self is seeing through all these perceptions, seeing that they are just constructions of the mind, of culture, of society. This "vision and knowledge," as the Buddha called it, frees us.

This idea of not-self is one of the most misunderstood and, in fact, abused teachings in Buddhism. The fact that there is no permanent core called "Kevin" doesn't mean that I have no feelings or that, most important, I have no karma. The Buddha said that I am the "owner" of my karma. This seems contradictory, since he says that I don't own my body or my thoughts, not my memories or my consciousness, not my house, my car, or my cat—pretty much all the things that I think are mine, he says, are not. But then he turns around and tells me that I do own my karma—maybe the one thing I wish I *didn't* own, at least the negative parts of it.

Guy Armstrong, a Buddhist teacher in the Theravada tradition, explains this by beginning with the Tibetan Buddhist teaching on the "mind stream." Instead of having some solid core, we are more like a stream of thoughts, feelings, words, and actions. Like a stream, our "self," or our personality, is constantly flowing, changing, twisting, and turning. Yes, there is some individuality, each stream is unique, but within the stream there is nothing solid, just these ever-changing elements. These elements are the results of our karma, our past intentional thoughts, feelings, words, and actions.

As Guy points out, if we *had* a solid self, we wouldn't be *able* to change these karmic conditions. It is only because of *anatta* that I can grow. This, again, is the power we tap into with not-self. The power to change is dependent upon this truth.

We cling to all sorts of identities, personal, familial, national, cultural, and more. These serve to define us, to set us apart from the rest of the world. When I began smoking pot in 1967, it put me into a subculture that I identified with. Many of the musicians I admired were taking drugs, and that was seen as a rebellion against the many problems and hypocrisies of the mainstream culture. I remember a warm summer evening in the Pocono Mountains of eastern Pennsylvania, not far from my hometown. My band was set up outside on the covered deck of a mansion overlooking the Delaware River. Teenagers spilled out onto the broad lawn where fireflies flashed in the humid air. Between sets, the lead guitar player and I snuck into an outbuilding and smoked a joint, then wandered back in time to pick up our guitars for the next set. We started with "Where Were You When I Needed You?" by the Grass Roots, and when we came to the guitar solo, we both stopped, thinking that the song was over. Marijuana can distort your perception of time, and to us, it seemed like the song had gone on for a long time. The rest of the band kept playing, of course, and we immediately realized our mistake. We were sharing a microphone, our faces close together, and we cracked up, barely able to keep playing. The keyboard player gave us a quizzical look—*What's up with you guys?*—and we simply laughed some more.

From our standpoint, he was out of it. And we were in. Our identity as pot smokers made us different and special, we thought. That innocent, playful moment was the beginning of forming an identity that would become an addiction. Soon, I wasn't just somebody who smoked pot, I was a pot smoker—I'd gone from someone who *did* something to someone who *was* something. It's a lot harder to change when you see your essence, your very self, as tied up with some behavior. Even as that identity stopped working, it was hard to let go of. When I came to the point of getting clean and sober, this was an underlying resistance, the sense that I was losing myself, that I would somehow become a drone or an empty vessel. It's curious to me now, looking back, that I thought that what was unique and special about me was my drug and alcohol use. The path of recovery has shown me the much more essential parts of me, the deeper parts of the stream of identity that flow through my life.

When we stop acting on our addiction, who we are changes. Over time, as we address our "character defects," write inventory, make amends, become more aware and compassionate, the whole mind stream begins to turn, moving toward wholesomeness, toward joy.

Not-self is directly related to another vital Buddhist idea, the interconnectedness of all things. When we realize that we are not some solid, separate self, we see that we are in fact intimately related to everything around us. Our bodies are birthed from other human bodies. Our genetic makeup is barely distinguishable from that of other humans, not to mention many other living things. The molecules of air we breathe have been in the lungs of millions of other people. We depend on other people for almost everything in our lives.

This realization of interconnectedness, along with the understanding of corelessness, of no solid self, helps us to stop clinging to our identity as we perceive it right now. Because there is no solid self, because we are in a constant state of flux and there is no core, when we try to hold on to identity, we suffer—we're trying to grasp something that doesn't exist. How frustrating. It's constantly being undermined and altered. We wind up spending so much time and energy trying to shore up this illusion. Fear and self-protection, judgment and shame all come out of this false perception.

Just as with impermanence, when we see the Truth of Not-Self we naturally let go. We see that there's nothing solid to hold on to, no satisfaction to be derived from being somebody.

In the Twelve Traditions of Alcoholics Anonymous, it says that "anonymity is the spiritual foundation" of all the traditions. This is referring specifically to not revealing your identity on a public level because, when the traditions were written, there had been some occurrences of people breaking their anonymity and then later going back to drinking. When this happened it hurt the image of A.A. But I think that the tradition has a more profound meaning: it points to the freedom awaiting us when we loosen our attachment to identity. Anonymity on the public level has become an insignificant matter 70 years into A.A.'s history, as its image is well-established now. But anonymity as the idea of not clinging to any idea of who we are is still a vital teaching. One of the ways this is formalized in the Buddhist tradition is that each monk or nun is given a new name when he or she is ordained. The old "self" is dead now. If changing identity is as easy as slipping into an orange robe, then how solid could it be after all? In Twelve Step groups, we use only our first names, another way of dropping identity. It's important to remember that neither of these rituals is the essence of letting go of identity. Lots of monks and lots of sober people still cling tightly to a sense of self. The real letting go happens inside and takes vigilant attention to the ways that we keep creating ourselves moment to moment.

As we practice mindfulness and insight meditation, we come to see these creations, these selves, as they take shape. With practice, we learn to recognize when different identities are arising and realign our relationship to them. We all have multiple personalities, and wisdom helps us to see them and use them toward skillful ends.

Prayer: I open myself to the flow of personality, without attachment or aversion. May I be free from clinging to limiting ideas of who I am and open to changing and growing in ways that will serve me and all beings.

Exercise: My Many Selves

In this exercise you will explore the ideas you have of who you are.

1. Gather pen and paper, then sit quietly for five minutes, following the breath and relaxing.

2. Now consider the roles you play in your life and write each one down. Who are you at work—your job title? Who are you at home and in your family? What other roles do you play? Hobbyist? Friend? Helper?

3. After listing these formal roles, start to look at the roles you play with your personality: the wit; the caregiver; the leader; the follower; the sexual object; the sexual prowler; the party animal; the mellow meditator.

4. Once you've written these all down, consider how these roles serve you or don't serve you. Is there suffering attached to any of your roles? Do you have to play that role?

5. Close your eyes again. Who are you now? Who are you if you drop all the roles?

THE HIGHER POWER
OF LOVE

*The Higher Power of Love is the underpinning of generosity
and service that drives human development. The power of love
weakens self-obsession and reveals our interconnectedness.
It is the source for joy, compassion, and fulfillment.*

The study of history can suggest to us that hatred is more powerful than love. Much of what is recorded is war and power struggles. Human beings have become more and more destructive, to the point that the 20th century was not only the most violent one in history, but the one in which we actually started to threaten the life of the planet itself with our actions.

And yet, when we look at our everyday lives, who is really remembered? Christ, Buddha, Muhammad, and other religious teachers are probably the historical figures brought to mind the most, as people perform their daily prayer and meditation and attend religious ceremonies. The teachings of the great religions are woven into our lives, our laws, and our cultures. It's clear that these beacons of love have had a great impact on human history.

The power of love in relation to hate is embodied in the Buddha's famous couplet from the Dhammapada: "Hatred never ceases by hatred, but by love alone is healed. This is the ancient and eternal law." The resolution of World War I shows the futility of punishing hatred. The Treaty of Versailles, which imposed severe hardships on Germany, only planted the seeds for the arising of Nazism and Hitler. On the other hand, the Marshall Plan after World War II, in which the Allies aided the aggressors of the war, Germany and Japan, wound up bringing those countries into the community of peaceful, democratic nations. The Truth and Reconciliation Commission in South Africa is another example of how a wronged people who could easily have tried to punish their former oppressors instead found a way to move beyond the hatred of apartheid.

This attitude works the same way in our daily lives. Most of us have had experiences with customer-service people on the phone: we call up to complain about some product or service, and the reaction of the person on the other end has a huge effect on how we proceed. Are they defensive? Uncooperative? Dismissive? If so, we're likely to get more frustrated and angry. Are they helpful? Empathetic? Conciliatory? Our attitude will become much more relaxed as we have the sense of being cared for.

On the other hand, if I call up in a rage, I don't usually get a lot of help. Who wants to help someone who is yelling at them?

Everyone gets criticized now and then, and how we respond to that, with love or with hate, with acceptance or resistance, has a big effect on the outcome. In the months leading up to my giving up drugs and alcohol, my girlfriend more than once pointed out my problems. She was smart and insightful and saw me more clearly than I saw myself. But I wasn't ready to absorb her insights.

We were living in a little bungalow in Venice Beach, California. The kitchen was just big enough for two people; the dining room barely held a table and chairs; the living room felt crowded with just a small couch and rocking chair. A narrow staircase led to the one bedroom upstairs. Cute as it was, the place could feel claustrophobic. When she said something to me that I didn't like, I'd feel the walls closing in. I'd strike back, yelling and even knocking over furniture. I'd try to get away from her, but the place was too tiny—there was nowhere to run. Finally, I would explode out the front door and dash down the street to the beach. At least the more extremes of violence from my 20s were past, but the same snarling rejection of the slightest whiff of criticism kept me edgily defensive.

This behavior is like protecting the walls of a fortress that is actually rotting from within. While all our attention is focused on the perceived threats outside the walls, the place is collapsing behind us without our even knowing it. Meanwhile our friends and family—and maybe therapists and spiritual guides—are trying to tell us, "Look inside yourself!" Instead of heeding their warnings, we keep blaming them for the way things are going: "If they would just stop criticizing me I'd be okay."

As long as I kept pushing back, as long as I let anger and resentment dominate, I stayed stuck on the wheel of self-destruction and emotional immaturity. When I finally surrendered to the truth of my condition, instead of being destroyed or wiped away by the admission of my addiction, I felt a huge relief. Acceptance, nonresistance to the truth, is one of the aspects of love, and I only discovered that when I dropped my resistance to seeing my own failings.

When I tapped into this aspect of love, my life began to change— finally. My efforts before were futile, partly because they were motivated by aversion and defensiveness—"I don't like this; I don't want to hear that." Not only *hatred* will not cease by hatred, but life itself can't be conquered with hatred. If we want happiness in our lives, we need to live in harmony with the Higher Power of Love.

Someone came up to me after a class I taught recently, obviously agitated, and said, "I really don't appreciate the way you talk about other religions. I think it's disrespectful." I was on the spot, standing there in front of a large Buddha statue in the role of a spiritual teacher. And, of course, I didn't like what he was saying. First I felt defensive, and I tried in my mind to pull out some parry to the thrust of his criticism. Then I felt a surge of anger: *Doesn't he know who I am . . . what an idiot . . . probably some kind of religious nut . . .* These thoughts and feelings passed through me as I tried to drop them and take in what he was saying. Obviously he was in pain, and I had triggered that.

As he wrapped up his comments, I knew I couldn't respond with defensiveness or anger—partly because, as I let those feelings pass, I knew there was some truth in his words, and partly because I knew that my role here was greater than my personal desire to be right or to look good. As a teacher, I have a responsibility to live out the teachings (which I obviously wasn't doing very well by judging other religions), and that means being as compassionate and non-harming as I can. He apparently didn't expect me to admit my error, because as I started to respond, he said, "You don't have to say anything." I can imagine how he felt. It must have been hard to get up the courage to confront me like that, and what if I came back with some blizzard of judgments or rationalizations? Instead I said, "You're right, and I'm sorry that I spoke in that way."

I could see the relief on his face. He'd been heard. And I felt relief in letting go of my own judgments and just admitting to my mistake— a Tenth Step, promptly making amends. His anger was immediately defused.

This points, in a way, to how the mere absence of hate is powerful. From a Buddhist perspective, then, it's not so necessary to try to make yourself loving; just stop hating and you will discover love quite naturally.

Addiction is an expression of hatred: hatred of our lives, our feelings, and ourselves. I couldn't stand the way I felt, so I drank and used drugs. I couldn't accept my life as it was, so I tried to blot it out. There's something essentially life-denying about addiction. When I try to escape reality, this present moment, I am turning away from life itself.

In 1984, the summer before I got sober, I was playing a gig at a hotel in Anchorage, Alaska. One day I got a call from a friend in California telling me that the leader of the band I had played with for several years, a percussionist and sax player named Lofty Amao, had been shot and killed in Venice Beach. The band he led, called Zzebra, had played African-based rock, and my time with him had transformed my understanding of music. It had also brought me closer to success in the music business than I'd ever gotten. That night, before the last set, I went to the bar and ordered a shot of Jack Daniel's, Lofty's drink, something I almost never drank. I chased it with a beer and had another shot. Then I walked on stage and told the band to follow me. I started playing a crazy bluegrass riff that I'd made up when I played with Lofty and that he loved. I was tumbling toward drunkenness, and the band members looked at me with worried expressions. But the audience ate up the riff, going into wild square dances, and we finished the night okay. I thought I was celebrating Lofty's life. But I wasn't; I was trying to kill my own life.

Some 20 years later, Lofty's wife, Mina, who was the keyboard player in Zzebra, organized a reunion. Their daughter was getting married, and she wanted her father's old band to play at the wedding. For a week we rehearsed in a farmhouse in Vermont, where we had originally formed. Far from the morbid grief I'd felt in Alaska, this gathering was full of love, joy, and intimacy. The wedding, in a broad meadow on the family farm, brought the past and present together in a healing celebration of Lofty's life and legacy. Rather than remembering him with self-destructive indulgence, this was an affirmation, an expression of the power of love.

The Higher Power of Love has to do with the actions that spring out of a sense of connection, caring, responsibility, and deep affection. When we act from these impulses, we change the world for the better. These feelings are natural human responses, but they are hard for the addict or alcoholic to access. Getting loaded cut me off from others, even though at times intoxication gave me that "I love you, man" sloppy affection. I cared about others only insofar as they could give me what I wanted, whether it was drugs, sex, money, or companionship. During those years when I was drinking and using—from 16 to 35—I was consistently irresponsible, doing only those things that satisfied my agenda. The blockage in my heart—I only discovered this when I began to practice lovingkindness meditation—rendered me disconnected and selfish, incapable of giving or receiving deep affection. As long as I couldn't really feel or express love, I couldn't understand what love really was. It's a vicious circle, our actions feeding our feelings and our feelings triggering our actions.

Ajahn Amaro says that in our culture we think of falling in love as the highest form of happiness. I remember times when I've been in this passionate trance. The feeling of intimacy I had with the object of my passion would bleed over into everyone I encountered. Walking down the street I'd feel a sense of connection with the toddler in the park struggling to walk, the homeless man going through the garbage for empty soda cans, the clerk in the bakery who gets me my muffin. When the heart is open, whether through a love affair or a lovingkindness meditation, the barriers break down and we recognize our innate interconnectedness.

The problem with passionate love is that it's temporary and conditional. As our emotions change, the whole sense of magic fades. Although this passion can lead to a loving and caring relationship, that sense of oneness usually passes. With Buddhist lovingkindness practices, what are called the *Brahma-Viharas* or Divine Abodes, we seek to make this spiritual connection—this falling in love with life—into something more reliable, not dependent upon illusory emotions but founded on our insight into interconnectedness and supported by our commitment to meditation.

The *Brahma-Viharas* include four emotions: *metta* or lovingkindness, *karuna* or compassion, *mudita* or sympathetic joy, and *upekkha* or equanimity.

Metta is the openhearted sense of loving connection. The practice of metta involves trying to send or spread lovingkindness to all beings, starting with ourselves (sometimes the toughest practice) and moving on to our loved ones, then to neutral people whom we have no particular feelings about, and finally to difficult people toward whom we feel some resentment, fear, or anger. This is a progressive process that helps us first get in touch with the basic feeling of lovingkindness, then start to become more and more generous with that feeling.

This practice can be naturally integrated into Twelve Step work as we move through the stages of recovery. The first stage of metta is starting to feel the heart. We breathe into it to gauge how open or closed we are. We are powerless over the state of our heart right now, so this is the first Step, the honest acceptance of where we are. Coming to believe and turning it over—Steps Two and Three—involve having confidence that the heart can be transformed and committing ourselves to the practices and life choices that make that possible.

As we open the heart with these practices, we see the history of damage and pain we've caused in the world—our inventory. As we stay with the practices, over time and with consistent effort, the heart opens—our "character defects" are removed, as Steps Six and Seven say.

Karuna—compassion—is also part of this process. Metta is fundamentally the wish that all beings might be happy and safe. Karuna recognizes that this isn't always going to be true. As we do our Step work, we open to our own suffering in ways we'd always resisted when we were getting loaded and trying to run from pain. It's important that we have a sense of caring for our own pain, recognizing that we have suffered. It's easy to judge ourselves and our actions; it's not that we shouldn't be held accountable, but when we understand the Noble Truth of Suffering, we understand that life is challenging, that it's full of pain and struggles. As we go through the Steps uncovering our inventory and our powerlessness, we need to take care that we are kind to ourselves, understanding and forgiving. We also need to take care of others, to see that there is nothing unique about the nature of our suffering, that it is shared, in one form or another, by all beings. This is the heart of karuna, the caring that arises in the open heart when we see suffering in others. When we have acknowledged and explored our own suffering, we realize that we aren't alone in the challenges of life, and when our heart is open, we naturally feel concern and empathy for others who are struggling.

Mudita is the flipside of karuna: where compassion is feeling with someone else's pain, sympathetic joy is feeling with someone else's happiness. This is another aspect of sensing interconnectedness. We instinctively feel mudita when we see a cute baby or a puppy; when our child comes home with a blue ribbon or our partner lands the job she was seeking; when we go to our best friend's wedding.

In other situations mudita might not be so natural. When our colleague gets the promotion we wanted; when the neighbor comes home with the new car we can't afford; when someone in our writing group gets the six-figure deal.

What I think the Buddha is telling us in his teaching on mudita is that envy and jealousy will only cause us more pain. If we understand interconnectedness, then doesn't another person's happiness belong to us, too? If we can feel other people's pain, can't we also feel their joy? If we wish other people happiness, we'll discover that we also feel happy—and the opposite is true, as well: If we wish failure for others, we create pain for ourselves. We gain no benefit by wishing others unhappiness.

Of course, this is an ideal. I can't pretend that I have perfected mudita for all beings, but I do try to see when my lack of mudita is hurting me. Mindfulness is always the key to change. When I see that I'm obsessing over someone else's success, I can at least defuse that negative energy by watching it carefully, even if I can't arouse a lot of joy for that person right now.

Jealousy is based on the belief that there is only so much success to go around—the zero-sum game. My first creative-writing teacher talked about viewing other people's success in the class differently. He said that we should realize that when other people we are working with get a book deal, it means we are in a place where people are succeeding, that these are the people we should want to be around. We're much more likely to benefit from being in a group with a successful writer than with one who isn't any good.

Beyond the specific form of mudita that encourages us to take joy in other's happiness, mudita also has the quality of appreciating life. Mudita reminds us to enjoy the simple pleasures, to drink in life's beauty and richness. The Big Book says that "God wants us to be happy, joyous, and free," and indeed, any spiritual work would be pretty pointless if it weren't fostering this.

These first three of the Brahma-Viharas focus on the sense of relatedness we have with all beings, loving them, caring about them, and celebrating life with them. Equanimity, on the other hand, reminds us of the limits of this connection. Our love, compassion, and shared joy can't fix anyone else, any more than another person's feelings can fix us. They are still responsible for themselves as we are for ourselves. Upekkha—equanimity—gives us peace because it means we don't have to be responsible for things beyond our control. It means we need to take care of ourselves, of our own mind stream. Equanimity gives us the balance we need to accept and hold the challenges of life; it means that we aren't knocked over by craving or aversion, by the pleasant or the unpleasant; it means that we don't get lost in our concern for others. In some sense, then, equanimity is really the love we give ourselves.

In equanimity practice, we start to notice how every moment of sense experience causes a reaction in us—pleasant, unpleasant, or neutral. These reactions, called *vedana,* are the automatic feelings that arise when we hear a jackhammer or a Mozart sonata; when we smell rotting fish or baking bread; when we see a homeless person or a movie star. We tend to be swept away by these feelings and to act on them without thinking. Addiction is like this: blindly following instinctive reactions to the point of self-destruction. When we learn to bring mindfulness to these reactions, we can open to a broader sense of experience, seeing that the pleasant doesn't mean *good,* that the unpleasant doesn't mean *bad.* These are just sense experiences that can be known with wisdom and let go. Sometimes wisdom will tell us we need to act, and other times we'll see that there's no need to do anything. We can just let it be.

The more equanimity we bring to our experience, the freer we are. When we can choose our reactions rather than stumble into them, we have a greater chance of making wise choices. Equanimity is perhaps the most admired quality in Buddhist teachings, as it embodies the essence of non-clinging, that which brings true freedom and awakening.

One of the things that makes love a power greater than ourselves is that it inspires us to do things that don't exactly serve any self-interest or personal need, but wind up serving others. When my daughter was born, I got this on the deepest level I'd ever known. She was delivered by caesarean section, and I stood by my wife in the operating room while the surgeon's boom box played Aretha Franklin singing, "You make me feel like a natural woman." I was focusing on my wife during the procedure, encouraging and supporting her as her belly was sliced open. I was a bit dazed when the baby came out and they handed her to me. I held her to my breast and carried her down the hall to the room where she would be weighed and measured. The overwhelming feeling of wanting to protect her flowed out of me as I talked continuously to her. When, in the middle of the weighing, her lips started to suck, a signal that she was ready to nurse, I scooped her up, despite the nurse's protests, and whisked her back to my wife, where she latched on just as she was supposed to. Everything I was thinking, feeling, and doing was for her. This instinctive response to my own child was what the Buddha chooses as the most profound example of love when he says in the Lovingkindness (Metta) Sutta, "Even as a mother protects with her life her child, her only child; so with a boundless heart should one cherish all living beings."

Love, then, according to the Buddha, shouldn't be limited to the personal; it should be universal. The Buddha tells us to cultivate this feeling within so that we can spread it to all beings. Although love is natural and instinctive, like mindfulness it needs to be developed in order to fulfill its potential. But once someone has developed a loving heart, it will touch people in all kinds of ways.

Certainly the love of a mother or father can be powerful. The Buddha says we could carry our parents around on our shoulders for the rest of their lives and it wouldn't repay them for the care they gave us when we were infants and children. The only way we can repay our parents, says the Buddha, is to teach them the Dharma.

Although this teaching may not resonate for someone whose childhood was poisoned by alcoholic or abusive parents, I think we've all encountered people in our lives who have acted with spontaneous love and generosity toward us. This kindness can take many forms.

My first English professor changed my life with just a few words. We were standing in the hallway outside the classroom on the last day of the semester, with students swarming around us. We'd been friendly throughout the term—we were probably about the same age, this community college teacher and me, the recovering alcoholic trying to start a new life. "Have you ever thought about being a writer?" he asked.

I don't remember my exact response, but I remember the feeling: *No! I'm trying to find a real occupation! Being a writer would be just another version of being a musician!*

Despite my resistance, though, I was flattered. I'd done well in the class and loved the exercises he'd given us. Even though I told him I didn't want to be a writer, I couldn't resist signing up the next semester for the creative-writing class he recommended.

He didn't have to do any of this. Community college teachers are overworked, with as many as ten courses to teach each year, 50 or more students enrolled in the classes. Taking the time and interest to encourage an individual student, one who isn't even asking for help, is not necessary. But I believe this was an expression of love, an act of generosity and caring, a spontaneous offering springing from his appreciation of writing, of my work, of human potential. That one suggestion set in motion the events that led me here, to writing this book. An act like that comes out of non-selfishness, a sense of caring and responsibility. And it changes the world.

Prayer: I open my heart to love. I vow to cultivate generosity and unconditional lovingkindness for all beings. I will seek to abandon hatred and meet anger with compassion.

Exercise: Triggers to Anger

Before we can love, we must let go of hate. Each of us has triggers that set off our anger. This exercise helps us identify and let go of those triggers.

1. Gather pen and paper and find a quiet place to sit. Begin with a few minutes of mindfulness meditation.

2. Now, reflect on what makes you angry. Each time you think of something, write it down. Begin with the personal: family, work, and friends. Then explore the social and political and other external influences on your anger. Write each one down.

3. Once you have the list, look at each trigger and ask yourself why it makes you angry. What in you is reacting to this stimulus?

4. Anger is set off by many things: our defensiveness, our sense of justice, our beliefs and opinions, and our sense of safety in the world. Some responses are logical and some are emotional.

5. Ayya Khema says that our reactions to triggers are never caused by the trigger, but are always coming from inside us.

6. As you look at the triggers, ask yourself how your reaction is serving you. If you didn't react in this way, what would happen? Is there another way to respond to this situation?

7. When you are done, choose one of the triggers to include in your mindfulness practice. For the next week, notice every time the trigger arises and make the commitment not to react in your usual, automatic way. See if you can break the habit of reactivity to this trigger.

The Higher Power of the Eightfold Path

The Higher Power of the Eightfold Path is the power that leads to the end of suffering. Its components reach into every aspect of our lives, challenging us to live wisely and kindly, and guiding us to freedom.

The Eightfold Path is the Buddha's prescription for freedom. According to his teachings, these eight factors have the power to turn us from what he called "worldlings," normal everyday people under the spell of greed, hatred, and delusion, into enlightened beings. Each of these factors has its own power.

I've already talked about Mindfulness, considered by Buddhists to be the crowning tool of the path. Now I'd like to talk about the Higher Power inherent in the other aspects of the Eightfold Path.

The Eightfold Path is traditionally configured in two different ways, depending on the *sutta* (the Buddhist discourses) where it appears. While structurally it is said to follow the order of *sila, samadhi, panna* (morality, concentration, wisdom), when its aspects are presented in a list, the wisdom elements come first, followed by the morality elements, and finally the concentration or meditative elements. I will use the latter order.

A note on language: the aspects of the Eightfold Path are often called "Right" or "Wise." The word in Pali is *samma,* which, according to Ajahn Amaro, "is a musical term meaning 'attuned' or 'well-tuned,'" a definition that fits nicely with the idea of living in harmony with a Higher Power. When we call something Right Effort, it's not so much that our effort is right or wrong, but rather that it is either in or out of tune with what is wise or wholesome. This allows for gradations, for being closer to being in harmony or further away. Most of us are at some midpoint on the path, our effort and mindfulness and intention mixed, not right, not wrong. The important thing is that we are on the path, committed to growing, aimed in the right direction. Having said all this, I admit that I'm so used to the terminology of "Right" that I find that easiest to work with, but I hope you will understand the word in the context of being attuned.

VIEW

Right View sees the truth and inspires us to follow the path. It connects suffering and its cause, showing us the root of our problem; it sees that actions bring results, thus inspiring us to live wholesomely, guided by spiritual principles. When perfected, Right View is synonymous with enlightenment.

Right View is, in the listed formulation of the path, the first step. Having Right View means that we understand the Four Noble Truths. It means that when we hear the Dharma we say, "That sounds right," rather than "I disagree" or "Huh?" The power of Right View guides us and inspires us to step onto the path; it energizes us to take on the arduous work of spiritual development. Without this vision we are blind to the truth of suffering and to the way out of suffering. Without this power we continue to react to the world in ways that lead to more suffering.

It's not easy to overcome a lifetime's, or perhaps many lifetimes', conditioning, to go against our own culture, and to take on the work of uprooting the hatred, greed, fear, and confusion that are so deeply embedded in us. To begin this work, a powerful vision of the futility of chasing pleasure must enter our hearts, together with the possibility of another way. In the same way, it is the insight into the suffering and pointlessness of our addiction that inspires our recovery. Right View is this vision, an awakening to the fundamentally unsatisfactory nature of life as it's commonly lived and a realization that letting go rather than accumulating is where freedom lies. This vision is the starting point of the path, the spark that ignites our commitment to seek another way, and it is the "moment of clarity" that brings us to Step One's admission of powerlessness.

I was living through a cold Vermont winter when I first encountered a book on Buddhism, Chögyam Trungpa's *Meditation in Action*. I'd just learned Transcendental Meditation and was meditating religiously twice a day. Crazy things were happening in the outside world, a mayor and city supervisor assassinated in San Francisco and 900 people poisoned by their cult leader in South America. But my world was the cocoon of a magical Afro-rock band, music that had helped to inspire me to begin a spiritual journey. My walk-up studio apartment was on the third floor of a building on the main street of Burlington, a block away from the club that our band played regularly. The old building had ten-foot ceilings and rattling radiators, and my place was barely furnished. I sat on the bed and worked my way through this short book with wide eyes. Something I'd looked for all my life had finally arrived: a way of seeing the world that made sense. A little chime went off in my heart with an arrow pointing "This Way." It was the beginning of Right View for me.

To have Right View about the Dharma isn't enough, though. When I read that book, I connected with the teachings and felt that I understood what they were talking about; what I didn't see was how my own way of living was so out of touch with Right View. While I saw the first Noble Truth, the Truth of Suffering, in my life, I didn't see how my addiction was causing that, and I didn't see how so much of my approach to life was unrealistic. While the Eightfold Path made perfect sense to me, I really only engaged in the meditative aspects of it, and even those in a limited way. I never embraced bringing the Buddhist teachings into every aspect of my life.

For the seven years between first learning about Buddhism and getting sober, an inner struggle took place between my increasingly wise view and my addictive, confused view. My spiritual hunger fought with the deeply conditioned impulse to act on my cravings. Against the background of my personal history, my family and genetic history, and the culture of drugs and alcohol I lived in with my music career, the eventual triumph of Right View over addiction is an indication of the power of the Dharma.

When I got sober, even though for a few years I was less engaged in Buddhism, Right View actually grew in me. Seeing the truth of my addiction was, of course, a vital breakthrough. Dealing with the basics of life, work, money, relationships, and living ethically and responsibly deepened my understanding of how karma works, and I had increasing clarity of view.

This refining of understanding goes on to this day. The layers of conditioned craving and ignorance continue to resist growth even as I work to strip them away. Right View is not just something we have or don't have. It can be cultivated. Practicing mindfulness, engaging life with openness and curiosity, being willing to challenge our beliefs and assumptions, all deepen our understanding of Right View. That's how we tap into its power. The "higher" or more in tune our view gets, the more clearly we see the truth, and the more wise we become. As we develop the rest of the path, view is developed as well. The culmination of Right View is enlightenment, the highest view. In this way, Right View is seen as both the beginning and the end of the path.

Prayer: I commit my heart and mind to the search for truth, to seeing the Dharma in all things. May I be free from ignorance.

INTENTION

*Right Intention gives clarity, direction, and resolve on the path.
With Right Intention, we are never entirely lost no matter
how much we stray. Right Intention guides us back to
ourselves and the values of kindness and wisdom.*

Right Intention is stimulated by Right View. When we see the truth of the way things are, whether of our addiction or just of our own human struggles, we know that we need to change our lives, and we begin to see how that can happen. We set the intention to follow the path. Once we have set our intention, we are clear in our goals and our means. This is the power of Right Intention: to set us firmly on the path, heading toward freedom and always knowing what direction we need to go. Each time we lose our way, or drift from our breath, when we wake up, our intention sets us straight again. All the factors of the path depend on and are driven by intention.

As I've explained, intention is the fuel for karma; the motivation we bring to an action is one of the critical determining factors of the result of that action. As we progress on the path and watch our own minds, we become more attuned to intention. At first we might think our intentions are straightforward, but as we begin to see more clearly, we realize that all intentions, except for the highest, are mixed. Even as we are doing service, we'll find some egotism or greed, some expectation of reward. Even as we express anger or resentment, we may also find that there is a trace of wisdom or piercing insight.

This mixture of intention may be what allows us to get sober. Even when we are caught in our addiction, there is some part of us that wants to change, some intention to heal. There's a way in which people demonize their pre-sober selves: "Before sober: bad. After sober: good." They attribute their recovery to the intervention of some external God, as though they did nothing themselves to bring it about. From a Buddhist viewpoint this makes no sense. We have to have laid some karmic foundation for change, and since intention is what conditions karma, then we must have had some intention to recover. For many of us, it's quite apparent that we had mixed intentions for a long time. My history of a spiritual search alongside a persistent drug and alcohol habit is an obvious example. It is, of course, a dangerous mixture because the positive intention may not win out, as we see in so many people who struggle to get sober.

The power of intention also has the quality of attracting assistance. As we gain clarity about where we are going, the universe seems to become more welcoming and helpful. A kind of snowball effect develops as both external and internal forces become more concentrated and focused. I've seen this at many stages of my recovery. Once I'd made the decision to go back to school, many things fell into place, such as scholarships and grants, guidance from teachers, and even jobs that suited my needs; at the same time, my own direction became more and more clear and my energy and motivation grew. When I committed to writing about Buddhism and recovery, friends helped me with both the business and creative ends of the work; at the same time, my own understanding of the subject deepened as I fixed my gaze on the topic.

The highest goal of the spiritual life is full enlightenment—and in Mahayana Buddhism, enlightenment for all beings—a word whose meaning can perhaps never be fully apprehended, but which points to a sense of freedom, serenity, and wisdom surpassing that of normal human experience. Certainly this was the intention that drove the Buddha through his years of struggle before his attainment. After his enlightenment, it's pretty clear that his intention became freeing people from suffering. That, I believe, was his sole remaining intention, if indeed a fully enlightened being actually has something we can call intention. (This is a question for theologians and philosophers, not alcoholic Buddhist authors.) The Buddha's example gives us a good idea what we ourselves might want to strive for.

Any change, any growth, any attainment must be preceded by intention. As we strive to stay sober and grow on the path, we keep referring back to intention: *What do I want to accomplish now? How do I need to change? What still stands in the way of my happiness?* As we answer these questions, we become more clear about what our intention needs to be. In my daily practice, I've found it helpful to put some time aside in the morning to set my intention both for that day and for my ongoing spiritual work. That way, as situations arise in the day that challenge me or give me the chance to work on the issue that I'm concerned with, I tend to remember because it's fresh in my mind. My intention acts as a trigger for mindfulness, and then the mindfulness opens up my awareness to the possibility of change, helping me avoid a conditioned response to a situation and instead make a wise choice based on my higher intention.

But, whatever our goals and intention, we have to remember that we just point ourselves in a direction. We don't get to decide where we actually arrive. In Step Three, when we turn our will over to the care of God, we're trying to align our intention with that of God, to live in harmony. There is always the risk, when we do that, of having expectations. It's easy to get caught in the idea that, since we're trying to do our best, God will, or should, give us what we want. When I started writing fiction after going back to college, it felt like I was just following the guidance of wise people, not my own ego. I finished a novel while still an undergrad, and one of my professors got his agent to represent me. Everything was falling into place, and I believed that I was "meant" to publish a novel, that it was inevitable. As months passed and the agent couldn't find a publisher, disappointment set in. Then I got accepted to graduate school in creative writing, and my hopes were revived. I went off to Southern California and wrote a second novel. Another teacher became my advocate and success was assured—or so I thought. When the rejection letters started coming in again, I began to lose confidence as I recognized the flaws in the novel. As graduation approached I was devastated. I hadn't reached my goal, and I didn't have a backup plan. It took a year of temp work before I found my way into an occupation—technical writing—that I could depend on. What had happened? Why had things gone wrong?

When I went back to school it was with a simple intention of becoming employable outside the music business. When I started writing I was relatively innocent about what I was doing, but over time, I tried to take over God's job—the results of my actions. The aspect of my intention that was *Right* Intention was the part that wanted to learn and grow. Right Intention means that we don't so much aim for specific results, but rather try to act in harmony with the Dharma, that we try to work toward kindness, wisdom, and service. How that will work out isn't our business, and if we get attached to results, we'll often be disappointed. Obviously, my writing career eventually worked out, but not in the way I planned. As the joke goes, if you want to hear God laugh, tell him your plans.

Prayer: I open my heart to the wisdom and power of my highest intention. May I stay attuned to it and follow it always.

SPEECH

> *Right Speech transforms our relationships, bringing*
> *harmony into social interactions. Through the power of*
> *speech we heal our wounds and give of our wisdom.*

Right Speech is the quality of speaking kindly, truthfully, and wisely. Speech is one of the most powerful human instruments—think of the speeches of Martin Luther King, Jr., or Hitler. Speech can transform our lives and those of others. When we speak we give voice to thoughts, and if we watch our thoughts for a while we will see the risks inherent in this enterprise.

As a Dharma teacher I have a privileged position from which to learn about Right Speech. When I sit in front of a group of meditators my responsibility is right in front of me. My experience speaking in Twelve Step meetings has allowed me to be comfortable sharing with a group of people, and over time I've seen that my own personality is more suited to relatively spontaneous teaching than tightly organized talks. This, unfortunately, creates other challenges. While my Twelve Step experience has taught me to speak from the heart, my earlier family experience embedded some less wholesome habits of speech. Occasionally that cynical and sarcastic conditioning pokes through the more gentle and kind words. When I'm teaching, it's obvious how out of place this is, and I get pretty quick feedback. Sometimes the words don't actually come out of my mouth, I just see them form in my mind and let go.

It's much harder for me at home to restrain my speech. Again, because my conditioning is so deep from my family of origin, I tend to pass that on to my new family, my wife and daughter. I have recently begun taking a daily vow at the end of my morning meditation to avoid teasing and sarcasm, the two things that they object to most strenuously. They probably haven't noticed a change, but I am aware now of many times when a sarcastic thought comes up, I see it, and instead of saying it, I just let go. Of course, I forget plenty of times and things slip out, but even then, because of the vow, I tend to notice it. It's very interesting to embark on an effort like this because when I have a sarcastic thought there's a strong pull inside to say it. When I restrain myself, at first it can feel unnatural, like refusing to shake someone's hand when it's held out to you. In that moment I get to feel the force of conditioning, of karma, and to see how my own choice in that moment allows that karma to begin to change.

It takes tremendous attention and care to develop Right Speech. Even in the monasteries it is said to be the precept most commonly broken. In Twelve Step programs, speech is perhaps the prime tool for healing. When we share at meetings we learn the power of telling the truth—and being heard.

Speech has the power to change our lives, inside and out. The words we use and the energy behind them also trigger our own emotional states—think of how you feel when you are shouting at someone versus speaking gently. In order to cultivate this power, we have to first explore the ways in which we habitually interact and how we harm ourselves and others with these habits. As with each of the elements of the Eightfold Path, mindfulness underpins Right Speech. In order to change speech, we have to pay close attention to thought, impulse, and intention. Then, instead of blurting out some unskillful words, we take the time—often just a moment, but a critical moment—to consider whether to speak and, if so, what to say.

This process points to the interaction of the different aspects of God or Higher Power. Rather than seeing God as a monolithic entity, we see that it has many facets. As we come to understand and cultivate the positive aspects of these facets, we "improve our conscious contact" with God and come more into harmony with the laws of the universe.

Speaking our truth in a group or ritual setting can have special power. When I first got up the courage to share in Twelve Step meetings, I was amazed how I felt afterward, lifted up, freed of a heavy weight. And once I let people know who I was, it allowed them in, it gave them the chance to connect with me.

Recently I had a powerful experience of using speech to bring change. I participated in a Toltec journey at an ancient pyramid site near Mexico City. We walked into this tourist spot, where dozens of school groups and people with cameras and maps were strolling through the ruins of the majestic city. Our first exercise was in a sunken plaza surrounded by stone walls, and as we moved into the space, the leader asked us to walk around the football-field-sized area and find an object that could represent something we wanted to let go of. As I started to walk toward the imposing walls, I looked down and saw the dried, trampled grass beneath my feet and realized that I didn't really want to look at that ugliness. I immediately thought of the ugly sadness in me that I don't want to look at—the roots of depression that I'm afraid to see. I stooped to the grass and picked up a blade of dried grass like a piece of hay. As I walked around some more, I spotted a toy arrow, the kind the local vendors sold along with bows for kids to play with at the site.

After a little while the leader called us together and we formed a circle in one of the corners of the plaza. He created a kind of altar with a few stones in the middle. One by one the participants moved into the middle of the circle and showed the rest of us the symbols of what they wanted to abandon, and each one spoke to explain what the symbols meant to them. The leader then did some energy practices, a kind of laying on of hands, to help them complete the letting go.

Standing there with my little strand of hay, I breathed and got grounded, letting myself feel into what I wanted to let go of, the knot in my belly and a lingering sadness. I felt more and more clear and more and more committed to the process, until I finally stepped into the circle and fell to my knees in surrender before the altar.

"This represents the ugly part of me that I am afraid to feel," I said, holding up the piece of hay. I tossed it onto the altar. "And this," I said, holding up the arrow, "represents the part of me that wants to escape, to see only the beautiful." I snapped the arrow and threw it on the altar. "I am letting go of my fear of sadness now!" I stated with vehemence and sincerity.

To complete the exercise, I had to tell a specific person what I was committing to, so I walked up to a friend in the circle, put my hands on his shoulders, stared into his eyes and practically shouted, "I'm ready to let go of my fear of sadness."

"I believe you," he said.

We hugged and I went back to my place in the circle. Breathing and grounding myself again, I realized that the knot in the belly was gone. All the sadness had now left my body. I felt happy and light.

While this was a more ritualized version of what happens in a Twelve Step meeting, it felt very similar to the relief of sharing in one of those meetings. It also had the quality of a vow, one of the practices in Mahayana Buddhism. The really transforming elements of the ritual, like those of a vow, were the sense of presence and mindfulness and the strength of intention behind my words. When made aloud, the vow adds the power of the witnessing community. Finally, the audible quality of a spoken vow, which engages our sense of hearing, has a distinctly different, and deeper, effect than words we simply say in our minds. The physicality of sound, the actual waves of air hitting the eardrum, tends to produce a stronger imprint on the memory than a thought.

The next day we prepared for a ritual that focused on death. The leader had two women who were experienced in these practices act as "Angels of Death" standing between the group and the plaza, which represented the earth. In this plaza we would each create our own expression of letting go of our physical body. But first we had to convince the angels that we were ready. As I walked up to the woman I had to go past, I felt a tremendous presence and power.

"Are you ready?" she asked me as we stood face to face, staring into each other's eyes.

I almost didn't recognize the voice that came out of me, deep, resonant, and forceful. "I am ready."

"You may pass," said the angel.

I walked mindfully to the steep stone steps that surrounded the plaza and sat down to watch the others complete the ritual. As I sat there I closed my eyes and immediately went into a deep meditation. These rituals had brought me into a place that I usually get to only after days of silent meditation. The Higher Power of Speech had freed me in ways I had never expected.

There are many ways we use speech, from the casual to the holy, and each one has power. While a million thoughts may pass through our minds, only certain ones pass our lips. If we use speech skillfully it can be transforming, bringing peace and harmony to our world and bringing freedom to our hearts.

Prayer: I vow to refrain from the use of false or harmful speech and to speak with love and wisdom; may my words bring harmony and freedom.

Exercise: Mindful Listening

Experiment with using this exercise in different contexts: sitting in a business meeting; in a Twelve Step meeting; standing on the sidewalk talking to a neighbor; working with a therapist. It's also a good practice to use when listening to a Dharma talk. Any time you are listening to someone else speak is an appropriate place to use mindful listening. If you have time, go through the whole exercise. If not, just focus in on your body for a moment.

1. First, take a discreet deep breath, not drawing attention to yourself, but allowing the breath to go further into your body. As you exhale, relax.

2. Now, find a place in the body where your attention can rest. This might be the arms or legs; the belly or back; your hands or feet; even your face. You might prefer to just feel your breath.

3. As your attention rests on this part of the body, be aware of the sensations happening there. Don't try to get too meticulous, just get a general sense of the constellation of sensations in that area of the body. Once in a while, take another deep, calming breath.

85

4. Keeping a large degree of attention on the body sensations, notice that you can still listen to every word being said. Having attention on the body doesn't diminish your ability to hear and comprehend.

5. As you listen, notice your own thoughts. Are you commenting on what the person is saying? Planning a response? Wishing you weren't here? Whatever is appearing in your mind, just be aware that this is a passing thought, and come back to body sensations and listening.

6. If you have a response to the speaker, see if this response appears in the body as well as the mind. How does judging feel? How does it feel to agree with someone? To disagree? All of these thoughts have corresponding physical manifestations. Instead of following the thoughts, follow the body and drop the thoughts.

7. Continue to listen in this way until it is your time to speak.

Exercise: Mindful Speech

Speaking mindfully is very similar to listening mindfully—only harder. It's very difficult to separate spoken words from thoughts, and thus from ego. This work requires great determination.

1. Before you speak, make the inner commitment to try to be as mindful as possible as you are talking.

2. Again, take a deep breath before you start, relaxing the body and trying to bring some calm to the mind.

3. Use awareness of the body to ground yourself in the present moment. Some people like to pay attention to a more or less neutral place, such as the arms and legs, while others find that watching the sensations in the belly and chest, where emotions are most evident, is more helpful. Experiment for yourself and see what works for you.

4. Now that you've paused and grounded yourself, begin to speak, keeping as much attention in the body as you can. As you speak, take time to select your words. Before you say something, quickly consider whether the thought you're having is one that can be communicated usefully. Is there a way to modulate your words for better effect? Be careful that your words are accurate. Words like *always, never,* and *should* are hard to prove; *usually, rarely,* and *might* are often more accurate.

5. Try not to rush, just keeping some attention in the body and some on the mind, noticing how your mind state changes as you speak. Notice how speech itself becomes a driving energy, and try not to be swept along by it. At any time, you can stop speaking, take a breath, and re-center your attention in the body.

6. Often when we are speaking, others interrupt us. If this happens, see how that feels. Is there a physical sensation that comes in response? A sense of incompleteness? Of frustration? Can you let go of that and move into mindful listening?

With mindful speech, compassion and love are aroused, and these qualities stimulate the deep, intuitive parts of the mind, allowing a free-flowing wisdom to manifest. Because we aren't speaking out of the place of asserting our identity, but rather from a place of openness and calm, mindful speaking becomes a form of investigative meditation.

ACTION

Right Action triggers the power of karma. It is a simple guide to God's will and puts us in harmony with the moral fabric of the universe. Right Action transforms our relationships with others by building trust and unity; it transforms our relationship with ourselves by building self-esteem, blamelessness, and clarity.

The term *Right Action* is just shorthand for the Five Precepts, the moral rules the Buddha taught as guides to skillful action in the world. Coming more into harmony with Right Action is perhaps the most direct way to change our lives, at least on the outside (which of course, has a direct effect on the inside).

The precepts start with not killing, probably the most universal law of human civilization. In Buddhism, though, these guidelines point to more than just how we behave. They are meant to help us end suffering for ourselves and others. It's pretty obvious how not killing keeps us from causing suffering to others. But it also benefits us, not just because it keeps us on the right side of the law, but because it helps us to let go of hatred, one of the three "poisons" the Buddha described as the cause of the endless cycle of suffering. Not killing is just the starting point, the gross external form in which we begin to address this poison. As we explore the impulse to harm other beings (not just humans), we open the door to the dark side of our nature. If we are ever going to overcome our own anger, resentment, and conflicts, we are going to have to see this aspect of ourselves clearly, to feel it, to taste it, to fully take in its implications. Touching these forces within ourselves, we see the pain that they cause us and others. When we explore this energy, we see its universal quality—the poison of hatred is not "mine," it doesn't belong to me, it doesn't define me, I am not hatred. It is something that comes over me unbidden—in a sense, I am powerless over hatred. This opens us to greater compassion for everyone who experiences hatred. This is why the Vietnamese Zen master Thich Nhat Hanh is able to write a poem in which he expresses compassion for a young girl, one of the boat people escaping Vietnam, raped by pirates *and* for the pirates who rape her. He understands that suffering is not just *being* harmed, but that *harming itself* is suffering. The fire of hatred and cruelty that burns inside a rapist is agony. This absolutely does not mean that rapists, or any violent criminals, do not bear full responsibility for their actions; they do. What it means for us is that if we have hatred for those who hate, we are causing ourselves suffering. If we profess a commitment to love and peace, then we only undermine that commitment when we selectively hate others and wish violence on them.

Ultimately, then, the power of the first precept is the power of love. The fulfillment of the precept is not just to refrain from killing, but to care for living beings.

The second precept, not stealing, also has layers of meaning. It serves a social purpose by keeping people's possessions safe. On a deeper level, it is the antidote to the poison of greed. This is the prime force that the Buddha says, in the Second Noble Truth, is the cause of suffering. Our continual grasping after objects, people, feelings, and experiences keeps us stuck on the wheel of *samsara*. Greed is the energy of addiction. As with hatred, we first address greed by coming to know it.

One of the first forms of Buddhist meditation I learned was the *noting* practice. In this practice, you make soft mental notes of thoughts as you notice them appearing in the mind. I learned to simply note whether a thought was one of greed (wanting) or hatred (aversion). Quickly I came to see that virtually every thought had some element of one or the other or both of these qualities, even if it was a "positive" greed, like the desire for freedom. As I came in touch with desire in this way, I saw how painful it was, that it contained the feeling of lack, of not having enough, of needing something else to complete me, make me happy, make me whole. Our culture makes a virtue of greed—"Greed, for lack of a better word, is good," says the rapacious Gordon Gekko in the film *Wall Street*. But when we look closely, we see that desire, greed, wanting, can never be satisfied. The simple rule of karma—that which we repeat becomes stronger—means that the more we act on greed, the more greedy we become. Instead of satisfying our desire, the ostensible purpose of greed, we in fact wind up with more desires.

The precept of not stealing, then, has the ultimate purpose of freeing us from the grip of this voracious beast. It is the beginning of letting go. It is the beginning of the end of addiction. In meditation practice we learn this in a simple way: We sit still. As we sit, desires arise and, at least for the period of meditation, we don't act on them—even though we may continue to think about them. As we continue this process and this practice, we cultivate the quality of renunciation, of dropping desire, and, ironically enough, we become more and more satisfied—after all, if we don't want anything, we are by definition satisfied. In this way we realize the flipside of the rule of karma: That which we don't repeat becomes weaker. This is the power of letting go that we cultivate by taking the precept of not stealing.

The third precept is the commitment to non-harming with our sexuality. This addresses a particular form of desire. When used for its primary biological purpose, sex is perhaps the most amazing and miraculous power in the universe: this body is able to join with another body to generate a new body. Wow! If that's not an expression of Higher Power, then I don't know what is. The challenge with our sexuality is how to use it skillfully. Monks and nuns don't act on their sexuality. That doesn't mean they aren't still sexual beings. They live with that energy without acting on it. As a young man, I thought that satisfying sexual desire was the way to happiness. Just as with greed and hatred, this only fed my craving.

But sex isn't like drugs and alcohol. I can stop drinking and using, but I can't stop having a body. For many people the obsession to drink and use disappears, but sexual energy, in one form or another, lives on even for those who completely give up sex. For noncelibate lay people the challenge can be great. What is skillful? What is normal? Single people are faced with the question of when to get involved sexually. For addicts this is a very tough question. Many of us find in recovery that we have no idea how to manage our sexual relationships. Once I was sober, this was perhaps the overriding issue of recovery for the first seven or eight years, at least until I met the woman I would go on to marry. But even then, negotiating a married sex life is not easy.

Our culture has such a confused relationship with sex. On the one hand, it's everywhere in the media. Just to go through the checkout line at the supermarket is to be faced with images that verge on the pornographic. On the other hand, authentic discussions about sex are rare. Whom do we talk about sex with? Our buddies in the locker room? Our girlfriends in the powder room? These aren't places where we'll find much insight. Sexual addiction is perhaps the most rapidly growing addiction because of the availability of pornography on the Internet. And pornography is the biggest business on the Internet. While alcoholism and drug addiction have become more or less socially acceptable—I can pretty comfortably say to someone I've just met at a party, "I'm a recovering alcoholic"—sex addiction still has the kind of stigma that alcoholism had in the 1930s. When I first heard the concept of sex addiction, I thought, *That doesn't sound so bad. I wish I could have enough sex to get addicted.* The term is confusing—it doesn't really refer to addiction in the strictest sense, but rather to the obsession with various behaviors and the compulsion to act on them. We can be completely obsessed with something and never actually do it; sex addiction takes many forms and is fundamentally about the suffering caused by that obsession.

Whenever I've brought up issues of sexuality in men's meditation groups, there's been a palpable sense of relief as people shared and realized that their struggles weren't at all unique. The best thing we can do to heal our sexual wounds is to connect with others and reveal our pain and our confusion.

The question, then, of how to turn our sexuality over to a Higher Power is a challenging one. Again, we begin by bringing mindfulness to bear. What feels right? What doesn't? Am I overwhelmed with addictive craving? Am I feeding that? How can I have a sense of comfort in my sex life? We pay attention to our experience—internal and external—and we set our intention to act skillfully. We do our best then to act in ways that seem right, and we try to forgive ourselves when we slip. We see that our sexuality is not ours, it doesn't belong to us, it is not who we are. It is universal, impersonal.

Some years ago I was working on a Dharma talk about what I called "positive precepts," essentially the opposite of what the precepts were warning us against—love instead of hate, generosity instead of greed—and when I got to sexuality, I began thinking that if sexuality's evolutionary purpose is to recreate life, then it is essentially creative. This seemed like a clue to how we could use our sexuality in a positive way. Perhaps our sexuality can be expressed beyond biology, as music, art, poetry, or sculpture. Creativity isn't limited to the arts, though. It comes out in cooking, in designing a business plan, in solving a math problem, in building a house. This power of creating goes far beyond reproduction to inform every aspect of life. How we work with this power goes a long way toward determining our happiness and awakening.

The fourth precept is the one on Right Speech, which I've already covered. This precept points to the ways that our speech can harm others. Lies, gossip, anger, and harsh words are just some of the ways we harm with language. Speech can also be one of the most healing forces, in therapy, in Twelve Step meetings, in words of kindness to one who is suffering.

The fifth precept suggests we shouldn't use intoxicants. For the person in recovery this is a reminder that intoxicants aren't just an addiction, but a fundamental impediment to spiritual development. I've come to see sobriety itself as a sacred state, one infused with power. Just as, day after day, week after week, my mind was confused and fragmented, my clarity distorted by drinking and using, at two years sober I began to have a sense of continuity I'd never felt before. I realized that waking up every day with a clear memory of going to sleep the night before was new to me—and refreshing. I started to feel as though I were accumulating experience, and out of that experience, wisdom, an understanding of life I'd never had before. Now I've come to see intoxicants as having a shattering effect on consciousness like software crashing. Each time I got loaded—especially drinking to blackout, but really any drug- or alcohol-altered state—I was rebooting, all the files lost. I never had a sense of accumulating experience or having any feel for how things connected in life because the connections kept getting broken. I know this explanation is impressionistic and probably insufficient; I'm trying to capture in words something that is subtle but powerful, something that exists beneath conscious awareness but has a great effect on that awareness.

Intoxicants take many forms. People address their primary addiction, say alcohol or drugs, and after they get cleaned up they realize that their smoking is really a problem; they quit smoking, and soon notice that they're eating somewhat compulsively; maybe they go to a program for eating disorders or are just able to deal with the food themselves; now they see other addictive tendencies. Our work on what we call intoxicants can seem to be endless. It may be that there is something we can call an *addictive personality type.* Or perhaps, as people who are acutely aware of the problems with addiction, we just exaggerate things that aren't actually addictions. I don't know, but this kind of multi-layered addictiveness seems common.

Thich Nhat Hanh points out the intoxicating effects of things other than substances. TV is certainly a prime suspect; the Internet is right up there, too. So too are things like shopping, sugar, overworking, and overexercising. All of these can become forms of escape. Why is that a problem? Don't we all need to escape now and then?

The problem with intoxicants is that they destroy mindfulness. And when mindfulness is gone, all sorts of bad things can happen. In the Buddhist tradition, breaking the fifth precept on intoxicants is not seen as having the same inherently negative karmic quality as breaking the other precepts, because it is possible to use intoxicants without becoming intoxicated (but don't tell that to an addict). However, the influence of intoxication is that *we tend to break the other four precepts.* My own violence, dishonesty, promiscuity, lies, and verbal outbursts happened mostly when I was drunk and stoned. The booze and dope lowered my inhibitions, let loose my reptilian brain, dissolved my moral boundaries. This may be the biggest danger of intoxicants karmically (besides killing yourself or others behind the wheel).

The power of this precept is the inner strength that comes with clarity. In meditation we are trying to learn to be fully present for our experience. Sobriety is about the same thing. In meditation we start to see the many strategies that the mind and heart use to avoid the present moment. When we have a commitment to sobriety, we are committed to facing these moments—one day or one breath at a time. As we stay sober, over time we become oriented toward catching the escapist tendencies of mind, body, and heart. We know the danger of feeding or even ignoring those tendencies, and we become vigilant observers, learning to let go of cravings and self-destructive impulses. This sustained, daily awareness is the foundation of wisdom, a wisdom that uproots the poisons of greed, hatred, and delusion.

We don't invent sobriety. We connect with it. We can't force ourselves to be sober; addiction is too powerful. Sobriety happens as the mind, body, and heart become aligned with the truth. As we struggle to solve our addiction, gradually the light of awareness begins to shine through the veil of confusion. As we point ourselves toward that light, it also begins to move toward us, a kind of spiritual magnetism.

This is how Higher Powers work: Our intention and effort become directed toward goodness or clarity or sobriety, and in that very intention and effort we begin to harmonize with the positive aspects of the universe. As we harmonize, those forces begin to work for us. It is in the *interaction* of the Higher Power within and the Higher Power without that change and awakening occur.

Prayer: Just for today, I vow to follow the Five Precepts, living with kindness and clarity. May my actions be of benefit to all beings.

LIVELIHOOD

Right Livelihood builds the fabric of a just, compassionate society. It puts the power of love into action and makes real our goals and intentions.

The work we do is another very direct and clear way that we affect our karma. Finding a way to earn a living without harming can be difficult. During my undergrad studies I took a clerical job working for a computer-science research institute in Berkeley. They were trying to advance the uses of technology, and I thought it was a positive place to work. One day I came upon some paperwork that showed that much of the funding for the institute came from the Department of Defense. Since then I've paid attention to the ways in which different jobs are tied into both destructive and constructive aspects of our society. As with intention, it is difficult to find perfect livelihood or highest livelihood. Possibly this only occurs in the monastic life. However, since monastics are dependent on laypeople, even they can be seen as somehow tied into the more complex economy.

Ultimately, however, what's most important in livelihood *is* intention, not the work itself. Have you ever seen a garbage collector who was totally engaged in his work, happy, positive, helpful? And have you ever met a doctor who didn't seem to care about you? It's hard to think of a more important service than the medical profession, and yet look at the harm that can be done by someone who is negligent. When our work is informed by love, attention, and wisdom, we raise almost any occupation to the level of Right Livelihood. There are some activities that are inherently harmful, of course, but even soldiers can be peacekeepers. It is up to each of us to examine our own hearts to see what we are bringing to our work. Greed? Generosity? Compulsion? Service? Uninterest? Mindfulness? As with most intentions, our motivation is likely mixed and will fluctuate. We can only do our best, then let go.

Livelihood doesn't just get us money or prestige, it also affects our inner life. It's where many of us get our sense of purpose in the world, where we find the greatest rewards. If we don't take this seriously, we can wind up adrift, disconnected. When our work is in harmony with the values of morality and service, the power of livelihood instills our lives with value and purpose.

Perhaps the greatest power of livelihood is the creation of society, of civilization, of culture. Typically each of us is focused on our own work, our own goals and concerns. But if we step back and look at the interaction of humans on earth, we can see that what is really happening is that we are creating our world together. Virtually anyone whose occupation isn't explicitly harmful or criminal is being of service to others. Sometimes this may seem somewhat mundane. I've worked as a technical writer for software companies for a dozen years, and at one point I questioned the value of my work. Then it occurred to me that the purpose of a technical writer is to help people to understand software; in other words, it's a service. Even this relatively banal work had helping people as its fundamental goal. That's when I saw that each of us is contributing to this web of human society. The clerk in the store, the farm worker, the chief executive, the doctor, the teacher, the truck driver, the garbage collector, each of them, each of *us,* is helping hold together this complex system that allows us to eat, have clothing, have a job, be healthy, learn, have goods, keep our homes clean. Livelihood is, at its root, *service.* Certainly we each have our personal needs that are satisfied by earning money, but even taking care of ourselves is service.

When we look at the world we've created, even with all its flaws and problems, we can see an amazing accomplishment. It's through the power of our work and our cooperation that human civilization has developed as far as it has. And each generation, while focused on its own needs, also works toward a future they will never see. Bridges and buildings are constructed that will outlive their builders; medicine is developed that will heal people far in the future; teachers give an education to students who will be around when they are gone. We are all part of something much larger than ourselves.

The power of Right Livelihood through the power of karma transforms our inner and outer worlds, changing the world around us, and even the future of that world.

Prayer: I vow to devote my livelihood to service, for others and for myself. May those efforts enrich my life and that of all beings.

EFFORT

Right Effort activates the power of karma, merging the power of will with the power of letting go. It creates the possibility of change and, when combined with Right Intention, moves us toward freedom and happiness.

Right Effort is one power that seems connected to will, not to God. If effort is about me trying to do something, then where is a Higher Power in that?

In one sutta the Buddha describes the effort he made to come to awakening. He is asked how he "crossed the flood," a metaphor for overcoming greed, hatred, and delusion and arriving at the safety of nirvana. The Buddha says, "By not halting, friend, and by not straining

I crossed the flood." Then he's asked how that worked. "When I came to a standstill, friend, then I sank; but when I struggled, then I got swept away. It is in this way, friend, that by not halting and by not straining I crossed the flood."

Anyone who has sat down to meditate with a lot of determination and said, *I'm going to watch my breath and I'm not going to be distracted at all. Nothing's going to stop me,* knows the futility of straining. The mind wanders; that's just what it does. The heart grasps at pleasure, pushes away pain; that's what it does. If, on the other hand, you've taken the attitude *I'll just sit and let it all happen,* you know the futility of halting, of doing nothing. The mind drifts, you fall asleep, boredom sets in, restlessness. In the same way, if we come to recovery with the attitude *I'm going to make this happen; I'm going to make myself stay sober,* we often burn out and fall back into addiction. But if we think that we don't need to do anything, just let it all happen, there's probably not going be enough energy to deal with the cravings when they arise. This shows the central paradox of effort in meditation and in recovery. If we try too hard, we simply wind up being swept away by the violence of our own effort; if we don't try hard enough, we sink under the weight of our own ego and craving mind. What's needed, then, is balance, what is sometimes called "effortless effort." This is where Right Effort connects with Higher Power.

When we make a steady, non-straining effort, we come into harmony with effort itself, with the power of effort. We start to work with this force and begin to be carried. It doesn't work if we don't show up—if we "halt"—and it doesn't work if we try to control the process, if we "strain." As with all the aspects of Higher Power, we have to work with effort, do our part, and let go. In the Twelve Step tradition we emphasize "showing up." In many ways, I see this as the key to recovery and spiritual growth: consistency. But showing up isn't just something we do with our bodies alone; we also have to show up with our awareness and our energy.

Right Effort isn't a prescription. You can't simply say, "Do this and don't do that," because each moment is unique and calls for its own effort. Jack Kornfield tells how as a new monk he complained to Ajahn Chah that his instructions were inconsistent, that he didn't give people the same answers to questions. "It is as though I see people walking down a road I know well," he told Jack. "I look up and see someone about to fall in a ditch on the right-hand side of the road or get off on a side track on the right so I call out to him 'Go left, go left.' Similarly if I see someone about to go off on a sidetrack to the left, or to fall in the left-hand ditch, I call out 'Go right, go right.' All of practice is simply developing a balance of mind, not clinging, unselfishness."

Ditches appear in all kinds of ways in all kinds of places. The fundamentalist approach to religion is to say that there is only one answer. This provides people with a sense of safety in a frightening world. They don't have to figure out for themselves what's right and wrong or what to do in a particular situation. But unfortunately this approach overlooks the complexities of the world, of life. The mindful approach requires that we be attentive, mindful in each situation, and that we develop and use discriminating wisdom to address life's challenges. Over time our mindfulness and wisdom grow and we become more skilled at dealing with the difficult situations that we face. We come more into harmony with the power of Right Effort.

If I'm going to talk about Right Effort, it's important that I address another teaching that is spelled out in a more structured way: the Four Great Efforts. The Buddha says that there are four things we need to do in our practice: avoid unskillful states that haven't yet appeared; abandon unskillful states that are already present; cultivate skillful states that haven't appeared; and maintain skillful states that are already present. This seems like a fairly mechanistic approach to effort. What he's doing, though, is giving us a road map for what to pay attention to. In any given moment, then, we can ask ourselves what we need to address, what we can do to improve our state of mind. Sometimes we need to be looking at the unskillful, difficult, or painful states and trying to let go; sometimes we need to be working on our positive states.

Effort is the foundation for any change, for any growth. With wise effort we show up, draw on the resources available, the people, the literature, and the practices, and do what's suggested without a lot of expectations. This implies a trust, an understanding that our effort isn't the sole determining factor in the results, that there are other forces at work. With Right Effort we see the subtle and paradoxical nature of the path as we learn to strive with diligence at the same time that we "let go and let God."

Prayer: May I find a balance of mind in practice, neither struggling nor halting. May I have the wisdom and strength to cultivate the good and abandon the harmful.

CONCENTRATION

> *Right Concentration increases the power of the mind to be*
> *present and to look deeply at what is true. The power*
> *of concentration brings calm, coolness, and clarity.*

On those miserable days during my addiction when I ran out of pot, I suffered terrible anxiety, a visceral sense of agitation that seemed unbearable. I would wind up scraping out a pipe or crushing up seeds to smoke; at one point I ground up pain pills and smoked them to get a buzz.

I had many days when my craving to drink was just as painful. The sense of built-up pressure made me feel as if I'd explode if I didn't get loaded. When I'd finally get a hold of a six-pack, I'd chug two or three just to take that edge off.

This restlessness and angst is a typical symptom of addiction. The obsession and compulsion it triggers power our addiction and spin it out of control. When I was caught in that hell, I didn't know any other way out than to drink or use.

Meditation, and especially concentration, or *samadhi,* is an antidote to this anxiety, but when we're caught in addiction the idea of sitting still and following the breath can seem unimaginably difficult. The Twelve Steps guide us out of this agitated state. When we admit our powerlessness, we let go of the compulsion to control our drinking and drugging; naturally this brings relief. Step Three, turning our will and life over to a Higher Power, is a further relief, as we now start to let go of the compulsion to control everything else. As we write and share inventory, try to let go of our defects of character, and finally make amends for the harm we've caused, a great deal of weight is taken off our shoulders. Our life starts to come together. The Big Book states that at this point many "promises" will come true for us, one of them being "We will comprehend the word serenity and we will know peace." Largely what I think this refers to is the relief one feels after being freed from a destructive addiction and the lifestyle that came with it. When we start to live morally, with a sense of kindness, service, and surrender, life is much simpler.

However, I've also gotten the impression from the many Twelve Step meetings I've attended that what I would call peace and serenity, what I've tasted in meditation, is rarely achieved through the Steps alone—not *never,* but rarely.

Concentration is the strongest raw power cultivated in meditation. It's this power that brings peacefulness and relaxation. In its deeper manifestations, concentration leads to mystical states of bliss and a sense of union with the divine. For the addict, this is the closest thing to a drug in meditation practice. And that's where things get complicated.

Concentration alone has no special spiritual value. A cat burglar needs to be concentrated; athletes, scholars, and computer programmers are among the most concentrated people around; to perform any complex task, you need concentration. In order for concentration to have a spiritual value, it needs to be combined with mindfulness, which keeps the focus on the present-moment reality rather than some escapist state; intention, which directs the purpose of concentration to deepening wisdom and love; and morality, which keeps the uses of concentration on a wholesome level. When combined with these and the other elements of the Eightfold Path, concentration supports the arising of the most profound insights. Without a strong degree of concentration, these insights are rarely accessible.

Mindfulness, intention, and morality can be developed in many contexts, but for most people, concentration needs the special circumstances of intensive meditation practice to come to fruition. Concentration requires sustained stillness and quiet to grow. In our daily lives, getting even an hour a day of stillness and quiet can be difficult. So, most of us need a meditation retreat to deepen concentration. In the monastic tradition, three months out of every year are set aside for the "Rains Retreat." While few lay practitioners can take three months out of their schedules each year, many serious Buddhist meditators do so for at least a few years; others set aside some period, a week or two perhaps, for retreat each year, as well as occasionally going on longer retreats.

While developing concentration isn't the sole purpose of retreat, we could say that it is the sole element that can't be developed in the same way or to the same extent outside of retreat. However, the Buddhist tradition also has a long history of controversy over how much concentration is enough—and how much might actually be *too much.*

Concentration needs to be seen in the larger context of practice. I found my way into some of the deeper states not by trying to get there, but just by doing my vipassana, or insight, practice with devotion for years. If we strive for bliss states, we usually just create more agitation. It's much wiser to allow these states to arise in their own time out of the natural progression and deepening of meditation. This should always be done with the larger goal of insight and heart-opening that our practice is focused on. Otherwise, we will get sidetracked, and if we are addicts, risk recreating our addictive behaviors in our spiritual practice.

This open, accepting approach to developing concentration practice is founded in the idea of concentration as an aspect of God. We can't control concentration; it is a power greater than us. All we can do is work in harmony with concentration, taking the steps necessary to arouse it, then getting out of the way to allow it to arise as it will. Rather than thinking that "I" am concentrated (or not), we can say, "Concentration is appearing." There's nothing personal about concentration; it doesn't define me and I don't own it. As with all the aspects of Higher Power, my job is to make the intention and effort to cultivate or be in harmony with this aspect, then accept the results of that effort.

The issue of concentration isn't limited to intensive retreat practice. How we focus our attention influences every moment of our day. While we can arouse mindfulness in just a moment, to sustain it takes some degree of concentration. The way we concentrate is by continually bringing our attention back to the object, whether it's the breath when we're meditating or the traffic when we're driving, whether we're cultivating lovingkindness or gazing at a sunset.

Our culture and our society encourage a scattered attention. We're supposed to be multitasking, driving the car while talking on the cell phone; reading the paper while we eat breakfast; writing an e-mail while we listen to the iPod. Research shows that we can't actually pay attention to more than one thing at a time, and that, instead, our attention hops around, a moment of listening, a moment of writing; a moment of looking at the traffic, a moment of speaking on the phone. The net effect of all this shifting of attention is a state of stress, anxiety, and agitation. Even when we have a moment to relax, we are so much in the habit of jumping around that we fall back on the couch and start flipping through the dozens of cable channels or clicking from one website to another. For someone who has experienced the obsessiveness of addiction, it's all very familiar. We can feel the energy coursing through us, the compulsion to find more and more stimulation. This is dangerous for an addict, because our drug of choice was our favorite stimulation—or sedation.

The answer, then, is to make different choices in how we use our attention. Each day we need to find ways to sustain a mindful attention, if only for a few minutes, whether it's with formal meditation, taking a walk, listening to music, reading a spiritual book, or talking with a trusted friend. As we enter into these healing activities, we bring the tool of concentration, continuously bringing our attention back when it wanders, encouraging our mind to rest with the present-moment experience. The benefits are great.

Most of us have had the experience of being so wrapped up in reading a book that we stay up much later than usual to find out what happens. Even if we've had a tiring day, we may find ourselves completely alert as we follow the unfolding plot. This is the effect of concentration. What makes that concentration so strong is our interest in the subject matter or the story. When we can arouse interest in a subject, our concentration naturally follows. When we are interested and concentrated, our energy naturally follows that. This is why people who get very concentrated on retreat sometimes find they need less sleep than usual. When the mind is concentrated there is much less stress, so we don't get so drained. In our daily lives we can get the same benefit by bringing more sustained attention to our activities. When we aren't building up stress through the day, when we are taking each moment and each event of the day with a calm, focused attention, we find that our energy is much more balanced and clear.

In meditation practice we might find ourselves getting frustrated by our inability to stay with the breath, to stay present. Certainly one way to deal with this is to try directly to deepen concentration with some practice or other. However, the approach of mindfulness isn't so much to force our way into concentration, but rather to look at what is getting in the way of concentration, to become more present and accepting of what is happening, rather than trying to make something else happen.

A good place to start is with the Five Hindrances, the classic impediments to concentration. These are mental, emotional, and physical states—desire, aversion, restlessness and anxiety, sleepiness and dullness, and doubt—that cause agitation and fogginess.

Desire is, of course, a central issue in Buddhist teachings; it's identified as the cause of suffering. When we are trying to develop concentration, desire keeps pulling us away from the meditation focus to the object of desire. Craving has the effect of spinning our thoughts round and round in pursuit of some experience or thing that we feel will bring satisfaction. While we're meditating, sitting still with our eyes closed, most objects of desire will be unattainable, so the desire can actually become more intense than it would be if we could act on it.

Beneath the thoughts of desire, there is often a visceral feeling in the body that drives our craving. In meditation practice, we take our attention right to the heart of this sensation, letting the attention rest in the middle of the craving, just feeling it as it is, being present with the suffering that is desire. As we watch it, if we can drop the obsessive thoughts and stay with the feeling, very often the desire will fade.

The hindrance of aversion is simply the flip side of desire, *not* wanting. The mind and body react much as they do with desire, triggering thoughts and feelings that tend to be self-perpetuating. Again, dropping into the felt sense of the aversion tends to undercut its power. It's actually quite interesting to see the differences and similarities between the feelings of desire and aversion.

While desire causes grasping and dissatisfaction, it is, at least theoretically, founded in a positive emotion, a reaching for something pleasant. Aversion, on the other hand, is founded in the negativity of hatred. This makes it particularly poisonous. When we cling to aversion we create a negative energy around ourselves. Recently I was watching my daughter's softball team and they were playing poorly. As I sat on the bench with other parents, I picked apart each player's faults. Pitch after pitch, play after play, I ran a negative commentary. In the middle of it I became aware of what I was doing, the bitterness that I was creating. I felt the discomfort of the other parents as they inched away from me, and I tried to restrain myself. The next day, before another game, I made a vow to speak positively about the team. As I was watching them lose again, I found that there were just as many positive things to say as negative, and that my own experience was completely different, that instead of feeling frustrated and angry, I felt hopeful and happy.

The hindrance of restlessness and anxiety is very common in meditation. When we first sit down to practice, the momentum of life can make it very difficult to sit still. Again, dropping into the body, using non-judgmental, mindful attention, can help us ride out these energy storms. Anxiety, the mental element of this hindrance, is often driven by an emotion in the body. If we try to deal with it mentally by either figuring out a problem or just dropping the thoughts, very often the emotion in the body will keep triggering and re-triggering the anxious rumination. The only way around this is to face the physical experience driving the anxiety.

The hindrance of sleepiness and dullness, like restlessness and anxiety, has a physical and mental component. It often happens that as people start to slow down, as the anxiety fades, sleepiness takes over. We drop from one hindrance right to another, with no stop in between. And, indeed, a balanced meditative state combines alertness and relaxation, without either one becoming dominant.

It can seem odd to suggest we be mindful of sleepiness, since falling asleep is all about losing consciousness, not gaining it. But if we start to watch our energy carefully, we can often catch the sleepy feelings just as they arise, just as the head tips forward or the thoughts get dreamy, and at that moment, we can use some of the tools recommended for dealing with sleepiness: take some deep breaths, sit up straighter, and open the eyes. I often find it helpful to leave my eyes open for a few minutes when I get sleepy. Just by letting in light we naturally wake up.

The fifth hindrance, doubt, has many manifestations. In meditation it shows up as the thought *I can't do this* or *What's the point of this practice?* It's quite easy to doubt ourselves when we begin to meditate, because most people don't get the results they expect when they first try to practice. Instead of some lovely, relaxed, and blissful state, we find ourselves restless or sleepy, agitated or bored, caught up in dreams or worries or distractions. Whether it's your fault or that of the practice, you might not know, but there's certainly the sense that you're not getting anywhere. Without some trust in the process, this can be the end of your meditation experiment. If we don't have some larger sense of how this works, it's easy to just fold up our tent and go home. However, if we are able to place some trust in those who teach us and those we see who are obviously gaining benefit from meditation, we can ride out these difficult early days. It's important, too, to recognize the things that *are* happening. Even if it seems like your mind is all over the place for the whole meditation period, you might find that at the end you actually do feel more relaxed. If you are able to look at what's going through your mind, you're quite likely to get some insight into yourself, into your psychology and your habitual patterns of thought and emotion.

There's a natural tendency as the hindrances arise to try to make them go away, and ultimately that's a wise thing to do. However, the mindful approach isn't to immediately try to get rid of them, but rather to get to know them and to let them fade of their own accord. Since they are bound to keep showing up in our lives, it's vital, especially for addicts who tend to get triggered by these states, to learn to live with them. We must see them clearly first before we can begin to change; we must learn to be with them without reacting, to surrender to them and accept them, or else we create more struggle; as we watch them we'll see their changing nature, their impermanence, and understand that we don't have to be overwhelmed by them. They are just temporary problems. Finally, as we see them come and go, we gain the wisdom to see that we don't have to take the hindrances personally. They aren't who we are. When we see them as just visitors, our tendency to react, to run away or to strike out at these energies, is diminished.

The hindrances are part of life; they appear in meditation, they appear at work and at play. They come and they go. Even after his enlightenment, the Buddha was beset with these energies—although he seems to have gotten very good at letting go of them. Even during lengthy periods of intensive meditation practice they will keep popping up. Nonetheless, as we work with them, trusting ourselves, trusting our practice, at times they will fade away. Then, as the Buddha says, "Having abandoned these five hindrances, defilements of the mind that weaken wisdom, secluded from sensual pleasures, secluded from unwholesome states, the meditator enters and dwells in the first jhana [meditative absorption]." A delightful state of peace and clarity pervades our body and mind: the fruits of being in harmony with the Higher Power of Concentration.

Prayer: I commit myself to staying focused and allowing concentration to grow. I trust that if I am still and come back to the breath, serenity will deepen.

Exercise: Building Concentration

For many people, developing concentration is one of the biggest hurdles in meditation practice. The tool of mindfulness helps us to develop insight, but without concentration, the meditative experience itself can be frustrating as the mind flits from place to place and the body struggles for comfort. Concentration helps us to hold the mind steady and to relax into the body.

The essence of concentration is called "one-pointedness." This term is often misunderstood. It doesn't mean that the attention is narrowed down to a tiny "point." It simply means that the mind stays focused on only one thing. That "thing" can be quite broad and spacious, or it can have a quality of movement, like the breath.

The way to achieve one-pointedness is to choose one "object" to pay attention to and then continuously bring the mind to that object. If the mind wanders, don't pay attention to where you've been or get caught in analysis or judgment; just come back and try to remain as long as possible with the object. If things are happening in the background of your experience, just let them be.

Stillness of the body supports stillness of the mind. During the concentration exercises, try to remain perfectly still. Notice the subtle body movements that happen beneath your awareness.

Note: You may not want to do these exercises for the full period of meditation. Try using a concentration practice for the first 5–10 minutes, then going back to mindfulness practice.

Following are two simple exercises. The first comes from Thich Nhat Hanh, the Vietnamese Zen master, in his book *Present Moment, Wonderful Moment.* It uses a set of phrases or verses called *gathas.*

Gathas

Repeat the following phrases silently in unison with the breath, continuing to feel the physical sensations of the breath. Each pair of words or phrases corresponds to an inhalation and exhalation.

1. In-breath – Out-breath
2. Deep – Slow
3. Calm – Ease
4. Smile – Release
5. Present moment – Wonderful moment

If you lose track of which phrase you're on, simply start at the beginning again. As you repeat the phrases, also try to continue to feel the breath, either at the nostrils or in the belly.

Try adapting the meaning of the words to your breathing and your experience if that feels comfortable: letting the breath get deep and slow; becoming calm and easeful; allowing a slight smile to come to your lips; realizing the uniqueness of right now. Only do this if it feels right; it's not necessary to do it to achieve the benefits of the practice. Simply bringing the mind back to the phrases and the breath over and over will develop one-pointedness.

Counting Breaths

This simple practice comes out of the Zen tradition. If the Gathas don't feel right to you, but you'd like to work on concentration, try this: when breathing in, note "In" silently in the back of your mind. Breathing out, note "One." Proceed up to ten, then start back at one. If you lose track of what number you are on, simply return to one. Don't pay attention to anything else in your experience.

Exercise: Eightfold Inventory

In this exercise you will look at the ways that you are fulfilling the Eightfold Path and those ways you could further cultivate it.

1. Begin by writing down each of the eight aspects of the Eightfold Path. Go over each one and make sure you have an understanding of what it means to you. In the places you aren't so clear, try to get more information. Read up on aspects of the path that you don't fully understand.

2. Once you feel you basically understand the path, ask yourself how much you are living it. Are you acting on Right View? Is your Intention clear? How's your Concentration? Are you comfortable with your Livelihood?

3. Once you've reviewed each element of the path, pick one element that needs more cultivation. Ask yourself how you could more completely fulfill this part of the path.

4. If it's one of the meditation elements, mindfulness, effort, or concentration, consider taking a class or going on a retreat; if it's one of the morality elements, action, speech, or livelihood, look at the ways you can live differently; if it's one of the wisdom elements, view or intention, try to bring them more into your daily awareness by remembering the Dharma and by setting clear intentions. For any element, it can also be helpful to do more study and practice.

Once you've chosen an aspect of the Eightfold Path you want to cultivate further, make the commitment to work on this element for the next month. At the end of the month, review your progress and see if you want to spend another month on that element or move on to another element of the path for the following month. Do this for as many elements as you choose, one month at a time.

THE HIGHER POWER
OF FAITH

The Higher Power of Faith gives us the confidence to continue our practice and our program despite obstacles. It softens and opens the heart, inspiring us with the joy of knowing we are on the right path.

There are two basic kinds of faith, and I've had a hard time with both of them. One is faith in myself, and the other is religious faith in something outside me, a teaching, practice, or dogma.

As a child I believed in all the teachings in the Bible, the miracles and magic. It was exciting and inspiring to think these things had happened sometime in the distant past. I went to church, I confessed my sins, and I prayed. I took communion and believed I had the body of Christ inside me. I felt a sense of the sacred, the holy.

But my faith must not have been very strong, because when my brother Michael, who was three years older, got his driver's license, I started skipping Sunday Mass. We would dress up in coats and ties, wave to our parents, and get in my father's Buick convertible. Then instead of driving to church we'd drive out of town, off into the Pennsylvania countryside, putting the top down and turning up the radio. Michael liked to drive fast. He'd take the winding country roads like we were at Le Mans. The only praying I did was that we wouldn't have a head-on crash when he passed somebody on a blind curve.

My religious training was sidetracked when Michael started to mentor me. His critical analysis of Catholic doctrine swayed me. Over the next few years, I followed him in his cynicism and rejected the Church and the ideas I'd accepted for so long. Still, some part of me wanted salvation, a magical fix or transformation, and I think that's what drugs and alcohol became. I didn't have to take the risk of faith with pot—just smoke it and get what I wanted. Beer didn't require any commitment, just drink the stuff. Through my 20s I lived a largely faithless life.

In my early 30s, as I was beginning to delve into Eastern spirituality, I met a homeless guru named Ananda ("bliss" in Sanskrit) who told me that if I would just "live on faith" I'd get enlightened. By that time I'd decided that I needed some kind of spiritual magic to solve my problems. I'd been on a few meditation retreats and hadn't gotten what I wanted, and I felt a certain desperation. If I could just convince myself to believe in Ananda's teachings, then maybe I'd be okay. I tried to follow him, but in just a matter of months, I lost my faith—if I'd ever really had it. The skeptic in me was too strong; my belief in myself was too weak.

I still struggle with the outer reaches of faith. I hear stories from people I respect of miraculous events or beings they encounter on other planes, and I wonder. Is it possible? Are they deluded? Is it just some metaphor or myth? I've come to the point where I don't want to be dismissive of things I haven't experienced because I've seen how counterproductive that can be. I've seen that relying entirely on the intellect can be just as limiting as holding magical beliefs. There are limits to what I can know for certain, and if I try to claim that nothing is possible beyond what I can imagine, then I limit the possibility of what I can learn. Am I really so arrogant that I think that all the possibilities in the universe are already known by my little brain? Still, I don't want to be gullible or irrational. So my attitude toward magical-seeming stories is "Don't know." And the truth is, I don't have to know. What I've found in recovery and in Buddhist practice is that my faith doesn't have to be so extensive for it to be useful. In fact, one of the reasons I'm writing this book is so that skeptical people can connect with a Higher Power without surrendering their intelligence. Yes, you'll have to put trust in some things that you can't absolutely prove—like the Law of Karma—but not in what doesn't make sense.

Faith in myself is another matter. Being the youngest of five boys, I had a lot to compare myself to. Each of my brothers had special qualities: Dave his humor and leadership; Jerry his brilliant intellect and musical talent; Pat his charm and athleticism; Michael another brilliant intellect with a gift for design and making things. What did I have? Not that I was worthless, but I didn't feel that I could exceed my brothers with any special gift. Ironically, my way of acting out this lack of confidence was to aim for being a rock star. Because I didn't have any realistic faith in myself, I instead fell back on magical faith, that somehow—I didn't know how—I was going to be recognized for my specialness by some record-company executive and vaulted into fame and fortune.

This combination of ambition and insecurity tore at me—it's still an underlying theme of my character. I wanted so badly to express myself; for years I worked on songwriting everyday (as now I write books). But my lack of confidence repeatedly undercut me. When I was 21 I formed a band to perform my original songs. The music was interesting, subtle, complex, and anti-formula. It might have found a place in the market, but I didn't have the confidence and persistence that it takes to break through in the music business. A few setbacks were all it took to destroy my faith in the project. I broke the band up after six months.

Giving up so easily was indicative of another kind of magical thinking. I thought that if I were going to be successful it would happen overnight. If it didn't, then "it wasn't meant to be." This kind of fatalism can mask as faith, but it lacks the personal responsibility that faith requires. After all, as the Bible says, "faith without works is dead."

Faith, in the Buddhist teachings, isn't magical. It's the confidence that comes with Right View and Right Action: Our understanding of the truth inspires us to live wisely. When we live wisely, our actions are rewarded and our faith is strengthened. In this way we build a reliable faith.

Twelve Step recovery works in much the same way. We stop acting on our addiction for one day. We see the results. We stop for another day. Gradually we build faith in the program and in ourselves. We don't have to start with a strong belief. When I got sober, I thought, *Maybe this will work.* I was skeptical enough that I didn't do what they said I should; I didn't get a sponsor or go to lots of meetings. I just stopped drinking and using, read the literature, and dropped in on meetings, sitting in the back, watching and listening. I also practiced meditation regularly. For some people, I'm sure this wouldn't be enough. I'm fortunate that it got me through a year sober before I realized I needed more. By then I had developed enough faith in the program that I was willing to make a deeper commitment.

The Higher Power of Faith, then, is the power to continue on the path through challenges, doubts, and difficulties. The second summer of my sobriety, I was struggling. I'd been on the periphery of the Twelve Step world while traveling with a road band, and now I was back in L.A.; I'd gone from one unsatisfactory relationship to another, and I was lonely. I was confused and didn't know what to do. In the back of my mind there arose the glimmer of possibility: *Perhaps if I get more involved in a program I won't be so lonely and I'll be able to figure out what to do next.* I started going to meetings every day. That one act of faith triggered the beginning of my actual recovery. Soon I had a sponsor and was working the Steps. I got the confidence to start my own band and look for an interesting day job. I still didn't know exactly where I was headed, but I trusted something—I trusted in the path, and in myself. I trusted that if I just tried to do the right thing with openness and acceptance, I'd wind up in a better place, and I trusted that I could actually do this. These two elements of faith weren't leaps, but small steps. Those small steps unfolded over years and decades to the life I have today. I still don't have wholehearted faith; I'm still a skeptic. But I trust in karma and I trust in honesty; I have faith in surrender and acceptance; I have confidence in mindfulness; I believe in love, compassion, and forgiveness. These are great powers, and my commitment and faith in them gives *me* power.

In the Buddhist teaching on the Five Spiritual Powers, faith is said to be balanced by, and to balance, wisdom. The faith that I tried to arouse with Ananda wasn't backed with anything solid. We need to be careful that our inspirational faith isn't delusion. Magic can feel good, but eventually it leads to trouble.

The teachings on wisdom that I've talked about, impermanence, suffering, and not-self, can arouse fear. Faith is the antidote to that. It's natural to have some discomfort about impermanence; we're

112

threatened by change. When we undergo a huge life-transforming experience like breaking an addiction, we often feel a lot of fear about what this change will mean. Faith gives us the courage to overcome that fear and to trust the process. It's also natural to resist suffering. When we understand its nature, that insight can give us the confidence to be with it, to hold the suffering in a new way that helps us see it in the larger context of experience and our lives. Finally, when we find ourselves struggling with fears about identity and trying to protect our ego, if we trust in the insight that there is nothing solid to hold on to, that anxiety can dissolve into a sense of openness and freedom.

When we do "come to believe," we can enter a stage of "bright faith," what's called in recovery circles "the pink cloud." At this point, the power of faith really kicks in. We start going to meetings every day, working the Steps with a sponsor, volunteering and doing service; we also start to repair our damaged lives, making amends and being more responsible in our work lives, bringing more integrity to our relationships and our sex life, committing to honesty and reliability, and living with enthusiasm and vigor. With bright faith, everything clicks. The parking space is a gift from God; the flat tire is a teaching in patience. We meet someone on a bus who gives us a business card that leads to a new job, and we know that it was all meant to be. We are fully engaged and we have absolute faith in the recovery process. This is a wonderful and inspiring stage of faith. It was this kind of inspiration that led me to take four retreats in my first year of Buddhist meditation, culminating in the very challenging three-month Rains Retreat. It was this kind of faith that drove me to quit the road band I'd been with and start my own band at one year sober. The momentum of bright faith helps carry us through the huge transition from addiction to recovery and to establish us firmly on this path.

The risk with bright faith comes when it's placed in something less reliable than the ancient Buddhist teachings or traditional Twelve Step programs. Bright faith can be blind, as I found out when I was drawn into working with Ananda. As with many such teachers, to question his logic was to exhibit a distrust in him, and thus show your lack of commitment or worthiness. This is the perfect Catch-22 that cult leaders set up. I followed him because I wanted magic. He helped me to believe that if I just had enough faith, I would be transformed. For an addict, this is a setup. I didn't want to do the challenging, long-term work of spiritual development. I wanted "sudden enlightenment." This is, of course, what drugs and alcohol provide—not enlightenment, but instant, effortless transformation. So, bright faith, like all kinds of faith, needs the tempering of common sense and maturity.

Many people feel a letdown after a couple of years of recovery when the excitement and magic of early sobriety start to wear off. While bright faith shoots us out of the starting blocks, we realize now that we're in a marathon, not a sprint, and we have to find another level of faith. This is a critical point in recovery where some people lose their way. As addicts in recovery, that bright faith sustained us. It gave us the sense of magic that we lost when we gave up the drugs and booze. When that fades, though, there can be the fear that life is going to become gray and tedious.

The fear of boredom is one of the fears many addicts encounter when facing the prospect of getting clean and sober. "If I quit getting high, what am I going to do for fun?" Of course, for most of us, the fun ended years before, but we can't see that. And if we do engage a program, it's common to find that the sociability and support of others in recovery more than replaces the thrill of our addiction. When we get into recovery, we begin to realize how shallow our pleasure really was.

Many of us work all twelve Steps when we are in the bright-faith period. What we find, though, when that innocent trust begins to fade is that we have to return to Step One. If the lure of our addiction appears again, we have to remind ourselves of the bottom we hit in our addiction. As life settles down in recovery, we can begin to forget how bad things were. This is one of the reasons we work with newcomers and go to meetings. Even if we have forgotten, they haven't. Their stories are the reminders we need to keep our program fresh.

Our meditation practice can easily stagnate as well. The early intensity of my exploration of Buddhism gave me deep experiences of peace and stillness. The long retreats I took in my first year of practice opened many doors. After that, in my long slide into bottoming out on drugs and alcohol, I lost much of my inspiration. Although I continued to practice and have a strong sense of the validity of Buddhist teachings, I couldn't maintain the depth of concentration that had been so gratifying that first year. As an addict, I relied on that deep peace; it was very pleasurable. When my meditation became more distracted, doubt came up. Ananda had helped to undermine my belief in Buddhism, and now I fell into a more or less rote practice. I felt that I couldn't really fulfill the teachings, that I lacked something, and that, perhaps, the teachings lacked something, too. I didn't know what . . . Still, when I got sober, I picked up my practice a bit, and I did find that the clarity that came with sobriety helped my meditation. But it was only when I moved to Northern California at six years sober that things began to change.

I'd been going to school in Santa Monica for three years, getting my general-education requirements completed at community college. When it was time to transfer to a four-year university, I had the opportunity to choose between UCLA and Berkeley. Everyone in L.A. told me I'd love Berkeley, and they were right. There I found the kind of thriving, cohesive meditation community I'd lacked. I also found some of the Buddhist teachers and students I'd known when I first started to practice ten years before. My dormant faith was awakened.

Soon I was attending weekly meditation groups, going on longer retreats, and helping to lead a small Buddhist support group. I'd kept my practice and my faith alive, an ember in a dying fire, and now it burst back into flame. But this faith was very different from the bright faith of the previous decade. I didn't have illusions about magical transformations and fixes; I wasn't searching out every passing guru; and I didn't accept every word I read or heard from a teacher. I had my own understanding now, formed in the crucible of addiction and recovery and grounded in the deep roots of my meditation practice. I believed now, not just in Buddhism, but in myself. I trusted my own ideas and my own understanding. I could feel the forward motion of my spiritual growth—I could *see* it in my very life. More than ever, even more than when I was inspired by bright faith, I felt the imperative and the urgency of my practice. I knew now that practice didn't just mean going on a retreat or even meditating every day, but that it meant "practicing these principles in all our affairs," as Step Twelve says, trying to bring mindfulness, kindness, and wisdom into every facet and, hopefully, every moment of life. Suddenly it was as if practice had opened up, as if there was a great, broad landscape to explore and to play in. This was the power of faith growing inside me. This confidence would, over the coming years, deepen and broaden my practice so that there was no longer a barrier between Buddhism and the Twelve Steps; it would spur me into study of the traditional texts so that I could understand and interpret the Buddha's original teachings for myself; and it would finally guide me into offering my own insights to others and trying to be a guide myself.

Prayer: May my heart be open, and may I trust myself and my path. May I surrender to the Twelve Steps and the Buddha's teachings, the Dharma. May my faith inspire my efforts in my program and my practice.

Exercise: Exploring Belief in Yourself

What we believe about ourselves and the world has a great effect on our reality. In this exercise you will look at how your beliefs shape you and your world.

Begin with a few minutes of quiet meditation. Once you feel settled, begin to ask yourself what you believe about yourself. Reflect on how your beliefs about your own talents and weaknesses have influenced the decisions you've made in your life. What are the limits you place on yourself based on these beliefs? What would happen if you believed that you could have the life you want?

Exercise: Exploring Belief in God

Our spiritual and religious beliefs are critical to the way we interact with the world. What do you believe about God? Are you an atheist? Do you believe in an Abrahamic God? A mysterious God? A Dharma God? Reflect on how your beliefs about God influence your actions and reactions in the world. Consider whether these beliefs are serving you and whether you might be able to reconsider the less helpful beliefs you carry.

THE HIGHER POWER
OF PRESENCE

*The Higher Power of Presence is the power to be. It puts us in touch
with the oneness that is our true nature. Experiencing the power
of presence gives us deep insight, faith, and equanimity.*

The Higher Power of Presence is in some ways the simplest and
most essential aspect of God. It requires no understanding or extrapo-
lation. While the Buddhist teachings can seem dense and intellectual,
presence just *is*.

On one retreat I was struggling to connect what the teachers had
said with what I was experiencing. My meditation, instead of becoming more peaceful, was becoming more agitated. Instead of letting
things come and go, I was *looking* for something, waiting for a big
breakthrough or gift-wrapped insight.

One day I took a walk after lunch into the hills behind the retreat
center. A gate at the back of the property opened onto a steep dirt
trail. After climbing for several minutes, I came to a ridge. Breathing
hard, I kept to the trail, which then dipped into a valley and curved
around beneath a higher peak. Through a hole in a barbed-wire fence,
I found another trail that headed straight up. I didn't think I was going
anywhere, but I wanted to keep walking, keep climbing. The trail
edged a steep drop-off into the valley below. As I got higher, a strong

breeze came up from the hillside. Finally, as I reached the peak of the hill, I stopped and turned to see the view, back across the valley to the meditation center in the distance and, beyond that, a suburban development, a high school surrounded by sports fields, and a far-off freeway. Suddenly a huge buzzard appeared before me, swept up from the valley on the thermal draft. As I stood on this precipice, the bird was just a few feet away, dangling over the valley floor hundreds of feet below. I was actually looking down on it, a unique perspective that broke through my normal perception. Everything else I'd been looking at was common for me, so I was able to more or less ignore it. But seeing the huge wingspan of a buzzard on a thermal from above shocked me out of my blasé attitude into an intense feeling of now-ness. Nothing to figure out; nothing to understand; no insight or big breakthrough. Just this; just now.

I sat down on the cliff with a great relief. Maybe I would never be enlightened; maybe I'd never be as wise as my teachers; maybe I'd never understand it all. But what did I really need to know besides this? No one could take this away—and no one could give it to me. I didn't know if this had anything to do with Buddhism, but I knew that it had everything to do with life.

The idea of being present has little appeal for an addict or alcoholic. We drink to get "out of our heads"; on psychedelics we "take a trip"; on pot we get "spaced out." Anywhere but here. The pain or the craving we feel must be avoided at all costs. But, of course, life only happens here and now, so when we run away from the present, we run away from life. Further, it turns out that fully engaging the present is the gateway to real joy and freedom.

The Higher Power of Presence is associated with the mystical experience. Some people touch this power spontaneously, while most of us engage it only through spiritual practices. To make this connection we have to use the power of concentration, which then brings us to the stillness and peace that allow us the subtlety of perception required to sense "God" here and now. This sensing in turn brings us to a deeper peace as we come to see that we are never separated from God, as we are never separated from the present moment. It is only our misperception that creates this sense of separation.

When people talk about having "conscious contact" with God, as Step Eleven suggests we cultivate, I think they are talking about this aspect of God, its presence. And when people say that they are feeling distant from God, I also think they are talking about this presence. Given everything I've written, it should be clear that I believe there are many other ways to be in contact with God. In fact, I think that the idea of God as presence is overemphasized, often leaving people with a feeling of lack or failure, even when they may be quite in harmony with other aspects of God.

It helps to think of God as having two aspects: doing and being. The doing God is the Law of Karma, the Truth of Impermanence, the power of Right Action, and all the other ways that God functions in the world; the God of doing guides our behavior and helps us to understand the difficulties and challenges of life. The God of being is the God that we *know*. This is the God of "conscious contact." The God of being gives us the ineffable scent of the absolute. This God inspires the spiritual journey and shows us the ultimate futility of trying to find satisfaction in the realm of *samsara*. The God of being allows us to touch our deepest nature and to sense the vastness and mystery of mind and spirit.

The challenge of finding this God is the task of *not-doing*. Our lives are so oriented toward action and distraction that it's difficult to even begin to approach stillness and being. We go to work, where we are bombarded by calls and e-mails and tasks. If things slow down for a moment, we go online and read the news or play a game. After work we get in the car, turn on the radio, and perhaps make a phone call during our commute. We get home, turn on the TV or radio, start chatting with our family or roommates. Anytime there's a lapse of interaction or entertainment, we fill it with thoughts. We're so used to having some kind of stimulus that when we do stop doing, we're flooded with anxiety or sadness. The idea of sitting down to meditate can be intimidating.

For an addict or alcoholic, this whole process is aggravated. We feel the need not only to control our outer environment, but to control our inner life as well with drugs or alcohol. The idea of just being with ourselves as we are is incomprehensible. Our inner life is a tangle of self-hatred, craving, fear, resentment, and confusion. The only way to deal with this mess is to get loaded.

Some recovering people don't even try to practice meditation—Step Eleven—until they've been sober a while. And, unfortunately, it seems that many people never try it at all. I've found, though, that even people freshly in recovery can benefit from meditation. I teach at treatment centers where people are often just days away from their last drink or drug. In a short guided meditation I take them through some conscious relaxation, then help them to connect with the breath and notice when the mind has wandered. Oftentimes they are surprised by how relaxed they become. In a setting where there's nowhere to go and nothing to do, a place that's all about healing—about being—they find that the living presence inside them is surprisingly accessible. Much like going on retreat, time in rehab takes you out of your normal life, lowers the stress and stimulation, and gives you space to be with yourself.

In our daily lives, we can find ways to get out of the realm of doing as well. We can set up a space in our home that's for meditation. Here we place sacred or special objects on a table, creating an altar, and place a cushion or chair in front of it. When we sit in this place we move out of *doing* time and into *being*—the timelessness of ritual. We can enter this same world simply by reminding ourselves to be present—when walking down the street, when doing the dishes, when making love, when listening to music. The Higher Power of Presence is accessed through mindfulness. When we practice mindfulness, we bring ourselves into that presence.

Recently someone asked me the classic question: "Is there a goal in meditation?" Of course, there are goals in meditation, like finding peace, gaining insight, and opening the heart. Ultimately, enlightenment (whatever that is) is the goal of the Buddhist path. But the problem is that any goal requires "doing" to attain, and that action or desire conflicts with the essence of practice, which is just to be, to open to what is with a sense of allowing and acceptance. Karen Armstrong quotes a great mystic who says that "every concept grasped by the mind becomes an obstacle in the quest to those who search" for God. Not only is the doing of action an impediment on the path, but so is the doing of thinking.

The non-dual Buddhist and Hindu traditions offer guidance—of a sort—on this problem. For instance, Suzuki Roshi, in *Zen Mind, Beginner's Mind,* says that "you should not be bothered by the various images you find in your mind. Let them come, and let them go." But then he admits that this is a tough challenge. Somewhat enigmatically, he tells us that finding the way to balance doing and being "is the secret of practice."

Ajahn Chah appears to raise the ante when he says, "The Buddha-Dharma is not to be found in moving forwards, nor in moving backwards, nor in standing still." Well, now it seems that even *being* is a problem if we can't find truth in standing still. Ajahn Amaro says that "Ajahn Chah was trying to push his inquirers up against the limitations of the conditioned mind, in hopes of opening up a space for the unconditioned to shine through." So ultimately this is where being takes us—to the unconditioned, nirvana. When we come into stillness we are, in a sense, trying to imitate this unconditioned state. We're doing nothing, creating no karma. This then makes a breakthrough more possible. As the Zen saying goes, "Enlightenment is an accident, and meditation makes you accident-prone."

A friend said to me recently, "I'm having trouble with my Higher Power. I don't know if I'm really connecting with that."

I asked him, "But you're still staying sober, right? You're working in harmony with the Law of Karma. Your livelihood is skillful; you're trying to live a moral life, non-harming."

He said he was, and when I said that these were also part of his connection with God, he understood. I could have listed other things—his service work, his meditation practice, his appreciation of impermanence and suffering. All of these are expressions of a connection to a Higher Power. The trouble is, sometimes we don't *feel* it.

When I teach the Dharma, I'm not usually experiencing the things I'm talking about, but I have confidence in what I'm saying because I've been there. The insights I've had don't necessarily stay alive for me in every moment, but all those experiences have changed me and informed my life. I don't always feel them, but I remember them and they guide me.

We may not always be on top of the mountain, but if we go there we are changed, and when we come back down we remember the view. It stays in our hearts.

The truth is that we become attached to spiritual experiences the same way we get attached to drugs and alcohol and sex and food and TV and all the rest. If it's pleasant, we want more. And an important part of spiritual growth is letting go of our attachment to those peak moments. They can, and hopefully will, continue to have meaning in our lives, to guide us and to act as touchstones that we return to again and again, but we can't get those moments back. Our initial experiences of recovery may also have this quality as we first taste the freedom from our addiction. After a while, though, we might settle into a routine and feel that we've lost something, some magic or some special status. The initial breakthrough, taking Step One and admitting our powerlessness, is a transforming insight, but it has to be kept alive if we want to stay clean and sober. Ayya Khema says we have to "practice our insights," and this is true of recovery. Even if we aren't *feeling* magical, we need to remember the preciousness and, yes, the magic of recovery. It might not be so important to always feel that way, but it is vital that we remember. When we forget our disease, when we forget our powerlessness, we open the possibility of falling back to that state, to reliving that truth.

In the Buddha's story, we hear about his night of enlightenment, and then he goes on and teaches for 45 years. We don't hear about him having another enlightenment experience. It's pretty clear that his meditations are on another level of depth from those of the typical practitioner, but we also hear that at times he's still troubled by Mara, the Tempter, who tries to make him angry or disturb him in some way. Mara is a symbol for the Five Hindrances. He is the embodiment of all that agitates our minds and bodies. When he appears, the Buddha usually just sees him and, as he shines the light of awareness on this energetic disturbance, Mara slinks away. Apparently the Buddha's power of mindfulness is so strong that just by noticing a hindrance or some troubling thought or feeling, he is able to dissipate it. But the larger point, to me, is that *he's still attacked.* Even though he's attained complete enlightenment and Buddhahood, difficult things still appear in his mind. So you might say that it's not that he has perfected his mind, but that he has perfected his *reaction* to his mind. And I think we could say that this is the key to peace: not attaining some permanently blissful inner state, but developing the ability to be okay with whatever is happening.

Prayer: I open myself to the presence of God, and I trust that when I can't feel God, It is still here with me.

THE HIGHER POWER OF
SPIRITUAL AWAKENING

The Higher Power of Spiritual Awakening is the transforming power of insight and enlightenment. The ultimate goal of the path, it frees the heart by uprooting the poisons of greed, hatred, and delusion.

The culmination of the spiritual path is enlightenment or awakening. The definition of this experience varies greatly across different traditions—even the different schools of Buddhism have conflicting ideas of what enlightenment means. Nonetheless, in theistic and mystical traditions, these experiences are often said to be connected with God, whether in the sense of being in the presence of God as I've just described, being one with God, or actually experiencing God. In whatever way we understand them, such experiences are clearly profound and potentially transformative. However, if we say that enlightenment, the absolute, is God and everything else isn't, we create a problem. I believe that it's more accurate to include both the relative and the absolute in defining God. They depend upon each other and, if God encompasses all of reality, then they must both be included in our understanding of It.

The Buddhist term for enlightenment, *nirvana,* is another one of those Sanskrit words whose definition has been corrupted in translation. It probably doesn't help that the word was used as the name for a band led by a heroin addict who shot himself. Indeed, in the West, nirvana has often been associated with blissed-out drug states. It's also

123

thought of as a place, like heaven. However, neither of these comes anywhere close to the way the Buddha defined it.

The Buddha talked about nirvana (*nibbana* in Pali) as being like a fire that's gone out. According to Thanissaro Bhikkhu, a Buddhist monk and scholar, for an Indian of the time this would be "a metaphorical lesson in how freedom could be attained by letting go," because Indian physics viewed fire as "clinging to its fuel." This, then, gives us the easiest way to understand nirvana: letting go. The Twelve Steps, too, are about letting go. First we let go of our addictions, then we work at letting go of our character defects.

When I began to practice meditation, I envisioned nirvana as a distant, unattainable goal. Then, when I came to the Twelve Steps, I was confused to see that they said you could have a spiritual awakening just by working the Steps. But once I'd gotten through the Steps I didn't feel that I'd attained any high state of consciousness. Eventually I came to believe that there were different levels of spiritual awakening. Just realizing that I was an alcoholic and addict was an awakening. I was coming out of the denial, the delusion of my disease. And every stage of recovery has had some element of awakening. Buddhadasa Bhikkhu talks about "little nirvanas," how every day we have moments of letting go that are small tastes of nirvana. I think it's important to hold this view as part of our understanding so that we don't live with a perpetual sense of inadequacy in our spiritual life. We need to see the ways that our practice is valuable, the ways it is bearing fruit here and now.

For my purposes, what I want to know is, what is the power of spiritual awakening? It seems to me that the Higher Power of Awakening has two elements: the internal and external transformations. The internal transformation has to do with our relationship to the world, and it's this aspect that is typically referred to when we describe enlightenment: You're no longer attached to the world. There's no clinging to self or other, no craving for pleasure or objects. This is the total uprooting of what are called the three poisons or *kilesas*: greed, hatred, and ignorance. Obviously such an experience would be incredibly powerful, since it would change everything about your relationship to yourself and to life.

The external transformation is the one that Step Twelve mentions, the urge to serve. Enlightenment reveals the illusory nature of "I," which naturally turns us toward service to others. Step Twelve says that "having had a spiritual awakening as the result of these Steps, we tried to carry this message to alcoholics . . ." In other words, spiritual awakening isn't a selfish experience—as soon as it happens, we'll want to give it away. This is what happened to the Buddha. Once he was enlightened, after some moments of doubt as to whether anyone would be able to understand what he had seen, he set out to teach the Dharma. And that's what he did for the rest of his life. The power of that external manifestation of his enlightenment is still resonating through the world today.

These breakthroughs, enlightenment or spiritual awakening, can be categorized in different ways. One is the sudden, out-of-the-blue type and another is the cultivated "educational variety." I have met and read about many people who've had the former; sometimes it sticks and sometimes it doesn't. The power that comes from a sudden experience really depends upon the follow-up by the person who's had the experience. If it's taken as a prompt for a spiritual journey—someone like Eckhart Tolle, the author of *The Power of Now,* is an example of this—then it can open into a full-blown transformative experience. However, it also happens that people have an awakening experience and, instead of trying to learn from it, keep trying to repeat it or get it back; some people get overwhelmed by a mystical moment; and some people just ignore it.

The educational variety of awakening is more common. Step by step we open up, become more wise, more kind, more skillful in our lives. One day we look back and realize that we are completely different people. No single moment defines this transformation, but it is authentic and deep. Once attained, this doesn't have the slipperiness of the sudden awakening, which may or may not take. The gradual awakening is a thorough transformation that involves all three elements of the Buddhist path, morality, meditation, and wisdom. The sudden variety is usually oriented toward wisdom, but until the other two elements are cultivated, the wisdom isn't grounded.

Devoting ourselves to the quest for enlightenment may be the most meaningful thing we can do with our lives. The power that comes through this experience is the most transformative force a human being can engage. All spiritual paths ultimately aim for this awakening.

Prayer: May my efforts in practice bring spiritual awakening. May my awakening be of benefit to all beings.

THE HIGHER POWER
OF THE GROUP

The Higher Power of the Group is the power of community,
of human support. It frees us from shame and absorbs our suffering.
Through the group come wisdom, love, and companionship.

There you are, thinking about going to your first Alcoholics Anonymous meeting. *Everyone there is going to know I'm an alcoholic when I show up,* you think. The idea of being exposed to a community as having a drinking problem is painful. A sense of shame and embarrassment comes over you. Still, after the DUI and the fight with your wife, not to mention the years of trying to control it, the blackouts, the hangovers . . . it's time.

Driving across town you're still torn. *Maybe I'll just go home and watch some football.* But somehow you resist the impulse to run. The meeting's in the basement of a church you've driven by many times. You never knew that all these alcoholics congregated here. As you come up the walk, a few people smoking cigarettes and laughing nod and say, "Hi." You grunt and look down.

You step into the room, fluorescent-lit with folding chairs in a circle. You find a spot with no one nearby and sit. When you look up and see all the other faces in the room, no one is staring at you. No one is pointing fingers or whispering. Suddenly it hits you: *They're alcoholics too! They can't shame me if they're just like me.* A wave of relief comes over you as you breathe deeply and settle in for the meeting.

The first thing we discover at Twelve Step meetings is that we're not alone and that we don't have to hide anymore. While addiction has many torments, the sense of isolation and shame is one that tends to grow stronger the deeper we get into our disease. This can be one of the final blocks to recovery when we come to the point of acknowledging our addiction and a desire to change arises. While we might be ready to admit to ourselves that we have a problem, and perhaps to some intimates as well, to go into a room full of strangers and say, "My name is Kevin and I'm . . ." is a big step.

But when we do enter that room, when we raise our hand, when we say those words, we experience the Higher Power of the Group.

If I think that it's me against drugs and alcohol, against my craving, my obsession and compulsion, the task of recovery seems insurmountable. But when I realize that there are many, many people sharing this work, something changes. I see that others have been able to do it; they tell me that I can call them any time I need to talk; they tell me their stories, and I realize that I'm not unique, that, in fact, my condition is rather common, not nearly as dramatic or tragic as I'd thought. They tell me how they did it, and the whole process of recovery starts to look like something that makes sense. It's not mysterious or particularly complicated: go to meetings and don't drink or use in between; find a sponsor and work the Steps; be willing to take suggestions and to look critically at the way you're living. Be willing to change.

When we go to meetings and hear people's stories, then see that they are living productive, happy lives, we realize that we can be like them. We remember the person we were before the disease of addiction took over. We see the goodness in ourselves because the group and its members show it to us.

One of the Buddha's similes explains the way the group can take in our suffering. He compares dropping a pinch of salt into a glass of water, how that would make the water undrinkable, to putting the same amount of salt into the River Ganges, where it wouldn't even be noticed. In the same way, if we depend on one person, a partner or friend, to be our sole confidant, to absorb all our pain, that person can become overwhelmed, whereas when we share the same thing with a group, the group is unfazed. No one in a meeting has to bear the burden of our pain. They are silent witnesses, which is exactly what we need. When we hear ourselves speak to the community we hear ourselves in a different way, with the ears of one who cares, with the ears of compassion and wisdom. Many times, right in the process of sharing, I've learned something I didn't know. Somehow, the group's presence, its openness and acceptance, allowed me to discover something about myself that I couldn't seem to find any other way.

In both the Buddhist and Twelve Step traditions the community is seen as one of the central forces for support of spiritual growth. In Buddhism this is called the *sangha,* a term that originally meant the community of monastics but is now used more generally to refer to all the followers of the Buddha. Sangha is one-third of the Triple Gem or the Three Refuges, Buddha, Dharma, Sangha. By surrendering yourself to the sangha you let go of self-centeredness, immerse yourself in service, and reinforce your faith in the efficacy of the path. In the recovery world, the community is even more valued. Many people use the fellowship as their Higher Power, and meetings, gatherings of the fellowship, are the main form of Twelve Step ritual.

Community gives us inspiration, showing us that the Steps and the Buddhist practices work. Community helps us through the times when our own power is weak. Community is also a place where we can give of ourselves, where we can be of service and see our value in the world. Many people find their meditation to be more powerful in a group. And sharing in a meeting is one of the most healing spiritual practices I know of.

Besides the power of community, both traditions show the need for a spiritual mentor—a sponsor in the Twelve Steps or a teacher or guru in Buddhism. This personal connection with a person more experienced on the path is critical to our spiritual development. Getting through the Steps virtually requires a guide. In early sobriety, a sponsor is vital in helping us to learn not only how to stay sober, but, for many of us, how to live. Having a teacher also tremendously facilitates learning Buddhist meditation. While books hold lots of information, there's nothing like the right word at the right time to help us through the struggles of spiritual practice.

Sitting in a Twelve Step meeting, we hear dozens of opinions and everything from wisdom to insanity. It's not so much the individuals in the group that guide us, but, as the acronym GOD suggests, the "Group Of Drunks." While the Buddhist world is more hierarchical, it too depends on the interrelationships between teacher and community, and among community members, to thrive.

Turning our will and our lives over to the care of the group means showing up and being "part of." The isolating tendency of addicts is insidiously destructive. We start out avoiding one meeting and wind up shut off from the world. To be in harmony with the Higher Power of the Group means something of a submersion of identity in the group—placing "principles before personalities." The group supports us, but it also gives us the opportunity to do service; both are healing.

The Twelve Step tradition refers to a "group conscience," and while this sometimes simply means a majority vote, it also is talking about a kind of collective wisdom that arises from the group. We might not want to listen to the advice of each individual member, but if we hang around and pay attention, we start to hear the common threads that run through the sharing in the group. The foundation of Twelve Step sharing is to talk about our experience, not our opinions, and we find a great deal of helpful guidance in these stories.

Being open to the power of the group gives us a huge resource to draw upon. Our whole life has been made possible by others—starting with our parents and all the people who have been a part of our lives and our growth. Letting in and drawing on the power of others expands the possibilities of our own lives; giving of our power *to* others expands the meaning and value of our lives.

Prayer: I commit myself to being a part of my recovery and practice communities. I open myself to the wisdom of these groups and I offer myself in service to them.

THE MYSTERY

Some people object to the very idea of talking about God because they feel that it's so unexplainable that it's better left as a mystery. Obviously, if I felt that way, I wouldn't be writing this book. But I want to acknowledge and honor that viewpoint. And I can say that in certain ways I feel the same. When it comes to exploring the questions of presence and nirvana, and going further to what might (or might not) be behind the powers I'm looking at, we venture into the unknown. Any ideas in this realm are merely conjecture.

It's the human longing to *know* that leads people to muse on these topics. From a Buddhist standpoint, this longing is just another form of desire, and thus a cause of suffering. This is why the Buddha discouraged certain lines of inquiry. When he was asked about first causes, he wouldn't answer; when asked about how karma worked, he said that trying to unravel the strands of karma, trying to figure out all the causes that created a particular circumstance, would drive you crazy. "What's the point?" he asked. "What I'm interested in is suffering and the end of suffering." Answering metaphysical questions wouldn't end suffering, so he wasn't going to spend his time trying to do it. One thing you can say about the Buddha is that he didn't try to drum up business by telling people what they wanted to hear.

Nonetheless, there are powers, what we can call "aspects of God," that are evident. While I recognize that some aspects of God may be a mystery, that doesn't mean we can't look at the elements that we can see and try to understand how they work. What's important about God isn't to explain it, but to live in harmony with it.

Part II

THE PATH OF RECOVERY

A couple of years ago I decided to teach a workshop that focused on those Steps of the Twelve that mentioned God or Higher Power. I'd been teaching about Buddhism and the Steps for a while, and questions about God were the most persistent and troubling that came up in my retreats and workshops. I looked at the Steps, which of course I'd already written a book about, and was surprised to find that six of them would fit into my workshop. I'd somehow thought that there were only three, maybe four God Steps. The Steps I included in the workshop and that I want to talk about now are Steps Two, Three, Five, Six, Seven, and Eleven.

As I explored the idea of God, I learned that all three of the Western monotheistic religions, Christianity, Judaism, and Islam, traced their roots back to one Biblical (and Koranic) figure: Abraham. So, when referring to these religions, I sometimes use the shorthand "Abrahamic religions" or the "Abrahamic God." While this is almost certainly the God that the authors of the Twelve Steps were referring to and the God that those in the West think of when they hear that word, other vital world religions such as Hinduism, Buddhism, and Confucianism have completely different conceptions—or no conception at all—of such a creator God. While we in the West might take for granted that God is God, much of the world would disagree.

One of the ways that I came to think of God was as "It." God is not a He or a She, but an It. When I say that I "turned my will and my life over to the care of God, *as I understood It,*" there's a shock of insight that happens; a new conception of God flashes through the mind, like the answer to a koan I didn't know I'd been asked.

Each of the God Steps suggests we take an action or actions in regards to God. It's these actions that interest me and that I want to explore.

From Despair to Hope: Step Two

"Came to believe that a Power greater than ourselves could restore us to sanity."

CHANGE IS POSSIBLE

The months leading up to my final drink were desperate times. Part of me knew now that I was an alcoholic and addict. But I couldn't see what to do about it. The idea of going to a program was anathema—in my mind that was the end of the line for losers. Surely I hadn't fallen so far. But that resistance to change only made things worse. When you're miserable but you see a way out, you have hope. When you don't see any escape, all you have is despair. And despair only leads to more destructive behavior. Why not drink and drug myself into oblivion if there's nothing to look forward to? Why live a moral life if there's no benefit? I'm past salvation anyway, so I might as well enjoy myself in the only way I know how.

These are the painful thoughts of a person caught between Steps One and Two. Step One is the complete admission to ourselves of our problem, the recognition that despite all our efforts, we can't control our addiction. This recognition is essential to any kind of recovery—until we see the problem clearly we can't begin to solve it. But sometimes we get stuck on the negative aspect of the Step and it makes things worse. In fact, we might misunderstand the Step to mean that we are helpless victims of our addiction. And if we don't believe in God, then the further Steps may seem unattainable. This is a dangerous place to be.

During the six months leading up to my getting sober, this was the state I was in. Having at least vaguely realized I was an alcoholic after taking the "20 Questions," I knew I had a problem, but I wasn't ready to deal with it or didn't understand how. As a result, I abandoned caution and my values and went on a final binge. I couldn't see a way out of my situation; I couldn't see what I needed to do. When I'd been able to convince myself that I wasn't really an alcoholic, I'd had some sense that I was managing things. Now I realized that I really wasn't in control, which in turn made me give up even trying to control my addictions.

The antidote to despair is hope. There are two kinds of hope. One kind is when we *hope* something will happen, even though we aren't doing anything about it. These hopes are more like dreams or fantasies. I used to have them in my music career. I'd be sitting around smoking dope and writing songs *hoping* that I'd be "discovered," as if someone were going to parachute into my bedroom and say, "Kevin Griffin, *you* are the next rock star!" The other kind of hope is when we *have* hope, that is, we believe that change is possible even though things look bad. We understand that if we take the right actions things will probably improve—no guarantees, but there's a good chance.

This is what Step Two is suggesting when it says we "came to believe that a Power greater than ourselves could restore us to sanity." Recovery is possible, the Step is saying, although in language that suggests an Abrahamic God. But if we look at the Step from a practical viewpoint—*What is supposed to happen here?*—rather than a theological one, we can see that the benefits of the Step don't depend on a belief in a monotheistic Higher Power. They do, however, depend on hope.

The fundamental flaw in the state of despair from a Buddhist perspective is the idea that change isn't possible. If everything is impermanent, then change is not only possible, but inevitable. Still, this is not necessarily reason for hope. Things might change for the worse. Or we might believe that things are bound to change, but that we are fated to live in misery. When you're stuck in an addictive cycle, one that may have been going on for many years, it can certainly seem that you'll never escape, that recovery just isn't meant to be for you.

This reveals another flaw in the state of despair: the lack of belief in the Law of Karma, the truth of cause and effect. If there's no possibility of escape from addiction, it means that my actions have no effect, and this is clearly not true. The Buddha called not seeing the truth "ignorance." Not seeing that everything is impermanent and that actions have results is ignorance, misunderstanding how the universe works. Most of us, when confronted with the question of whether everything keeps changing and actions have results, would agree that both ideas are true. But that's when the question is posed to our conscious minds. Unconsciously, we act out our ignorance. Unconsciously, we think that we are stuck, that things are hopeless, that our lives are pointless. These feelings of despair can be so powerful that they overwhelm any innate wisdom we might have. Sure, we might believe in cause and effect, but we still can't dig our way out of despair.

When I teach meditation and the Steps at treatment centers I often find people resistant to the God Steps. I begin by asking, "Why are you here?" And the answer is usually something like, "To get help for my X, Y, or Z" (drinking, drugging, eating, and so on). So I say, "Then you believe that this treatment center, the people here and their program, can help you to recover?" And the response is "Yes." Then I tell them that they've taken Step Two: they believe that a power greater than themselves—the center, its staff, and its program—can "restore them to sanity."

"But don't I have to believe in God?" they might say.

And I'll respond, "What's God?"

The people who created the Twelve Steps—Bill Wilson, Dr. Bob, and the other founders—had one perspective on how the Steps worked. That perspective came out of their own religious conditioning and cultural context. In some ways, they didn't understand what it was that they had discovered, this remarkable approach to healing addiction. I think that in many ways they *did* believe that you needed an Abrahamic God to do the Steps. But I don't think that what *they* believed about the Steps is as important as what *we* believe.

Our culture, and certainly our religious culture, has changed vastly since the 1930s, when the Steps were written. At that time there was almost no religious awareness beyond Christianity and Judaism in our country. The 1960s began a huge transformation. Many people started to turn away from the religion of their upbringing and search for other ways to engage the spirit. By the 1970s, Buddhism, Hinduism, and the entire New Age movement were opening up our understanding of what God and spiritual growth meant. We now live in a time when perhaps the most respected religious leader in the world is a Buddhist: the Dalai Lama. Teachings on meditation have become mainstream through well-known practices like yoga and mindfulness.

In this new cultural context, the meaning of Higher Power also takes on a broader meaning. We can look at this Step and ask how it's trying to help us. What are we supposed to do with this Step?

Simply put, the Step asks us to trust something other than our own self-will to solve our problems. Our self-centered, reactive, ego-driven mind has gotten us into this mess by trying to control what we feel, get what we want, and do whatever we like; we can't expect the thing that created this problem to solve it.

When I woke up that June morning with the acceptance that I couldn't drink—Step One—what I believed was that a Twelve Step program could help me stay sober. You could say that my first Higher Power was the program itself. I didn't know anything about the Steps, but I knew a couple of people who'd gotten sober, and I assumed it worked. That was enough to get me started.

The people I meet in treatment centers have mostly taken a similar Step by going in for treatment. They may not have a lot of confidence in themselves, or even in the program they're in, but they have enough to get started.

As the Twelve Step saying goes, "more will be revealed," and our beliefs about Higher Power will often evolve, as will our understanding of how the Steps and the recovery process work and what's required. But we don't have to figure all that out in the beginning. To get started, we just have to believe that some process, whether it's the Steps, a treatment center, God, meditation, Buddha, or *something,* can help. And once we've gotten started we can begin to build on our sobriety and on our spiritual understanding. Once we believe that change is possible, we've overcome despair and gained hope.

THE EVOLUTION OF GOD

When Step Two says we "came to believe," it implies a movement, a "coming." And this process of growing into our beliefs is ongoing. Our spiritual lives are dynamic, changing things that are conditioned by many of our experiences, going back to our earliest encounters with God and religion and leading up to the present moment. Exploring this evolution can be a helpful way of deconstructing our belief system and understanding how we got where we are. What we learn in this exploration can then help us to more consciously develop our beliefs.

My own experience with religion began with a Roman Catholic upbringing. Like most kids, I was often bored in church, but I also felt, at times, a strong sense of devotion and faith. The mystery of the Mass, communion, confession, the incense and prayers all created a powerful belief system for me. I became an altar boy in fourth grade and was inspired by being admitted into the ritual.

But all of that was a child's understanding. My intellect wasn't engaged, and when, as a teenager, I began to question my beliefs, they pretty quickly disintegrated. It was the mid-60s and the world was changing. Our country was fighting a crazy war, rock 'n' roll was sweeping through my life, and the struggle between generations was forming. My generation was rejecting the old ways, and one part of that was a rejection of the old religion. By the time I had my driver's license I no longer believed in God.

But it's probably not surprising that someone raised with strong beliefs sought out some replacements. I became interested in whatever new spiritual trend I heard about, Scientology, Edgar Cayce, astrology, I Ching. None of these really took. I didn't develop any discipline or study anything very deeply. By that time my real gods were drugs, alcohol, sex, and rock 'n' roll. Still, there was clearly a part of me that wanted some more vital connection.

By my late 20s I finally did develop a discipline, Transcendental Meditation, or TM. It had taken over ten years from the time I first heard about meditation through the Beatles' studies with Maharishi Mahesh Yogi till I actually got around to doing TM. This was typical of my alcoholic/pothead behavior. I always meant to meditate, but I just never took the practical steps to learn. One of the reasons it took so long was the requirement that you stop smoking pot for two weeks before learning TM, and that seemed an insurmountable requirement.

In any case, I took on TM very diligently—one case where the addictive personality was actually helpful. I did it for 20 minutes twice a day, just as prescribed. I was great with the form, but I'm afraid my actual practice was lacking. Soon after learning to meditate, I went back to regular pot-smoking, and it wasn't unusual for me to do my evening meditation under the influence of drugs or alcohol, a pretty pointless exercise. The practice never went very deep at all, and that disappointed me. I thought that the mantra was supposed to do some magic, make me happy, enlightened, levitate, whatever, not realizing that I actually had to put my heart into the effort for it to work. One day when I complained to a friend about my lack of progress, he told me that smoking pot was sure to stunt my meditative growth. That surprised me—I thought you were only supposed to quit for the first two weeks. Surely they couldn't expect someone to quit smoking pot for good?

By the time I was 30 I was ready for something new, and that's when I encountered Buddhism. My meditation finally began to deepen on retreat, and I felt I was making real progress. Amazingly enough, though, it didn't pierce my alcoholism. I still drank and took drugs regularly between retreats. And when I didn't achieve some totally transforming spiritual experience on the three-month retreat, I became restless.

Up to this time, my belief in God had been pretty much dormant. I probably wasn't an absolute atheist anymore as I'd been as a teenager, but I didn't have any real belief. When I met the homeless guru who called himself Ananda—a guy from Detroit in jeans and a polo shirt—I was open enough to taking on a renewed faith in an Abrahamic God, mainly because I desperately hoped that doing so would bring the transforming enlightenment experience I craved so deeply. I was sure that somehow this experience was going to solve all my problems and make me happy for the rest of my life.

My time with Ananda was short, but it made a big imprint. Even after I left him I carried with me the magical beliefs he taught. Over the next three years I lived with this hodgepodge, a mixture of New Age, Buddhism, Christianity, Hinduism, Kabbalah, and I don't know what all, till I finally got sober. Ananda's teachings fit my alcoholic personality better than the discipline of Buddhism. He promised more or less instant enlightenment and taught a non-dual perspective that essentially tossed out moral guidelines as irrelevant to an enlightened being (like him—or me). The gradual path founded on principles of non-harming and ancient teachings was all old hat to him. The convenience of his teachings, along with his confidence and charisma, convinced me.

One effect, though, of being with Ananda was that when I first saw the Steps, unlike many people, I didn't have a big problem with the word God. I was able to slide by with the Steps, saying prayers, turning it over, and all the rest, based on the conditioning of my previous life, all the way from my earliest Catholic upbringing through Ananda's jumble of teachings.

When I arrived at the program and "came to believe," this was my background. I see now that my entire spiritual history was influential in my ability to work Step Two. Of course, my spiritual experience and understanding has continued to evolve, as I described in the beginning of the book, so Step Two is different for me today than it was then, but what was important at the time was that I had some way into the Step, some way of connecting. When we engage Step Two, if there is a struggle, it's important to look at our history, our spiritual conditioning, to understand how we got to this place of resistance. If we see our problem as simply a conditioned response, we may be able to overcome it by putting aside our prejudices for the moment and "acting as if," just doing the Step to the best of our ability and seeing what the results are.

According to the Buddha, one of the great impediments to spiritual growth and wisdom is "views and opinions." Most of us have pretty strong views and opinions about God—positive or negative. Once we see the conditioned nature of our views, it becomes easier to let go into the process, instead of staying stuck in the critical stance that blocks us from doing the work necessary for transformation.

SEARCHING FOR SERENITY

Early in my recovery, the Serenity Prayer became my main spiritual support: "God, grant me the serenity to accept the things I cannot change, courage to change the things I can, and wisdom to know the difference."

I see myself in a bar in Odessa, Texas. I'm on the road with the Hollywood Argyles, a phony oldies band pretending to be the original one-hit wonder from 1962. I'd resisted going on the road with them, but shortly after getting sober, unable to find another gig in L.A., I took them up on their offer to tour.

The bar is called Champoux—too cutesy by half—and it's a former disco. Over the dance floor is the inevitable mirror ball. We're getting ready to rehearse and the singer and bass player are on stage bickering—their usual form of communication. I wind my way through the plush red chairs toward the stage and repeat the prayer. The words "God grant me the serenity . . ." remind me that peace is superior to any other mind state and worth doing whatever is necessary to acquire. Looking up at B.J. and Bobby, I realize that I have no control over their behavior. I'm in this situation this afternoon and I can either accept it and be serene or resist it and suffer. I breathe and let that truth settle over me. I feel relief right then and there.

This acceptance part of the prayer has always been the most important line for me. It resonates with the famous Big Book passage on acceptance:

> And acceptance is the answer to *all* my problems today. When I am disturbed, it is because I find some person, place, thing, or situation—some fact of my life—unacceptable to me, and I can find no serenity until I accept that person, place, thing, or situation as being exactly the way it is supposed to be at this moment.

When I say the words about acceptance to myself and step on the stage and pick up my guitar feeling relief and lightness in my heart, it isn't an external God that has helped transform my mind state. It is my own inner wisdom that sees the truth of the words and realizes that fighting the situation is pointless. The words pull me out of my reactive state of aversion to the bandleaders and remind me of the bigger picture—yes, this is unpleasant, but since I can't change it, standing in opposition to it, holding onto aversion, is pointless.

I didn't see it that way at the time. I did feel I was reaching out to something or someone when I prayed. But when I felt that serenity, I didn't feel that it was coming from outside. I wasn't really reflecting on the process, on the contradiction in my own understanding of my experience. So what? It was working, and that's what was important. I was sober—for just a few weeks at that time—and staying sober and sane was the priority, not figuring out how my prayers were working.

Today when I say the Serenity Prayer I still say "God," but only for convenience. Occasionally when I stop and think about it, I'll put it this way: "May I have the serenity to accept . . ." This is the phrasing that Buddhist lovingkindness and compassion practices use. It's not speaking to a particular being, but it's still opening to something beyond the small self.

The second part of the prayer, "courage to change the things I can," focuses on the work of recovery—and life. For me this tends to be less about a moment of stress, as acceptance often is, but about my responsibilities and goals and how I fulfill and attain them. Oftentimes it's not necessarily courage that I need, more determination and patience, but in any case, I find myself facing my own passivity and impatience with this part of the prayer. Many times it's easier to give up than to persist; to run away than to confront; to hide out than engage. And this part of the prayer helps me to address those shrinking impulses and to put in the effort that's needed to accomplish my goals.

At around two years sober my sponsor helped me learn how I might do this. I was working for an airport shuttle service, a job I really enjoyed. There was something exciting about it, meeting people at LAX or picking them up at the start of their journey, trying to figure out the best routes around L.A., getting tips, and being independent in my van. One night I was about to end my evening shift when I got a call to take someone to Palm Springs. This would be a three-hour trip each way, which meant a solid commission, plus a probable good tip. I took the call and wound up driving a soldier home to his family.

On the way back from the desert I hit the predawn rush-hour traffic and a long trip got even longer. By the time I got back to the yard with my van, I had just enough time to go home, catch some sleep, and get back for the beginning of my shift. I was anxious to be on time because the company was offering a free trip to Hawaii to any driver who had a spotless on-time record for two months.

A couple of rides into my shift, I was coming up La Cienega through the hills south of L.A., taking a businessman to the airport. I was looking a few cars ahead, so that I could anticipate any problems, when suddenly there was a big Cadillac stopped in front of me. I slammed on my brakes, but too late. I plowed into it. The businessman was flung forward in his seat belt while my wrists snapped back on the steering wheel. The front end of the van accordioned. I couldn't believe it. There was no reason for the Cadillac to stop as far as I could see. It seemed like it had just appeared there. I got out of the van and began the slow process of unraveling the accident. Shortly one of our other vans came along and took my grumbling passenger on his trip.

As I went through the motions of trading information with the other driver, getting our van towed into the yard, and filling out the report, I knew what it meant: My van-driving career was over. The company insurance policy required that someone who got in an accident be fired. The next day they let me go.

I spent the next two days in bed, nursing my sore wrists and my fear and disappointment. I played the accident over and over in my head, how the Caddy had appeared out of nowhere. I didn't want to accept that I had been overtired and made a mistake. But worse, how was I going to get a job? All those ads in the paper. It was too much. I just couldn't do it. Then I talked to my sponsor.

"Look through the paper and call three places each day," he said. "Then you're done for the day. Don't try to do it all in one day. Just keep showing up one day at a time."

What he was teaching me was just to engage in the process and not get caught up in getting immediate results. It was one of the simplest, and perhaps most obvious, lessons I ever learned. And it worked. I've used the same process for the last 20 years, to get through college, to find jobs, to deepen my meditation, and to write this book. The "courage to change the things I can" for me is mostly about showing up. So, oddly enough, the courage I need is to trust the process, to believe that if I just do a little bit each day, I'll reach my goal. Before I learned this lesson I would kind of rush at a problem and try to get it fixed right away. If it didn't get fixed, I'd give up with what I thought was a "spiritual" response: "It's not meant to be." That's magical thinking. What's "meant to be" is that which is and that which can be—and it's only intention and actions that determine what is and what will be (within the parameters of what nature allows). That doesn't mean that you can do *anything*, but it does mean that you don't know if you can do it until you've exhausted the process of trying. Everyone has a different point of exhaustion, of course, so this isn't a formula, but really a guide for our hearts.

Again, it isn't some external God that gives me this courage, this determination. It's something that is inside me that I have to awaken or develop. When I say the words, I remind myself of my potential. I remind myself that giving up leads nowhere and persistence may pay off—and if not, I can go back to the first part of the prayer and try to accept my disappointment.

The final part of the prayer, "the wisdom to know the difference," resolves it. What can I change and what do I need to just accept? Often I don't even get to this question because it's become obvious as I reflect on my situation what I needed to do. So when I do get here, it's often with a sense of relief: I know what to do. My wisdom has shown me already.

Wisdom can be an intimidating word. To call yourself wise can seem arrogant. Don't you have to live in a cave for 30 years and grow a long white beard to be wise? There's no doubt that life experience—and maybe a lot of spiritual practice—helps us to develop wisdom. One formula is "experience plus attention equals wisdom." If we really pay attention to life, we'll learn how things work. Attention is crucial; we can have lots of experiences, but if we're not viewing them through discerning eyes, wisdom won't develop, just a lot of stories. Once we've put attention together with experience, we will begin to develop a deep wisdom.

This wisdom, once again, comes from within. Is it already there— are we just awakening it—or does it have to be planted and cultivated in our heart and mind? I don't claim to know the answer to that. But what's clear is that when it does ripen, when it does appear, it appears inside us. It's not coming as some external voice or inspiration that tells us what is true.

The Serenity Prayer became the foundation for growth for me over those early years of sobriety. Gradually the magical beliefs faded away and were replaced by a practical, karma-based approach to God: keep showing up, doing the best you can, trying to be kind, honest, and aware. The mad search for salvation, for a fix, for bliss and escape, finally died away as life started to work. A simple faith in the Twelve Steps and in the principles of recovery, honesty, open-mindedness, and willingness carried me.

LOSING GOD, FINDING BUDDHA

During the first seven years of my recovery, I didn't worry much about philosophy, how the process worked, or figuring it all out. I continued to practice Buddhist meditation, but I didn't see how it was connected to the Steps, other than to Step Eleven, which specifically suggests meditating. In fact, in my limited vision, I thought of Buddhism as in conflict with the Steps, the God stuff, powerlessness, inventory—somehow I couldn't see the connection. All I knew was that I loved Buddhism and the practice and I loved and needed the Steps and recovery. I was also in therapy, which I didn't know how to connect to the other two either, so I thought of all three of these supports as a three-legged stool, separate, but working together to hold me up.

But recovery and spiritual development are not static processes. Many people, after solving the major addiction issues in their lives, start to go through other experiences. Sometimes people have a spiritual crisis at five or ten years sober; others, of course, go back to drinking or drugging when they think they've "recovered." Many people I've met feel in early recovery that they are being held or carried by some spiritual power, but that as they age in sobriety, that special feeling dissipates. Some wind up feeling spiritually barren or become atheists or cynical and bitter. This is a critical point in recovery.

Perhaps this kind of crisis occurs because once the surface wounds of addiction are healed, the deeper traumas begin to surface. Some addiction professionals these days point to early trauma as being a cause of addiction, and while I think it's hard to generalize about that, I do think that there are layers of healing that have to happen to stay sober. Is it childhood trauma, accumulated pain of addiction, genetic baggage, or even accumulated karma from past lives? I certainly don't know. And I don't think it's as important to figure out the causes as it is to have tools for healing and recovery. The Twelve Step literature says that we should use whatever other help we need and draw from professionals or spiritual teachers for guidance in our recovery. For many people, I think this is vital. While it's true that some find the Steps, meetings, literature, and fellowship to be enough support for anything they go through in recovery, others have crises that call for further help. Unfortunately, this is sometimes because some aspect of the program, especially the God part, becomes alienating. Some people start to feel disconnected from meetings and the fellowship, while others may feel betrayed by a sponsor or a sober friend. Whatever precipitates a crisis in recovery, whether it's anxiety, depression, alienation, or spiritual disconnection, if we don't address it we risk not only our sobriety but our very lives.

Earlier I described my own crisis, losing the ability to pray to an external God while I was on a self-retreat at seven years sober. I was fortunate that I had a core practice to guide me through this time. In fact, it was then that my Buddhist practice began to come back to me, to become more central in my life. I'd always known how important it was and how special the teachings were, but for those early sober years I also knew I just needed to get my life together, to learn how to live a normal life. Once that was established, though, my hunger for something deeper was aroused. Although I'd already been practicing Buddhist meditation for 12 years at that time, in some ways I consider that turning point to be the real beginning of my practice. Prayer to God became less important, while the direct experience of presence became more prevalent. I started to finally make the Buddhist connections with the Steps as my spiritual life became integrated.

Over time I came to see how all the powers associated with God were contained in the Dharma, and I arrived at what can be called Dharma God. Does this mean that I never think of God as external or magical anymore? No. There are still times, especially in moments of despair or fear, when I feel disconnected from everything, and in those moments God *is* outside me, at least separate from the overwhelming painful consciousness I'm caught in, so it makes sense to pray to "Him" at that time. Ultimately, the concept of God is something we use. The Steps are very practical, and that's my approach, too. How can I use the concept of God to help me in this moment? That's the question I ask, and then I use whatever concept is most useful. You might see that as inconsistent with my "beliefs," but beliefs *are* inconsistent. They develop, they change, they evolve, they backtrack. Like the Twelve Step program, the Buddha was very practical. He said that it wasn't really necessary to know everything about the creation of the universe and how karma works and all the other mysteries in the world. Instead he focused on suffering and the end of suffering—we could say, on addiction and recovery. What causes suffering and how can I end it? That's what he wanted to know, it's what he figured out, and it's what he taught. And, as I've said, one of the things that causes us suffering is being attached to our views and opinions, in other words, our beliefs. As our understanding of God evolves, these beliefs change. Sometimes that happens easily and smoothly, other times it precipitates a crisis in our lives. If we can see that "coming to believe" is an ongoing process, one that may continue to the end of our lives, then we may not struggle so much or worry about whether we are believing the "right" thing or that our beliefs are "true." Ultimately, I think we should be most concerned, not about the accuracy of our beliefs, but about their efficacy. Oftentimes I can't know if they are true, but I can usually tell if they are helping me or not. And that's what I want to know. Are my beliefs leading to the end of suffering?

DIVING IN:
STEP THREE

*"Made a decision to turn our will and our lives
over to the care of God,* as we understood Him."

BEGINNING THE PATH

Step Three starts by saying we "made a decision." For an addict or alcoholic, just making a decision—any decision—is progress. When you're out there drinking and using, you don't decide, "First I'll roll out of bed at 2 P.M., then I'll start the day with a glass of wine and a joint, then I'll flip out on my partner and run screaming around the house, then I'll eat something and purge, snort some coke, break down crying, and maybe shoot some heroin." You don't plan these things, you just act—*re*act, to every craving, every resentment, every trigger, every out-of-control feeling.

When we actually make a decision, that is, consider our options and choose the one that seems most sensible or practical, we are already moving away from addictive behavior.

From the time I was a teenager, I was reacting. I dropped out of high school because I didn't like the way school felt. I didn't care about the consequences, I just didn't want to feel that way, bored and oppressed. I became a musician because it felt good to play the guitar.

I didn't think about what kind of career I would have, what kind of life. Well, yes, I thought about it, but only in a completely deluded way: *I'm gonna be a star.* How was that going to happen? Who knows? It just was.

Eventually I became stuck in my identity as a musician. I didn't *believe* I could do anything other than play the guitar, so naturally I couldn't. I was afraid to try anything else, so naturally I didn't. More reactivity, and still no real decision-making.

Through the confused and chaotic final years of drinking and using, as I swung between intense spiritual practices and alcoholism, my reactivity started to go off the rails: *I'll do this meditation; wait, I'll follow this guru; no, wait, just let me get high; if I can just sell this song, I'll be okay; I need a woman, I need a job, I need a drug, a drink, a savior.* Even my decision to get sober was another reaction to the madness that had overcome me. Finally, though, that reaction led me to enough clarity to begin to make decisions. Not right away, as my first year of sobriety was still a bit of a pinball ride, from gig to gig and woman to woman. But when I finally got a sponsor and started to take the program seriously, I actually started to consider where I was in my life and what I needed to do.

I needed a job, as music wasn't cutting it, and now I was ready to do whatever it took. One of the side effects (*side* effects?) of marijuana can be a sensitivity that makes any conflict or difficulty unmanageable. When I was stoned I didn't want to do anything I didn't want to do—which is the definition of a *job,* isn't it? Something you do even though you don't want to because you need the money. (Hopefully, of course, we progress beyond this type of job, but in the beginning they are often like this.) With the dope and booze out of my system I had a lot more tolerance. I made a decision to get a messenger job because I had a car and a license and jobs were available: not an unreasonable decision, if I do say so. I also decided to start my own band because I had the skills to lead a band, I had connections for gigs, and I was tired of working for other bandleaders. More reasonable decision-making.

Finally, at three years sober I made one of the biggest decisions of my life: I was going to go to college. Such a decision would have been unimaginable for me before I was sober. My beliefs about myself, that I hated school, that I couldn't do it; my beliefs about school, that it was pointless, that it would take too long; all these beliefs and more stood in my way. But now it became clear that it was the most sensible thing to do. I didn't want to go on being a starving musician; there was an inexpensive community college nearby that I could enroll in; I was discovering that I did like to learn; and I was realizing that I had other talents than playing the guitar. All of this made sense. It's amazing, in some ways, to realize how *non*-sensical my earlier life was, how irrational and thoughtless I was. Amazing and sad. So many of us get caught in these reactive habits, never able to see clearly, never able to choose wisely, never able to approach life in any kind of a rational way. This is the disease of addiction.

When we "make a decision" in Step Three, ironically enough, given the thrust of the Step toward taking guidance from God, we are actually taking more rational control of our lives. Even as our lives become more oriented toward the spiritual, we are learning to be more practical as well.

TURNING OUR WILL AND OUR LIVES OVER TO THE PATH

The phrase "turned our will and our lives over to the care of God" can be one of the most troubling in the Steps. For those uncomfortable with the Western theistic tradition, the language here can be off-putting. It certainly has the tone of Christianity, and in our polarized culture, such a tone can be enough to send some people running out of a Twelve Step meeting. It doesn't have to be this way.

If we break down the phrase "turn our will and our lives over," we see that, first of all, it's talking about two separate things, *will* and *life*—motivation and action. In Buddhist terms, our will is our intention, and as I talked about before, "Right Intention" is one of the factors of the Noble Eightfold Path, the Buddha's prescription for freedom. Right Intention comes out of Right View, seeing clearly what causes suffering and what ends suffering. When we see these things clearly, we more naturally set our intention to do what it takes to end suffering. So, when we turn our will over to the Dharma, we are making a commitment to try to follow this path, even if it requires us to do things that go against our preferences or impulses.

Turning our lives over is about the actions we take based on our intentions. The most obvious factor of the Eightfold Path that this reflects is Right Action, the five precepts of non-harming. When we turn our lives over, we are saying that we are going to live differently,

153

to follow the set of moral guidelines that our spiritual beliefs set forth instead of acting on addictive craving.

When we change our actions, we change our karma. Simple as that. For teenagers—at least this teenager—I think this idea can be hard to grasp. If you have been well taken care of as a child, when you get to that crossover point as a teenager where you are old enough to make a lot of your own decisions and where you start to believe that you know more than the adults around you, it's easy to be deluded. The benefits you've had in your early life largely did not come from your own efforts; your food, shelter, clothing, and medicine were provided by your parents, who usually expected little in return. What I subconsciously learned from my comfortable upbringing was that everything just came to me without any work on my part. Today we call this a sense of "entitlement," and that's not an inaccurate way of describing it. But in my memory it's more of a deluded, magical way of viewing the world. I made bizarre logical leaps, such as, since the Beatles didn't know how to read music, then I didn't have to.

I remember distinctly sitting on the couch in our big living room, my parents facing me in one of those "We want to talk to you" modes. They were desperate to help me figure out a way I could be happy in school since I'd dropped out.

"What about music school?" my mother said. "We'd be happy to pay for that."

"No!" I screamed. "That would ruin it!"

Music school, as far as I was concerned, would turn me into a drone. I imagined playing muzak at a country club or being expected to play classical guitar. Really, I just wanted to do what I wanted to do—which was play around on the guitar, get high, and be a star. And the delusion was that, somehow since the Beatles had become rich and famous, I would, too. I had no fallback position. No Plan B. What if I didn't become a rock star by the time I was 21? My parents suggested that it might be a good idea to have a degree so I could do something else if need be. To me, that was just absurd. Why waste time studying stuff I didn't care about to get a degree I'd never use? That would just slow down my inevitable rise to fame and glory.

These decisions were the essence of *not* turning my will and my life over to the care of God—or of anything else. I was basing my decisions on a self-centered, reactive craving and aversion. Like the spoiled child I was, my response to my parents' generous, helpful, and sensible suggestion was to have a temper tantrum: *No, I won't go to music school and you can't make me.*

The years after this were spent mostly hanging out, getting high, playing the guitar, but not really working at it; writing songs, but without a rigorous discipline. In my 20s, I did get some discipline, and my songwriting developed. But when I listen to those old songs, I see that there is always at least one line that's weak or embarrassing. I never had the creative discipline to rewrite and rework a song until it really clicked. I had a fatalistic approach to songwriting, just as I did to much of life. I would stick to my first idea even if it wasn't that good. Again, this reflected a laziness, and also a fear of criticism, in this case just *self*-criticism. My songs were the one place in my life I felt as if I had control, so I didn't want to mess with them. And besides, all those songs were written when I was stoned, and being high on marijuana just makes you feel good, makes the songs sound good, and saps any critical energy. It was just too much trouble to try to improve on the first idea I came up with.

What's even more absurd about my attitude, is that even with the songs I did write, I rarely made any effort to sell them. Occasionally I would make a tape and send it to a record company. But it takes more than that to become successful. It takes some business sense and footwork. I just spent my time playing in Top 40 bands wondering why I wasn't a star.

Not taking action, but expecting results, is not to understand or live in harmony with the Law of Karma. I believed that just by thinking about something or wishing for it, I would get it: *I want to be a rock star, so I will be one.* This was flawed thinking, wrong view.

When I got sober and took the first Step, I saw how my approach to life, as Step One says, was "unmanageable." I realized that I needed to be open to other possibilities—my music career wasn't working, and not much else was either. The whole idea of seeking God's will suggested to me that I shouldn't just follow my impulses or do the first thing that came to mind. I should be more careful in my decision-making. Of course, this is what Step Three talks about—making a decision. I recognized that now, at 35, I hadn't built a life for myself, but that I still could. I saw sober people around me who were changing their lives, who were doing whatever was needed. I realized that my approach to life, which was that if I met any resistance to anything I tried I should just give up, was not reasonable. If something was difficult, it wasn't a message from the universe. It just meant that more time and/or effort might be necessary. Or perhaps a change of course. While in the past I had thought that I *was* following God's will by giving up if something didn't work out right away, I now found that by making more of my own effort to accomplish things, I was more in tune with God's will. That's because, God's will isn't some magical fate laid out beforehand, but, rather, the fruits of karmic efforts—as well as the "truth of the way things are."

Those fruits aren't always the ones we want. Sometimes we make a great effort, only to fail or to get some unexpected results. When I signed up for a creative writing class on the advice of my first community college English teacher, I was just trying to do "God's will," to respond to the wisdom of other, more knowledgeable people. But, much like my music career, my prospects as a famous novelist didn't pan out the way I wanted.

This is when the acceptance implied in the Step is so important. When things don't turn out as we'd like, this is where we need to place our heart. As the Serenity Prayer says, it is through acceptance that we find peace. Winding up as a technical writer wasn't glamorous, but it gave me a respectable profession, something I'd never had. And that profession came as a direct result of all the work I'd put into learning to write: it was the karmic fruit of my efforts.

Many people in recovery have similar stories, finding themselves living a life that they never imagined but that is satisfying and meaningful. This comes about not through forcing our own preferences or desires, but by accepting the cards we are dealt and doing our best to work with them. Turning our will and our lives over to the care of God is a two-way street: we let go of our self-centered desires as best we can; we show up and do our best, and, although we might not get exactly what we think we want, something good comes, usually something that actually makes our lives work better than our fantasies would.

TAKING REFUGE

In the Buddhist tradition, the parallel to "turning your will and your life over to the care of God" is taking Refuge in the Buddha, the Dharma, and the Sangha. This means committing ourselves to be mindful, awake like the Buddha; to living in harmony with the truth, with the Dharma; and living a life of non-harming, supporting and being supported by the followers of the Buddha, the Sangha.

In the Five Daily Recollections we are told that we "take Refuge in our karma." This doesn't mean that some magical force is looking out for us. It means that if we live well we'll be okay, and not even in a physical sense, but in a spiritual sense. When we take Refuge, we aren't expecting some beneficent God to care for us now that we've bowed down to Him. Instead, we see that if we commit ourselves to these principles, we'll be protected by the Buddha, Dharma, and Sangha. We are the ones who have to do the work in this relationship. We have to try to be mindful as much as we can; to seek out and live in the truth, accepting suffering, impermanence, and corelessness and trying to fulfill the Eightfold Path; to support others on the path and to give of our time and love to the community. The commitment is challenging, but the rewards are great.

In different Buddhist traditions there are formal ways of taking Refuge, some that involve becoming official members of a community. This ritual can be powerful and vital, but the real work is the daily commitment. One of the things many practitioners do is to take the Refuges each day at the end of their morning meditation. This can be done by simply saying to yourself, "I take refuge in the Buddha; I take refuge in the Dharma; I take refuge in the Sangha." I try to add a little to this prayer by saying, "I take refuge in the Buddha. I commit myself to being as awake and mindful as I can today." Then I might take a moment to absorb this commitment and imagine carrying this awareness with me through the day. "I take refuge in the Dharma. I will try to remember the truth as I go through my day." Ajahn Amaro expands the meaning of *sangha* to be a life of morality that is the natural response to the awake mind seeing the truth (the Buddha seeing the Dharma), so when I say, "I take refuge in the Sangha," I add, "I will seek to express awareness and truth through moral and caring actions today."

Taking Refuge in the Buddha, making this commitment to live mindfully, is the key to all spiritual growth, the starting point and the touchstone to which we always return. In the Twelve Step process, mindfulness is at the root of Step One, seeing and admitting to our addiction. Until we bring this awareness to our problem there is no possibility of recovery. Mindfulness also is required to take inventory, Step Four. Here we have to look at ourselves, our past actions, and our habitual patterns of thought and emotion in an unsparing way. As we deepen our mindfulness, we become more able to open to what can sometimes be painful admissions about ourselves. A commitment to mindfulness also means that we are trying to pay attention to moments in our day when we tend to shut down or check out.

When we "turn our will and our lives over" to mindfulness, we start to try to bring this quality of attention more and more into our lives. We try to apply it to everything, to our internal and external experiences; to our thoughts and feelings; to our relationships and social interactions; to our work and our creative pursuits; to our play and our entertainments. There's nothing that can't be engaged with mindfulness. This is the Buddha's lesson.

Meditation Retreats, 1980–81

Forty of us are crowded into a small building on a mesa on the outskirts of Joshua Tree, California. It's Thanksgiving weekend, the opening of a five-day retreat, my first, and the cook is orienting us to the weekend, which will be conducted in silence.

"We need some volunteers to do jobs," she says. "We'll need two veggie choppers." A few people raise their hands, and she takes their names. "And pot scrubbers." More hands go up.

Sitting against the wall with my knees pulled up to my chest, I try to be invisible so I won't be assigned a job. Washing pots just seems like it's going to be a distraction from the "real" work of meditating. I'm thinking, "Volunteering is for suckers."

Some months later, I'm on another retreat in the desert, and again I avoid volunteering for a job. After lunch on the third day, I go to drop off my dishes at the kitchen, and I'm shocked to see my friend Edward behind the counter wearing an apron. A tall, striking Englishman who has been doing Buddhist practice for years and is, in fact, starting to teach meditation, he smiles at me as he takes my dishes and starts to wipe off the plate. I quickly smile back and move away. I step out of the dining hall into the clear, bright desert spring afternoon feeling completely confused. Why would Edward be working in the kitchen?

After the retreat Edward tells me how much he enjoyed working in the kitchen, and I'm further confused. I'm someone who has avoided kitchen—or any other part of the house—work all my life. What could possibly be enjoyable about it?

The following fall, I'm at the registration table for the three-month retreat I've signed up for. A pretty young woman smiles up at me and hands me a small piece of paper.

"You'll be cleaning the men's shower in the Annex," she says.

I look at the paper with my job assignment and try to smile back at her.

"Okay . . ."

No volunteering here. Everyone is given a job, like it or not—sucker or not.

The next day, after lunch, I gather the cleaning supplies and go to the shower room. I'm dismayed to see a huge, dark, moldy stain on the wall. The center was bought just a few years before by some Buddhist teachers and practitioners, but it was owned for decades before that by a Catholic monastic order who, apparently, didn't assign anyone to clean the men's shower.

I clear the hair out of the drain, Ajax the floor, wipe off the shower handles. As I work, I'm trying to apply the tools of mindfulness that I've been studying for a year now. Even as I resist the job, I try to pay attention, to my arms, my hands, the smells, the movements of my body.

When I'm done, I look again at the big stain. I step up to it and rub. Not much happens. I lean into it again, and a tiny spot comes clean. "Hmm," I think. "Maybe I could clean this thing."

The next day, my meditation practice having deepened a bit, more calm and concentration developing, I look at the stain and decide to make it a project: in three months I'll try to get rid of the whole thing.

Soon, my resistance to working during the retreat dissolves. I find myself engaged, even entertained, by my daily work. Sitting in silence day after day with very few distractions—the daily amusements include eating, taking a walk, and listening to a Dharma talk, with the high point being an interview with a teacher every few days—I actually start to look forward to my cleaning job, just as a break in the routine and a time when I can do something.

Over time, the stain gets smaller and smaller, and my engagement in mindful cleaning grows deeper. Eventually, the stain is gone before the retreat ends, and I'm left in the ironic position of being disappointed that I don't have any more mold to scrape off the walls every day after lunch.

Of course, I have to acknowledge the gradual cleaning of the stain as a metaphor for spiritual practice, but that's not really the point of the story. For me, finding that when I surrendered to this yucky job it went from being unpleasant to pleasant is a vital lesson in the power of mindfulness, the Buddha, and in the possibilities that are available to me when I turn myself over to this power.

Taking Refuge in the Dharma, turning our will and our lives over, includes coming into harmony with the Law of Karma as I described earlier. It also involves coming into harmony with the Three Characteristics of Impermanence, Suffering, and Not-Self.

We naturally resist impermanence because of the insecurity it implies. In our search for stability and safety, humans seem to be in a constant battle with this truth. Our bodies age, buildings fall down, levees break, lovers abandon us, children grow up, the seasons "turn, turn, turn," over and over again. This can be cause for torment unless we come into harmony with it. When we deeply accept impermanence, change becomes a natural flow, an in-breath and an out-breath. Our perception of life coming through this lens of openness show us we don't have to *do* anything, just stop fighting. When we cease this resistance, life naturally becomes more easeful because we are working *with* the way things are instead of trying to change the unchangeable. This doesn't mean that loss isn't still painful, only that there is no confusion, no agitation around it. We begin to see the good side of impermanence, the excitement and possibility of birth, of renewal.

Much the same happens when we come into harmony with suffering or the unsatisfactoriness of life. When we stop striving for perfection, for that which cannot be, serenity naturally follows. When we see that suffering is a guide, a wake-up call, not a punishment, we can use it to remind ourselves to explore our experience. Instead of running from suffering, we face it directly and ask, "Where is the clinging that is causing this pain?"

When we come into harmony with not-self, we stop clinging to identity. Instead of trying to be someone, we just allow ourselves to be who we are in this moment. In its natural form, identity is fluid, adaptable. If I try to act the same with my wife as I do with my meditation students, it's not going to work. When I'm playing with my daughter, my "self" is different from the one that hangs out with my friends. When I got my first office job in sobriety, I realized that I was doing just what I'd always avoided, working a conventional, straight job. I'd always thought it would be horrible to do something like that, and it went against everything I thought about myself as a hip musician. But in that job I was happy. I felt relieved to have a paycheck every week and benefits. I realized that giving up clinging to an identity as a musician was the most freeing thing I'd ever done. I'm really not a musician or an office worker—or a writer or a meditation teacher. These are roles I play. None of them defines me. When I cease struggling with that truth, I find peace and happiness.

Taking Refuge is the devotional act of Buddhism. It is an expression of faith and gratitude, a deep appreciation of the tradition and all the gifts it has given us. It is the respect we feel for a man, Siddhartha Gautama, who through his tremendous inner strength and wisdom came to a breakthrough in consciousness that still reverberates today. The faith isn't the blind faith of belief, but the trust and confidence that comes through testing the teachings. Taking Refuge expresses the inspiration we feel when we've been touched deeply by the practices and the teachings of Buddhism.

EMOTIONAL KARMA

When we talk about karma and the results of karma, I think there's a tendency to focus on external things—jobs, relationships, money, getting stuff. We have the idea that "good karma" is success, health, and no problems in our lives. And certainly this is part of it. But as I've looked at my own experience I've begun to see it in a different way, to emphasize another aspect of karma, what I call "emotional karma."

According to the Buddha, karma is generated three different ways, through thoughts, speech, and actions, and is informed by the intention behind each. Taking the most obvious one, actions, let's say you do something nice like open a door for someone. What is the karmic result? Well, we might think that we've made a deposit in our karma piggy bank that's going to pay off at some later date or maybe in a future lifetime. That may very well be true. But what's more provable and relevant, I think, is that in that moment *you feel good*. That feeling is the direct karmic result of your action. We don't have to wait until our next lifetime to benefit; the benefit is right here, right now.

When I went back to school I thought that the benefit was only going to come in four years, which seemed like a vast amount of time to wait for a payoff. What I soon discovered, though, was that I loved school. I enjoyed every subject I studied (well, maybe not statistics so much). Here I was studying things I'd never been interested in, science, math, languages, and each day was a joy. The karmic benefit of my showing up for class was immediate—*and* delayed—two kinds of karmic result.

The same is true of negative karma. When we lose our temper and start swearing at someone, we may be laying the ground for some future negative karmic result. But what's for sure is that right now we are going to feel lousy. Anger hurts. Just stop and feel it sometime. That's why resentments are such an issue in Twelve Step programs. The pain of resentment can trigger our addiction.

When we look at the karmic results of thoughts we can see this even more clearly. When our mind is filled with thoughts of anger, we feel terrible; when we are filled with thoughts of love, we feel wonderful. When we let our minds go off into dreams and fantasies, we feel empty, lacking; when we focus on what we are doing right now, we feel connected and complete. The effort to control our thinking and our mind's focus is a fundamental aspect of turning it over, of making the commitment to live in harmony with the Dharma, and it is perhaps the heart of Buddhist practice.

Over a lifetime, our emotional karma is what comes to define our personality and, in many ways, who we think we are. When I talked with a therapist a few years ago about my long-term struggle with depression, he explained how psychologists now understand the development of this condition. When depression hits a young person, it creates a kind of pathway in the mind whereby that mood becomes easier to fall into—like the way water flows into a riverbed. Repeated episodes create a deeper and wider pathway, making the likelihood of recurrence ever more likely. At a certain point, at least according to this therapist, the condition becomes virtually irreversible—thus the reliance of psychotherapists on antidepressants. This description of the development of this painful condition parallels very closely the Buddhist teaching that the more we think or feel in a certain way, the stronger the tendency to think or feel that way becomes; the opposite is also true, that the less we think or feel in a certain way, the weaker that tendency becomes. This teaching is encapsulated in the Buddha's statement, "Whatever one frequently thinks and ponders upon, that will become the inclination of his mind."

While we may want to think that it is other people or situations that cause our state of mind—and they certainly can have an effect—it is our own inclinations that ultimately have the greatest effect. The subtext here is that the inclination of our mind is something we have some control over. While most of us certainly develop habitual ways of thinking and feeling at an early age before we are aware of our own part in creating those thoughts and feelings, it is possible at any time to incline the mind differently. This is how we change our emotional karma. This is one of the vital purposes of vipassana meditation: to clearly see our habitual ways of being, to see the ways that some of these cause us suffering, and to incline the mind—and body—in a more skillful way.

I sit here typing these words—it's the late afternoon of a sunny Northern California spring day—and it's quite easy to get my fingers to push the letters that tell you that all you have to do is "incline your mind differently" and you'll be fine. But you and I both know that this is tough, maybe the toughest thing we'll ever do. The work of a lifetime, or at least that part of the lifetime that's left after we figure out that this is what we need to do. This task doesn't just require that we go "against the stream"; it's more like turning the stream around and getting it to flow in the opposite direction.

Who knows whether we'll be able to complete this task? This brings us back to where we started: right now. To do this work, we have to engage in effort in this moment, but to benefit from it we need to do it in a way that doesn't create suffering as we try to change ourselves. This is a tricky proposition. If we think we need to change, then there's a judgment, and judging ourselves is painful. This is where the subtle awareness of meditation is so important, being able to make an effort to change that doesn't carry an aversive quality.

One way to cultivate this effort is to come at it with a sense of compassion for our own pain and forgiveness for our own imperfection.

These are two essential qualities to bring to our spiritual work. Compassion comes because we know that everyone, including ourselves, suffers; forgiveness comes because we know that no one is perfect. If when we observe an unskillful thought or feeling we can bring these qualities to bear, then our effort to incline the mind won't be aversive but loving, gentle, and kind.

Again, this isn't a process that we just switch on. It takes a commitment to begin to see ourselves through the lens of compassion and forgiveness. Sometimes I read a spiritual book and think, *Oh, I've got to do that now,* and immediately feel bad because I'm comparing myself to the ideal put forth by the text. At that point I might either just sink into a negative mind state or think, *I don't want to feel like this. I think I'll skip it.* Of course, neither attitude helps. The Steps can guide us here. We begin any process of change with an honest admission of where we are. We take Step Two when we see the possibility of change. In Step Three we make a commitment to the process. This process is open-ended.

Finally, I'd be remiss if I didn't talk about psychiatric drugs. There are those in Twelve Step programs who feel that taking any drug to help you with a mental or emotional problem is wrong, that it's essentially losing your sobriety. My response to that is, *Who am I to judge what someone else needs?* There are states of suffering, both physical and mental, that are so extreme that to deny ourselves medical help is just foolish. If the choice is suicide or drugs, there's no choice; you have to take the drug—prescribed, under a doctor's care, of course. My understanding is that contemporary antidepressant and antipsychotics have no pleasure element in them; they help maintain normalcy without creating euphoria or an altered state. This is a complicated and personal question. I think it's a mistake for a spiritual teacher to speak of the process in absolutes. The tendency when teaching about Buddhism and meditation, as well as recovery, is to talk about ideals, and that can be helpful and inspiring. But if the ideals become sources of self-judgment and fuel people's sense of failure, then they aren't helpful. If ideals are unattainable right now for someone, how do we help them? Do we just write them off?

At one retreat, I noticed that the woman with the seat in front of mine was often not there for the meditation periods. I would see her outside moving rocks around for a drainage system that was being redirected on the hillside of the center. Since the retreat was supposed to be about silent meditation, not playing with rocks, she was clearly not fulfilling the ideal of the retreat. When we broke silence on the last day of the retreat, I spoke with her and found out that her son had recently died and she'd come on the retreat to work on healing her grief. The teachers, seeing that when sitting silently she sank into overwhelming feelings of loss and sorrow, suggested she work outside and meditatively move the rocks for the drain. This helped her to stay grounded and in her body, in the present moment. I thought this suggestion showed great compassion on the teachers' part and modeled a way of responding to an inner struggle. Rather than pushing the woman to practice the traditional form, they wisely looked at the reality of her situation, living with the immensity of losing her child, and guided her toward a more skillful way of being in the silence.

Working with emotional karma takes wisdom, and it's helpful to learn about what tools are available without thinking that one tool suits every job. Carefully watching how each heart/mind state arises, seeing its causes and its results, is the secret to learning how to respond in a way that doesn't create more harm. Attending to our inner emotional karma, moment by moment, is soon reflected in our outer karma, helping to bring healing and happiness into all aspects of our lives.

KARMA OF NON-ACTION

As I said before, the word *karma* means, literally, "action," and karma is associated with activities, be they mental, verbal, or physical. But all actions aren't active. When we sit down to meditate we are taking an action that is, at least apparently, *inactive*. Meditators are sometimes accused of being passive, usually by people who haven't tried it. The internal experience of meditation is far from passive, as the Buddha's teachings on effort make clear. He even says that if we've tried to let go of harmful, lustful, and hateful thoughts and have failed, then we should clench our teeth and "beat down" the thoughts. Not a very gentle image for this proponent of nonviolence.

Nonetheless, meditation, even while being internally active, is essentially non-action. It is a non-action that has powerful and far-reaching results. When an addict first engages in meditation, she'll often see how strong the impulse to act is. Of course, this may be true of anyone trying meditation, but I think that addicts are even more used to acting on impulse than non-addicts. This energy has been running us our whole lives. We've been pulled around by our craving and our aversion. And the habitual submission to these forces has developed into addiction. Just stopping, just refusing to act on these impulses, watching them come, feeling them in the body and mind, and, eventually, watching them fade, is one of the most important things we can do as addicts.

From the outside it may look as if we're doing nothing—and, from the outside, that's true. Internally, our world is moving in seismic shifts. Giving up an addiction, after all, is not taking on something new, or even doing something. It is *not doing something*. A great deal of the process of recovery is learning to not do things: don't go to the bar; don't call the dealer; don't go to the refrigerator; don't see the ex; don't try to fix anyone. And how do we learn not to act? Well, meditation is a great crucible for forging this power. We sit down and close our eyes and "do nothing." We sit with the feelings; we sit with the thoughts. We let it come and go, and we develop what is sometimes called "personal power," the ability to be fully present with whatever is going on inside us without acting on it or being overwhelmed.

The karmic results of this process are key to recovery. First, we get to see that we don't have to act on that thought, feeling, or impulse that has been running us for so long; we can live through it. Second, we gain confidence that we can manage to stay sober because we're learning to be with those feelings. Third, the energy of those impulses becomes weaker because they aren't being fed. Over time, what used to be an obsession may become just a passing thought or finally fade away completely, as does the craving to drink and use for many people in recovery.

This sea change in our hearts and minds comes through *doing nothing*. What a powerful lesson. We begin to see how being non-reactive, developing acceptance and inner peace and balance, is transforming in many ways. Not only is our addiction healed, but our relationships become more harmonious when we don't act or speak on every impulse, but allow ourselves to consider and process things. Our willingness to participate in the world grows as we become less stuck in our preferences and more open to other activities, other forms of work, other interests.

In the classic Buddhist teachings, this non-doing is called *renunciation,* a word that doesn't have much appeal in our you-can-have-it-all culture. But what is recovery, after all, but renouncing our addiction? Letting go, a term that seems to have more positive connotations, is essentially renunciation. And how do we let go? Well, very often by not acting.

Another powerful form of non-action is silence. A few years ago I was commuting to a teacher training retreat for a few days. One evening I came home feeling centered, peaceful, and loving. As my wife began to speak, I saw the impulse to disagree with what she was saying. Instead, I just listened and let my own thought pass. We spent a harmonious evening. Right in that moment I saw how I could have destroyed that harmony with just a few words. I also realized that over the years of our relationship, I've tended to think it was my wife's fault when we bickered. Or I've thought that we at least needed to work on our relationship *together* if we were going to have a more peaceful home. Instead, I got to see that all I had to do to bring more harmony was to restrain my tongue. I could change our relationship *just by changing myself.*

In meditation practice, we can develop a third kind of karma besides non-action and non-speech, and that is non-thought. This, of course, is the most subtle and probably the most difficult form of non-karma to develop. As we learn meditation, at first we just notice the thoughts after they've carried us away. With practice (and retreats help this a lot), we can sometimes notice thoughts just as they are coming up, and that gives us the chance to drop them. As our concentration develops, thoughts begin to quiet down so that fewer thoughts are even appearing in the mind. Thoughts are so powerful, and—while it's wonderful if we can learn to incline the mind toward more skillful, kind, or wise thinking—when we can just drop thought altogether for a moment, it conditions a spaciousness, a brightness, and a natural flow of lovingkindness.

SELF-REVEALING:
STEP FIVE

"Admitted to God, to ourselves, and to another human being the exact nature of our wrongs."

ADMITTING TO GOD

Sts. Simon and Jude Catholic Church, Bethlehem, PA, 1959

I'm standing in a line along the side of the pews in the back of the church waiting for my turn to go into confession. This is a normal ritual I perform every few weeks on a Saturday afternoon, a purification so that I can take communion on Sunday morning, swallowing the body of Jesus.

As usual I'm having a hard time figuring out what to say to the priest because I can't think of too many sins I've committed over the last couple weeks. Did I steal anything? No. Lie? Well, maybe a fib, but not really. I didn't really disobey my parents or swear. So I decide I better make some stuff up.

Finally I'm at the front of the line and the confessional opens and an old woman steps out. I quickly move over and go inside, kneeling in the darkened booth. It smells like old-lady perfume, incense, and wood. I feel my heart beating as I bow my head to my hands held in prayer. A little wooden window slides back and I see the outline of the priest as he leans his ear to the screen that separates us.

"Bless me, Father, for I have sinned," I begin. "I said bad words three times; I disobeyed my parents twice; and I told a lie." This short litany of supposed sins is the best I can do.

The priest says a few words, then gives me a "penance" of three Our Fathers and five Hail Marys.

Now it's time for me to say the Act of Contrition: "O my God, I am heartily sorry for having offended thee . . . " It's a powerful prayer that tugs at my heart. I feel really bad about sinning—even though I don't know what my sins are.

The priest blesses me and absolves me of my supposed sins, and I leave the confessional. I kneel at the railing in front of the altar and say my penance. When I leave the church it's with a light heart and happy mind. I feel relieved. I'm not sure if that's because I've been absolved or just because the whole ordeal is over.

Confession is a beautiful and vital part of many religions, so it's unfortunate that it can become so ritualized that it loses its meaning. Buddhist monastics have a similar ritual, which, I am told, has also lost a lot of its vitality. For me, it was only when I took a fifth Step in recovery that I actually experienced an authentic confession.

This Step follows the difficult and sometimes long process of writing an inventory—the fourth Step. For some the writing is the tough part, while others cringe at the "admitting" that happens in Step Five. Either way, it's challenging work.

In the Catholic ritual, confession is very much tied up with a belief in God, and Step Five tells us at the very first that we "admitted to God . . . " It's easy to understand what admitting to ourselves and admitting to another human being is, but for a Buddhist who doesn't believe there is some being with ears up there who can hear our inventory, how are we to understand this part of the process? Before I began to teach and write about God in the Steps, I largely ignored this question. But as I consider it now, I have some ideas.

It's risky to say that we are admitting to our "higher selves," as some might suggest. This idea, like the idea of "Buddha nature," can easily drift into solidifying a concept of self that Buddhism rejects—rejects on lack of evidence, not on the basis of some belief system. But we can certainly say that there are different aspects to our "mind stream." We are made up of many elements, some wise, some not so wise. So, we could say that the less wise part of ourselves is admitting to the more wise part.

Another way to come at this question is from the standpoint of a moral universe. When I talked about the Higher Power of Karma, I made the point that the universe seems to have a moral fiber woven into its structure. When we admit our wrongs to God, we see clearly how our mistakes, failings, and harmful actions broke those moral rules, seeing the contrast between our actions and the karmic guidelines the Buddha, and many other spiritual masters, have laid out. We see that relationship and its dissonance in a way that allows us to feel the harm we've done. We see how out of harmony with the universe we have been, how we have been standing outside the moral laws and doing them and ourselves damage.

This moral framework is expressed in what we call our *conscience*. Our conscience is our connection to God's law. A healthy conscience knows right from wrong, and when we admit the nature of our wrongs, our conscience is what hears us. The difference between "admitting to ourselves" and "admitting to God" is that admitting to God is impersonal. We aren't the ones who define the moral guidelines; we can't bargain with or rationalize our karma. There isn't even forgiveness or lack of forgiveness. There is only what is, the stark truth and its consequences. Admitting to ourselves and another human being opens up the possibility of compassion and forgiveness. What happened, what we did, is seen in a context; a wise response and future actions, including amends and the possibility of change, are all included in this part of the Step. But admitting to God, to the unfettered truth, is the starting point. Without that we risk short-circuiting the process and trying to avoid full responsibility for our actions. We must see this truth with honesty and integrity if we are to truly move on.

LOOKING BACK, LOOKING FORWARD

When we look at the Steps, it can seem odd in a way that after taking Step Three, turning our will and our lives over to the care of God, that we would then have to take "a searching and fearless moral inventory." After all, if we've turned everything over to God, why do we have to do anything else? Shouldn't God just take care of everything from here?

171

In fact, when we take Step Three, we are charting a new course in our lives, making a commitment to live in a more kind and wise way, in harmony with the Dharma. When we make that commitment, what immediately becomes apparent is that up to now our whole outlook and way of acting has been skewed toward self-centeredness, greed, resentment, all kinds of negative qualities that have fed and been fed by our addiction. Turning our life over to God doesn't mean that all those things go away. We've spent a lifetime building up these habits, and we're going to have to do some serious work to change them.

Step Four—"Made a searching and fearless moral inventory of ourselves"—is the beginning of this change. What we are doing, in a sense, is looking at the karmic patterns in our lives. If we want to change, we need to see what needs *to be* changed first and foremost. We need to see how we got here. The inventory shows us all the ways that we harmed ourselves and others, all the habitual ways of being that led to our downfall. This then gives us a blueprint for change.

Of course, this isn't easy. To write this all down can be painful and difficult. To read it to another human being can seem overwhelming. The fear of public humiliation and shame can make it look like a cruel joke perpetrated by some Twelve Step sadists. And yet, once we follow through, the sense of relief is palpable. Most people feel that a huge burden has been lifted from their shoulders. The bogeyman of our secrets has been let out of the closet and seen for what it is: a thought, a feeling, an illusion.

When, in Step Five, we look at the "exact nature of our wrongs," we are seeing the patterns, not just the specifics. By sharing it with another person, we now have someone who can keep us honest as we move forward, someone who knows our story and understands our tricks, our deceptions, our evasions, and our games. After I read my inventory to my sponsor, the process of change began. He saw my tendency to give up on things, so when I was about to drop out of a class in college, he called me on it. He saw the way I operated in relationships with women, and he guided me to new approaches. He saw that, even though I wanted a permanent relationship, I was letting my lust lead me instead of my love. He was able to give me specific suggestions for how to break those counterproductive habits.

It was only through first looking backward that I was able to move forward in a way that could bring real change. As long as I was just living reactively, I couldn't break the existing patterns. Only when I took a careful, honest look at those patterns was it possible to develop the strategies I would need for letting go in Steps Six and Seven.

Preparing for Freedom:
Step Six

"Were entirely ready to have God remove all these defects of character."

ENTIRELY READY TO LET GO

Being ready and willing to change is a huge challenge. We often find that even though we think we want to change, when it comes down to what we have to let go of, it's not so easy. But for someone with a Buddhist orientation or someone who just doesn't feel a connection with the Abrahamic God, there's a problem that comes even before that willingness: belief that this Step can work. The language here, again, is so Biblical, implying a dualistic relationship with a patriarchal God who's going to fix you if you just let him. That approach doesn't work for many people, including me. So how can we understand this Step and engage it from a Buddhist perspective?

When I first did this Step, I followed the instructions as laid out in the Big Book. I came home from reading my fifth Step to my sponsor, got out the book, went over the Steps, and asked myself if I was ready to let God remove my shortcomings. As far as the book is concerned, if I can say "Yes" to that question, I'm done with Step Six. However, the *Twelve Steps and Twelve Traditions,* Bill Wilson's commentary on the Steps, elaborates. And in the first paragraph of that commentary is a key word: *repeatedly.* While the Big Book and the Steps can make it sound as if all you have to do is be willing and ask God to remove your shortcomings and *poof,* you're done, the *Twelve and Twelve* is more clear about the reality of this process.

As Bill elaborates that process, he says that we'll never achieve perfection of this Step, being *entirely* ready, but if we aim "for the perfect objective which is of God," we'll know that we are striving for the highest ideals, and we will remain humble and ready to keep growing.

If we translate this idea to Buddhist teachings, we can say that we are striving to fulfill the Eightfold Path, to achieve the highest form of View, Intention, Speech, Action, Livelihood, Effort, Mindfulness, and Concentration. Being entirely ready to do this, being committed to this kind of spiritual work, is certainly as challenging as achieving "God's" objectives. The result, I would say, is the same.

When I began to engage in a spiritual life in my late 20s, years before I got sober, my willingness to change was pretty limited. I was willing to work at meditation, though, so that meant I was ready to make an effort toward concentration, with a limited interest in mindfulness.

As I became more serious, I thought about, though I didn't do much about, livelihood. As for the precepts of action, I was interested in them mostly in very superficial ways, like trying not to kill bugs. I didn't really engage in them—obviously, since I never considered stopping drinking and drugging though it was apparent that the fifth precept stated I should. I excused myself when I heard that the precept said not to use intoxicants "to the point of heedlessness." I don't know if this is an accurate translation, but it's how it is often presented. Somehow I was able to convince myself that I wasn't being heedless, even though I was still having blackout episodes, driving drunk, and all the rest.

As for view and intention, they too were very limited. I saw what I wanted to see and intended what was convenient, mostly ideals of enlightenment that had nothing to do with my real life.

All of this points to the fact that I wasn't really ready to change. I wanted the prize but I didn't want to do the work to get it. To go back to an idea I've talked about earlier, this was because of *ignorance,* my own lack of understanding about how things worked. We can debate how much of that ignorance was willful, but the fact is, my conscious mind at least didn't understand what I was doing. I was caught up in my own fantasies, in my own delusion that change would happen magically. I didn't understand that the Law of Karma demands that I take action if I want to change. Or, more accurately, I didn't understand what actions I needed to take. I thought that meditation was a magical process that would bring about change in all areas of my life without my having to make any other effort.

A few years ago I was talking with an acquaintance, a Buddhist practitioner, who was having employment problems. As we talked about what he was going to do, he said that he was going to go on a retreat, and then he'd be able to get a job. He seemed to think that a retreat would magically bring work. I thought, *If you want a job as a meditator, that might work, but I don't know of anyone who will hire you to sit on a cushion.* The attitude reminded me of myself years ago, confusing cause and effect: go on a retreat, get a job.

When I did Steps Six and Seven, even though I did them just as prayers, something had changed in me, I think both because of being sober for a while and because of working the Steps up to that point—especially Steps Four and Five. At that point I did start to take the actions for change that I had resisted for years, actions that went against my habitual tendencies, against my self-image, and against my preferences.

As I write this, I realize that I'm mostly talking about external things, about changes in work and relationships. And the Twelve Step literature points to the internal, to issues around self-centeredness, resentment, envy, and other emotional qualities. I suppose I talk about the more practical outer issues partly because they are easier to describe, but also because they tend to be the results of the internal changes. When I went back to school at three years sober, for instance, I did that as a result of changing my self-image. I was a musician; that's what defined me. I clung to that image even when it no longer served me. I clung to it despite the misery and humiliation that came along with it when it no longer served me. To let go of that was a huge spiritual and emotional surrender. Out of that letting go grew a new life, which included enrolling in college.

Similar changes happened for me around relationships. I had to let go of lust as a driving force if I wanted to have a healthy, long-term relationship. I'd clung to the idea that satisfying my craving was essential to my happiness. The result had been one failed relationship after another. When I let go of that, I started on the path to actual, not imagined, happiness.

Lust wasn't the only impediment to successful relationships. The unwillingness to be wrong, to look at my own failings, had an even more destructive effect on intimacy. At some point in every relationship, from the time I was 16 until my late 30s, I had reached a point where I began to blame my partner for what I was feeling, for how I was acting, and for the problems between us. I virtually never took a look at my own role. It was only through the Step process and sharing at Twelve Step meetings that I began to be able to admit to my own part in these problems. I was ready then to begin to accept my failings, and that made all the difference in dealing with another human being. It meant there was a basis for a conversation, for some give and take.

Many, if not all, of these issues, these struggles to resist change, came out of fear. We are afraid that if we give up what we know, we'll be left with nothing, or worse still, with what we don't want. Something has to happen—like hitting an alcoholic bottom—to make us willing to change. The root of this fear seems to be clinging to *I*, to a sense of self. We could probably say that all our "defects of character" derive from this one point. This is actually what the Twelve Step literature already says: "Selfishness—self-centeredness! That, we think, is the root of our troubles."

Buddhism takes the idea that self-centeredness is our problem to another level when it says that the very idea of a self, this *I*, is a delusion—so we're clinging to something that doesn't even exist as a separate, solid entity. Now *that* is a problem.

Who we are, our identity, our personality, is a conglomeration of memories, feelings, thoughts, conditioning, genetics, all of the stuff of the mind/body. It's a dynamic, living, constantly changing *process* more than it is an entity. In the same way that we are afraid of our bodies dying, we are afraid of ego death, of the death of identity. And in the same way that we try to protect the body, we try to protect the ego. It's pretty self-evident that the body is constantly changing and that ultimately it must die. Still, people spend a lot of time—and money—trying to at least make it look as if the body isn't changing, or if it is changing, that it's changing in good ways—getting stronger, more attractive, younger. We also try to make the ego look good with the right job, the right car, the right partner and kids, prestige, popularity, all that makes us appear to be on top of the world. If these qualities happen to be harming others, or even harming us, so be it. The possibility that this self, this identity, will die is too threatening. To admit our failings, to see through our attachments, to admit we are not the alpha being, is a kind of death for the ego. If we are going to become willing to change, we are going to have to allow this demise.

This sounds pretty dramatic, and we may get the sense that being a Buddhist means becoming a drone who doesn't have a personality or any preferences. But it's not that we stop being ourselves. The mind stream continues on. It's more about our relationship to that stream. Do we think it is who we are and must be protected at all costs? Or do we see it as an aspect of ourselves, one that is flowing and changing, that could stand some improvement, and probably also has some good qualities? If we can stand outside ourselves, view ourselves in an objective—or reasonably objective—manner, then change, admitting failure, letting go of identity, all of this is manageable.

To talk about death of the ego isn't so accurate; we should say, rather, death of the illusion, seeing the truth of the ego, seeing that it's a functional construction and not a permanent piece of the landscape. When we understand ego, our identity is working for us; when we don't, we are working for it.

To become ready to stop clinging to an identity, to let go of our defects of character, we have to work with the Higher Power of Dharma: cultivate the Eightfold Path; contemplate suffering, impermanence, and corelessness; and live in harmony with the Law of Karma. These are the things that will help us to "remove our shortcomings."

When I get to Step Six in my workshops, I often ask people to do an exercise in which they ask themselves what makes it easy to let go and how they could cultivate this quality. They then discuss this in small groups in a mindful-speech exercise. A couple of years ago I was taking a group through this process when a woman near the front of the class raised her hand.

"I realized that what made it possible for me to get sober was hitting a bottom. That's what made it easy to let go. But I don't want to cultivate hitting bottom."

For a moment I was taken aback. "Good point," I said, which is what you say when you don't know how to respond. I took a breath and considered. And this is what I told her: "When we practice meditation, we start to notice our suffering much more quickly. We become more sensitive to suffering and less willing to hold onto the things that cause it. So, what we are doing, in a sense, is raising our bottom, making it easier to hit bottom without it being a disaster. That way we can grow and change without our lives falling apart."

The Buddha said that the appropriate response to the Noble Truth of Suffering was to "understand" suffering. When we experience suffering clearly, we are motivated to change, to let go. So what the Buddha might be doing by pointing us toward seeing our suffering is helping us to become more sensitive so that we'll more quickly release the suffering.

When people get sober, a lot starts to clear up. After a while someone might say, "Now that I'm sober, I see that this smoking thing really isn't working for me," and they'll quit cigarettes. Soon they might become aware of their unhealthy diet and begin to eat better; they'll notice that their body doesn't feel very good when they don't exercise, so they'll take up a sport or exercise regimen; they'll realize they're feeling stressed and explore meditation. So, just in the way the Buddha suggested, as we stay sober we become more sensitive to our suffering, to what isn't working in our lives. This inspires us to change. In the words of the Step, it helps us to become "entirely ready" to change.

This approach to spiritual growth is typical of the Buddha's teaching in its counter-intuitiveness: pay attention to suffering in order to get happy. But, after all, when do we become willing to change? Surely not when everything's going well, or when we perceive things to be going well. That's why when people are in denial about their addiction, they refuse to do anything about it. When you are able to ignore your pain, you can avoid dealing with it.

In meditation our pain often becomes very clear. We can't ignore it, so our next tendency is to try to make it go away. Many of the questions that come up in a meditation class are about how to get rid of difficult experiences like pain in the knees, sleepiness, or rambling thoughts. We have the idea that meditation is supposed to be pleasant, peaceful, relaxing, and instead we've got all these problems. We want to push the problems aside and get to the good stuff.

When the teacher suggests exploring these things rather than giving some antidote for them, it can be even more frustrating. Here they've been talking about all the good things that come from meditating, but we're not getting any of them. We're sure, as we watch them meditating in front of the class, that they are having a wonderful, blissful time, so why won't they tell us how we can get some of that bliss, too?

It turns out that the good stuff is inside the problems rather than on the other side of them. We let ourselves become absorbed in the pain in our knees and eventually find stillness and concentration; we let ourselves feel the fullness of our fatigue, and we move through our resistance into a new level of energy; we open to the barrage of thoughts assaulting us, and we find that we can just let them pass through the mind with no friction.

This truth is even more apparent when dealing with emotional pain. Once we see our sadness, anxiety, anger, or fear, we can't help but want it to go away. But how do you make sadness go away? Isn't that how we got into trouble in the first place? Wasn't our addiction all wrapped up in trying not to feel something? If we try to think it away, we wind up feeding it with our aversion. The more you think about your problem the worse you feel about yourself: "What's wrong with me that I've got this problem? Where did it come from? Why won't it go away?" Rather than trying to think your feelings away, mindfulness says to open to them. Go into the body and feel where the emotion lives. Trust that holding the feeling with kindness and patience will allow it to pass. Impermanence is your friend in this case. Once an emotion gets triggered, it has a kind of half-life that has to be respected. If we aren't mindful, we keep reacting and feeding the feeling. The less you react to the feeling, the shorter the half-life. The feeling fades, the situation changes, your day goes by, and sooner or later you find that the feeling is gone, washed away by the tides of time with every other experience in your life.

And about those teachers in front of the meditation hall: it's not that they're experiencing bliss all the time (at least not this teacher), but rather that they've learned not to fight with suffering. This is the First Noble Truth: as long as you have a body and mind, there are going to be difficulties. How you respond to those difficulties largely determines the level of suffering in your life. To embrace Step Six in its entirety is to recognize the persistence of dukkha. To work Step Six fully is to meet each difficulty with readiness.

When we see our life as a spiritual journey, this process is ongoing. We realize that it's unlikely we'll achieve perfection, so there is always something to work on, always something to cultivate or let go of. And while this can sound like a burden, to me it's just the opposite: it is the purpose and the joy of life to keep exploring our potential and keep learning and growing. To quote an unlikely source, the Jefferson Airplane, "Life is change; how it differs from the rocks." Not that we have the choice, but if we did, would we really choose the relative stasis of a mineral over the dynamism of life, even with all its problems and pain?

LETTING GO:
STEP SEVEN

"Humbly asked Him to remove our shortcomings."

ASKING GOD TO HELP US GROW

Step Seven is where we again run into the stumbling block of how God is supposed to change us. Again we're faced with the idea of a magical process, of being fixed by some external entity or force.

Ajahn Buddhadasa addresses this question when he analyzes the Biblical saying "Ask and it will be given you; seek and you will find; knock, and it will be opened to you." He says about this passage:

> From the Buddhist point of view, this too is a matter of karma; we must act, that is, we must ask, seek, and knock for God to be moved. Mere faith is not enough. Even if one sits down to pray, it still will not be enough. In this context, the word "ask" implies an earnest effort to bring about a desired result, that is to say *we beseech the Law of Karma through our action and not merely with words.* [Emphasis added.]

Change happens through action, not through magic. When I stopped drinking I stopped getting drunk. When I stopped smoking pot I stopped getting stoned. When I went back to school I got an education and a degree. When I practiced meditation I developed calm and insight. Karmic actions and their fruits are what allow us to change, to remove or diminish our shortcomings.

Buddhism as we've received it in the West focuses on practices, and that's certainly what drew me to it. It's the practices that transform us. When we talk about "beseeching the Law of Karma through our actions," we're not just talking about following the precepts, although this is foundational. We are also talking about taking on the formal practices the Buddha and his followers taught—and teach. While the words *recovery* and *spiritual growth* can be fairly vague, when it comes to Buddhist practices, things get pretty specific. These practices depend on a commitment—the third Step—and discipline that are challenging. I've heard many people say that it was difficult for them to establish a meditation practice, and for addicts this certainly can be a problem. On the other hand, we can use our addictive and compulsive tendencies as supports for that kind of daily activity. While a great deal of growth can happen through other means, if you want what meditation offers, there's no alternative to doing the work. And this includes serious retreat practice.

My first attempts at meditation weren't very productive because I didn't understand the mechanics of what I was supposed to do. I was on the road with a Top 40 band in July of 1976, playing a hotel in South Hill, Virginia. This was a period of time when I'd stopped drinking for several months and was on a health kick, jogging two miles every day, a distance that seemed vast to me at the time. In South Hill, I'd found a red clay track behind a middle school to jog in the mornings, and this day I had a book by Alan Watts with me. When I finished my jog, I opened the side doors of my banged-up olive-green van and sat there with my feet dangling. I don't recall now what I tried to do, but I know that my understanding of meditation was extremely vague. I closed my eyes and nothing happened. So I gave up. This kind of quick-to-quit behavior was typical of me. I didn't attempt to meditate again for another two years. Then I learned T.M.

It wasn't until I learned vipassana meditation in the fall of 1980, though, that I began to see my meditation practice deepen. I was introduced to an array of practices that are at the center of the Buddha's teaching on liberating the heart and mind. They are the ways that we beseech the Law of Karma to remove our shortcomings. I want to talk about four different approaches to practice: mindfulness/insight, calm/concentration, love/compassion, and contemplation. These practices tap into the Higher Powers I talked about earlier. And, while I'm going to talk about them separately, I also want to talk about how they intertwine, supporting and depending on each other.

Mindfulness/Insight

Mindfulness is the foundation practice of all Buddhist meditation. It is what makes Buddhist practice unique. It is the logical tool for a practice that seeks to wake us up, because mindfulness is about being present to our experience just as it is. This isn't about a mystical or religious experience; there is no focus on devotion or faith; we are not trying to transcend anything with mindfulness. We are trying to penetrate as deeply as we can into reality.

Mindfulness, then, leads to insight. The term *insight* in our culture mostly means a wise thought, but in the context of Buddhist meditation, it implies something more nonverbal, an inner knowing or a transformative experience. These breakthroughs are said to uproot the underlying causes of suffering and eventually free us completely. While these insights are associated with meditation and the Buddhist path, an alcoholic who has lost the desire to drink can be said to have experienced such a transforming insight, a deep letting go.

The process of developing insight through mindfulness is laid out very clearly by the Buddha. He talked about four different areas of experience that we can be mindful of—body, feelings, states of mind, and phenomena—called the Four Foundations of Mindfulness. In these practices there's a quality of observing and investigating what's happening inside and outside us, our experiences and our reactions to them. We try to bring an objective attitude that asks, "What's *really* happening here?" In this way we can go beyond our conditioned and habitual ways of seeing the world and ourselves and come closer to the truth.

Mindfulness of the body, the first Foundation, is the most common form of mindfulness practice. Developing this aspect of mindfulness brings our sense experience alive in ways that can make it feel as if we're awakening from a lifelong state of half-sleep. I first saw this on retreat. One of the practices I was taught was mindful eating, in which the whole process is slowed down and you pay exacting attention to every step. It was as though my taste buds had been covered over with grime and suddenly I'd washed them off. Even the simplest of flavors, like brown rice, was captivating. Each mouthful of food I delivered slowly and mindfully, noticing the smell, the texture of the food in my mouth, the movement of my jaw and tongue, the action of swallowing, even the sensation of the food going down my throat to my stomach, was a delightful exploration.

I recall an early morning sitting during that desert retreat when, sometime into the meditation period, the birds awoke and started their busy morning activities. I took my attention off my breath and just listened, enthralled by the rich concert of sounds.

All of these experiences, and many more, are cultivated by simply placing our attention on one or another of our senses and patiently returning again and again. To bring our attention to some sense experience is one of the quickest ways to come back to the present moment, because we can only feel our bodies in the present moment. We can't feel them in the past or future.

Usually the first sense experience that's taught in meditation is the sense of touch: feeling the breath. The breath is always with us. It embodies the life force, the continually changing and rhythmic nature of existence. It has the unique ability to both stimulate and calm the body and the mind. It is how life begins—the first breath and first cries—and how it ends, as the final exhalation rattles out of the body. We can find the breath everywhere in the body if we look closely enough. It is subtle and complex, yet obvious and simple. It offers us an ongoing focus rich in sensation. The Buddha's first instruction on mindfulness is to explore the range of qualities of the breath. Once he explains this practice, he suggests that we notice how breath comes and goes, its impermanence. This means that we are seeing the reality of the breath in two ways, as physical sensations and in the greater context of its changing nature.

The Buddha teaches awareness of the body not only to help us to be mindful, but also to help us to let go, as when he suggests contemplating the unpleasant aspects of the body as an antidote for lust. Nothing like seeing your lover's excrement to turn you off. His "charnel ground meditation," in which we seek out dead bodies in various states of decay, is perhaps the most intense practice he suggests, again for helping us to let go of the idea that there is something permanent about this life. This practice is meant to remind us of how short life is and inspire us to make the most of it through our spiritual work.

Mindfulness of body has been adapted and developed in the West in many ways, including integrating mindfulness with yoga, qi gong, and martial arts. One of the most skillful ways of using mindfulness of the body is in working with emotions.

When I started having difficulty with focusing my attention on a long retreat, my teachers suggested I start working more with emotions. The instructions for doing this involved taking my attention into my body. This became, and remains, one of the central tools in my practice. I often focus on the chest and belly areas, feeling the tumult of emotion that moves through there. As I feel these energies, I breathe, relax, and try to let go. Sometimes this calms the feelings and sometimes it takes a while for them to pass. The practice of focusing on the physical experience of our emotions can bring about powerful changes in our response to our feelings, helping us to be less reactive. We can simply be with feelings, noticing how they are dynamic, ever-changing. We come to see that just by accepting and focusing on them, we can get through them; they don't have to be overwhelming or destructive.

I'm talking, now, about the kinds of surface feelings that tend to move through us in the course of the day, not the deeper, more chronic emotions that might be more embedded in our psyche. While these too can benefit from, and indeed need, this kind of gentle, focused attention, they also may need other forms of care, like therapy, bodywork, or even psychiatric medication. I'd certainly been an emotional person before I learned these practices, but it wasn't until I learned to engage my emotions in my body that I was able to work with a psychotherapist in a way that penetrated my feelings and let me open deeply. The Big Book tells us that we shouldn't limit our healing and spiritual work to the Twelve Step program, and I think the same can be said about Buddhism. I think it's important to stay open to the range of healings that are available to us.

Meditation practices don't work like medicine; they don't have an instantaneous effect. They take patience, persistence, and repetition. Over time they can be transforming. This doesn't mean that you can't miss a day of meditation or that you need to become perfect at catching every emotion and processing it through your body, but it does mean that you regularly do these things, that they are in the forefront of your consciousness as coping strategies.

The second Foundation of Mindfulness is feeling (*vedana* in Pali). Here the Buddha is referring not to emotions but to the more or less automatic responses we have to any stimuli. These are three: positive, negative, and neutral. A positive feeling might come when we smell baking bread. That smell conditions desire, and for someone with a an eating disorder, for instance, that desire can lead to clinging and suffering because desires can never be satisfied. The negative feeling we experience when someone yells at us conditions aversion, which also leads to clinging and suffering, because anger is painful and unfulfilling. The neutral feeling we experience when we brush our teeth conditions ignorance, which also leads to clinging and suffering because we're simply not paying attention. When we bring mindfulness to these reactions, we break the cycle of suffering. When we notice the pleasant feeling aroused at the sight of the bottle of wine at the grocery store, we can let go, come back to the body and the breath or to our emotional energy.

Occasionally I'll catch a whiff of marijuana at a concert or on the street. That's a smell that connects me with a deep, sensual craving. But because I've contemplated the ways that marijuana crippled me, and I've lived with that understanding for decades, along with that pleasant feeling comes a moment of mindfulness—I awaken to the danger. That makes it pretty easy for me to just notice the enjoyment and subtle craving and let it go. If we don't notice these reactions, we can get pulled into the whole round of addiction. When we practice noticing these reactions, we start to hold them differently, as passing moments of experience, just little blips on our sensory radar, and a balance develops that helps us to stay calm, peaceful, and at ease as we move through our day. This practice of watching reactivity is called "Guarding the Senses," which doesn't mean that we try to block things from our perception, but that we don't get drawn into every stimulus that comes along. If we bring mindfulness instead of unconsciousness to these feelings, we develop the habit of responding with clarity rather than reacting with ignorance.

Reacting to stimuli is natural to even the simplest organisms that move toward food and away from danger. This reactivity is a tool for survival. But for humans, it is at the root of addiction. When a squirrel is frightened by a dog, it can't relieve that stress with a bottle of booze. But a human being who gets home from a stressful day at work can. When there are few limits on the ways that we can soothe or please ourselves, we have to learn to place those limits on ourselves. For the non-addict, this apparently isn't a problem. But those of us who are drawn to alcohol, drugs, sex, gambling, food, relationships, or anything else in addictive ways must train ourselves to let go when we are hit by a pleasant or unpleasant stimulus.

I started drinking at 16 with a Seven and Seven—Seagram's Seven and 7-Up. I loved it—there was never any doubt that I was going to keep on drinking. My life quickly became centered around getting booze on the weekends so I could get loaded. This was an automatic response, with little attention to the actual experience of craving, just a reaction. A year later I smoked marijuana for the first time. It didn't work at first—one of the oddities of pot—and my brother's friend, who was giving it to me, suggested I hyperventilate, taking ten deep breaths rapidly, then holding the last breath. I passed out on the kitchen floor, and when I woke up I was stoned. From that moment I was a pothead. I liked it, I did it. No question, no thought, just reaction.

Both alcohol and drugs were pleasant experiences at first, and I simply took them because I liked the feeling. But soon enough, I was taking them because I *didn't like* the feelings inside me. This points to the two ways that addiction operates: one, as the search for pleasure, and two, as the avoidance of pain. Both of these start with vedana, the pleasant and the unpleasant, which, when unrecognized, become desire and aversion.

On a retreat a few years ago my mind was becoming quite still, and I started to just pay attention to vedana, noticing each time some sense experience evoked a pleasant or unpleasant reaction. This occurred fairly naturally; I didn't set out to do it. As I noticed these reactions, I would simply say to myself, "Pleasant" or "Unpleasant." When I did that, the reactions couldn't take hold; desire and aversion simply didn't arise. I went into an interview with my teacher, Jack Kornfield, and told him about what I was doing. "That's equanimity," he said, "the great peace that comes when the heart is no longer swayed by the worldly winds." This may sound like some kind of zombie state, but in fact, it was tremendously freeing. When my mind wasn't getting pulled into every desire or negative state, it was free to enjoy the moment. The sense of lightness and presence was delightful. In that state I saw how much of a victim I was in my typical daily mind, just pulled from grasping to pushing away every time anything engaged my mind or body. In the same way that I'd woken up to my slavery to drugs and alcohol, it felt like I was waking up to another level of enslavement, to the "worldly winds" that buffet the heart.

Of course, when the stillness and concentration of the retreat ended, so did this balanced state. But the glimpse of that balance has informed my understanding of my experience ever since.

Becoming attuned to the arising of feeling, whether pleasant, unpleasant, or neutral, is one of the ways that mindfulness helps us to remove our shortcomings, freeing us from the habitual patterns of reactivity and opening us to new ways of engaging the world.

The third and fourth Foundations of Mindfulness aren't as easily defined as the first two, but they essentially cover our thoughts and emotions and how we view them. The way the Buddha talked about these things was somewhat different from our modern approach. I'll try to honor his original teachings while also adding a more contemporary understanding.

The third Foundation can be called "states of mind," which covers moods, like joy or sorrow, and also things like our level of concentration or agitation. Our mood colors our perception of the world and can insidiously poison our experience. If, when we're stuck in some emotional reaction, we ask ourselves what state we're in, we'll often realize that things are not as bad as we think they are. Observing our state of mind as we move through the day is a great way to keep tabs on our experience and stay present and honest about what's happening.

I often suggest at the beginning of a guided meditation that people check in with their state of mind to see what mood is dominant. There's a tendency to think of meditation as some specialized activity that has no relationship to our usual mind states. When we think like this we can often miss the obvious backdrop of our meditation experience. However, if we acknowledge the energy that's present as we begin our practice—anxiety or sadness, sleepiness or restlessness, calm or ease—then we'll be more understanding and accepting of what arises as we sit, and we'll often have a better idea how we need to approach that period of practice.

Besides observing these mind states, we can also look at the contents of mind, our thoughts and feelings. Applying mindfulness to this enterprise means shifting from identifying with our experience to investigating it. Seeing thoughts and emotions as objects, rather than as facts or things that belong to us, is one of the most important changes of orientation that we can make and one that opens us to tremendous insight. Viewing thoughts impersonally makes it much easier to take criticism or write inventory. You don't have to defend yourself because you realize there's no self to defend. Viewing moods as just passing clouds in our consciousness means we don't have to react to every change in the emotional weather.

When we first learn meditation, we're usually instructed to just drop thoughts and keep coming back to the breath. This is the ideal, but rarely does it happen, especially in the beginning. Naturally enough, our minds wander off into memories and plans, stories and judgments, calculations and fears. In the vipassana tradition, as I described in the Mindfulness of Thoughts exercise, certain approaches suggest labeling thoughts when we notice them: "planning," "judging," "wanting," "aversion." This is the beginning of seeing the habitual patterns of thought that pass through the mind. At first this can be quite painful as you realize how destructive your thinking is, how unproductive and pointless. But this is also part of the process of dis-identifying with the contents of mind. Just naming these thoughts puts them in their place. As you begin to see how certain types of thoughts appear over and over, you see how, to some extent, you create our own reality. You can see how your focus on criticizing others in your thoughts leads to conflict in your life or how your focus on dreaming about the future undercuts your present. And if you are an addict, you can see how addiction arises, with obsessive thinking leading to the compulsion to act out.

The question of thoughts creating our reality is a tricky one. Some people take this too far and claim that our entire life is a projection of the mind. Then they'll tell us that we can have exactly the life we want if we'll just think the right thoughts, that thoughts directly manipulate physical reality without us taking any actions. This is a popular notion that lets people think that there are shortcuts to change and to having what they want. I'm afraid it doesn't have much basis in reality, and worst of all, it can be used by people to blame themselves for things they really aren't responsible for.

Nonetheless, the Buddha said:

> All experience is preceded by mind,
> > Led by mind
> > Made by mind.
> Speak or act with a corrupted mind,
> > And suffering follows
> As the wagon wheel follows the hoof of the ox . . .
> Speak or act with a peaceful mind
> > And happiness follows
> Like a never-departing shadow.

Is he saying that our thoughts create our reality? Not quite. Instead, he's saying that our thoughts lay the foundation for our experience of reality. Most directly, the point is that a "corrupted mind" is painful and a peaceful mind is pleasurable. But more important, the mind leads us to words and actions that cause either happiness or sorrow in our lives.

If we watch our thoughts, we'll see what lays the foundation for our experience of reality, but changing our thinking won't automatically change our lives. There's work to be done.

My first vipassana teacher taught me the noting practice and told me to label each thought of desire or aversion. I set out to do this with determination and devotion, thinking that there would be all kinds of other thoughts passing through as well. Pretty soon, though, it seemed I could identify some quality of wanting or not-wanting in every single thought. Some thoughts, like "My knees are killing me" or "I hope I can sell my new song," were obvious in their orientation. But then I saw that even subtle thoughts like "Some tea will be nice after this" or "I wonder if I'm doing this right" were also pulling in one direction or the other.

I've suggested this practice to people, and sometimes they debate whether certain thoughts really fall into one of the two categories. Perhaps not. But seeing at least that *a huge percentage* of thoughts did had a powerful effect on me. Initially I was disappointed—*Is that all there is to my thinking?* But then it became an inspiration to let go of thinking. I had always believed that "my thoughts" were mine, that there was something unique and purposeful about them. But seeing how they were all (or almost all) oriented in one of two directions took the originality and "Kevin-ness" out of them and made them seem much more generic. If all my thoughts are just programmed habits, why should I believe them? Why should I invest so much energy into them?

My relationship to thoughts started to change. Instead of accepting them as true, I began to question them. Now I had a choice in how to react to the thoughts—to act, to speak, or to simply drop them.

Mindfulness of emotions is more tricky than noticing thoughts. What are emotions, anyway? Early in my practice one teacher told me, "Emotions are a combination of thoughts in the mind and sensations in the body." That sounded good. When I mentioned this to another teacher, he said, "That's not quite right," but didn't elaborate. My own sense is that, while emotions certainly have a mental and physical component, there is something else, what's sometimes called the "emotional body," a sense sphere in and around the body but not quite fully physical. When I bring mindfulness to emotions, it's first through the body. Then I notice the related thoughts. What we call *mood,* then, is like an overlay that infiltrates both body and mind. This can be the most powerful and potentially difficult aspect of emotions because of its pervasiveness. Emotions condition thoughts so that the way we feel blends with the way we are thinking to create a sense of a solid reality. When the mood is good, no problem. But when it's bad, we can really get stuck. As I noted in the section on "Higher Power of Impermanence," we often have the sense that a mind state will stay forever. Depression is like this. It takes a great deal of persistent attention to break this view.

The authors of the book *The Mindful Way Through Depression* point out that when we are struggling with a bad mood, the tendency is to try to think our way out of it. The problem is that *"focusing on the mismatch between our idea of the people we want to be and our idea of the people we see ourselves as makes us feel worse than we did in the first place"* [Emphasis in original]. So, our self-judgment—*I'm screwed up and I need to get fixed*—just makes us feel worse. The antidote, they suggest, is to open ourselves beyond the limited view of our own thoughts and experience, to see our thoughts as passing "mental events," to break the habit of trying to fix things using what they call the "doing mode" and instead cultivate the "being mode of mind," which is, simply put, mindfulness. Instead of jumping in, trying to solve problems, worry about them, fight with them, we step back and observe, just allowing ourselves to feel things as they are. As we develop mindfulness and concentration we become more adept at moving into this observing space, getting out of the tendency to identify with every thought and feeling that comes along.

Changing our relationship with thoughts and feelings from identi-fication to mindfulness is what allows us to remove the shortcomings inherent in them. Mindfulness of these energies is the first step—and sometimes the only one necessary—in letting them go.

When the Buddha says we should be mindful of "phenomena," he's taking us completely out of the realm of the personal and into the realm of the universal. He suggests that we start to view our expe-rience, the phenomena of mind and body, through the lens of his teachings, the Dharma. In particular, the sutta on the Fourth Founda-tion of Mindfulness gives us several of the classical lists to reflect on, and I want to highlight three of these: the Five Hindrances, the Seven Factors of Enlightenment, and the Four Noble Truths. Exploring these fully could take another book—or two—and I suggest you seek out more information on them. But for now, I'll try to talk about them briefly.

There's a tendency to identify with the Five Hindrances, to think "I am wanting" or "I am hating." However, when we put them in a less personal context it can take the sting out of them, letting us realize that desire, aversion, and all the rest are just energies or natural forces that come and go. Have you ever known someone who didn't have these hindrances at some point in his or her life?

Mindfulness of the hindrances means that we try to notice when one of them appears, to acknowledge it, accept it, and let it be or let it go. This is a challenging process at every stage. To even notice a hin-drance is difficult because we are conditioned to react to them, not be aware of them. So, when we want something, our typical response is to try to get it. Interrupting this habit is one of the first goals of medi-tation: If you are committed to sitting here for some period of time, then when you want something you *aren't* going to try to get it, which means that your desire will be right in your face. Then what? Well, I know I've spent many meditation periods lost in desire, dreaming of a vacation, a lover, or a better life. But sooner or later I wake up and see what's happening; I taste the bitterness of desire and feel its compulsion in my blood.

This becomes another critical moment in the process. When I see the suffering I'm causing myself, how do I react? It's easy to go into another negative state. Many times, I've seen my mind caught in a hindrance, whether desire, aversion, some dull mind state, or an anxious feeling, and immediately had the thought *What's wrong with me?* or just an underlying feeling of frustration: *I'm meditating to get peaceful and happy; I don't want to sit here absorbed in craving.* This becomes another point at which we need to bring to bear wise attention, seeing the process clearly, breathing, and allowing. When we've been practicing for a while and we've seen these traps enough, we come to understand what's happening and catch ourselves. This is just another place where the mind is acting out of negative conditioning. *Acceptance* of the hindrance means that we understand that we are powerless over the arising of the hindrances, that they are a natural human response, and that they don't reflect any personal failure on our part. If we watch them enough, the tendency to judge ourselves can dissolve into laughter at the absurdity of the wanting beast, the reptilian mind that seems to be nothing but hunger and hatred.

Once we come to this place of accepting the hindrances, then we are ready to let go. We see the uselessness, even destructiveness, of the hindrance; we see our role, the tendency to feed the hindrance with our judgment or resistance; and we see that just allowing the hindrance to have its life, to play itself out, will many times be enough to let go.

In contrast to the focus on the negative qualities of the hindrances, mindfulness of the Seven Factors of Enlightenment is like a "positive inventory," taking a look at how our practice and our spiritual work have developed. For many people, looking at their positive side is more difficult than looking at the negative. Somehow the negative stuff gives us something to work on, a problem to solve. Focusing on the positive might seem prideful, or even bad luck, as though we are tempting fate by reveling in our good qualities.

But the Buddha often talks about the value of seeing our own goodness. Part of being happy, he says, is recognizing our positive qualities. The Factors of Enlightenment focus primarily on our meditation development: mindfulness, investigation, energy, rapture, tranquility, concentration, and equanimity. In the same way that we notice the hindrances, we can notice these factors. This is also a kind of "meditation inventory." The Buddha suggests that we ask ourselves whether these qualities are there in us and that we consider how they come about and how we can develop them further. At times I reflect on which of the factors is strong in me and which is weak. Then I try to increase my effort around the weak factors. At the same time, I try to take some pleasure in the ways that some of these factors are present and well cultivated in me.

The Buddha's core teaching on the Four Noble Truths is the final focus he suggests for mindfulness. He tells us that to cultivate this focus a meditator "understands as it actually is: 'This is suffering'; he understands as it actually is: 'This is the origin of suffering'; he understands as it actually is: 'This is the cessation of suffering'; he understands as it actually is: 'This is the way leading to the cessation of suffering.'" One could say that this is the essence of the practice: seeing our suffering, its cause, our potential to end it, and what we need to do to end it. Keeping these four truths in mind means that we are seeing our problems, our failings, our clinging; that we are seeing how we are creating those problems; that we know we don't have to stay stuck in them; and that we remember what we have to do to change.

When, a few years ago, I had a sudden back spasm that put me on the floor in writhing agony, it wasn't long before I put the experience in the context of the Dharma: this was the First Noble Truth, the Truth of Suffering. There is a sense of relief, of ease, when you see the truth of something, even something painful. You're not struggling in confusion. You get it. Acceptance and equanimity come out of this understanding. This points to the importance of actually studying the Dharma so that these ideas are clear and primary in our minds. Western Buddhism has a streak of anti-intellectualism in it, as though all you had to do was meditate and everything would become clear. And, while meditation is essential—better to only practice than to only study—an intellectual understanding of the Dharma informs our practice and makes us more broadly aware of the workings of the Dharma.

The Four Foundations of Mindfulness are the foundations of letting go. They give us a vast range of options and opportunities for paying attention to our experience, the ways we cling and cause ourselves suffering. We "beseech the Law of Karma" to remove our shortcomings by engaging life, moment to moment, in these ways. The Higher Power of Mindfulness is our guide and our support.

Calm/Concentration

When people ask me about how I work the Steps, I often tell them that I use meditation as a gateway into each Step. One of the most obvious ways that this works is in Step Seven. Almost every time I meditate I let go. Mindfulness, of course, is one way this happens. Calm and concentration are another. Many times I've sat down in a state of agitation, anxiety, or resentment and found, as I follow the breath and become more focused, that those feelings simply dissolve. I don't have to figure them out, write inventory about them, or otherwise deal with them, just let the Higher Power of concentration melt them away.

This is a wonderful tool for a person in recovery to develop—especially in early sobriety, but also later on as well. Many of us alcoholics and addicts seem to react to life with more stress than others, so having a reliable tool for dealing with that edginess and craving on a daily basis is precious. In the suttas it says that concentration cools the passions and in this way helps us to let go of clinging because we don't feel so driven when we are calm. A craving or resentment that seemed so important just dissolves under the soothing qualities of relaxing and stilling the mind.

The fact that quieting the mind helps you let go of disturbances is commonly understood, as when someone tells you, "Breathe," when you're upset. It's not that you aren't breathing, but rather that if you focus on a relaxing breath, calming the mind and body, the disturbance will often pass on its own.

While it's true that just a moment of calming breath can help us to let go, the most beneficial effects of concentration come with concerted effort. When people first start to practice meditation, they often find it difficult and frustrating trying to hold the mind still. Unfortunately, for most of us, just setting aside a few minutes a day for meditation doesn't give the opportunity for the more effective levels of concentration to develop. That's the province of retreat.

197

The essential elements of concentration are quiet, stillness, and repetition. A silent retreat, with alternating periods of sitting and walking meditation, gives us all three.

The transition from daily life to the retreat environment can be difficult. We're so used to being able to change the channel, figuratively or literally. When I went on my first retreat I imagined that I'd be accessing all sorts of bliss states and peacefulness, but instead my knees hurt, my mind wouldn't stay still, and I kept falling asleep. It was as though I thought that in going out to a meditation center in the desert I would be leaving myself behind in Los Angeles. But of course I came along, with all my physical and mental issues.

Coming into a real state of meditative concentration for the first time is like breaking through some invisible membrane. Inside the membrane is your usual noisy self, but when it pops, you open into something spacious and still. Some thoughts may still be there, but they aren't taking up all the space; they're just part of a much larger landscape. Until you break through that membrane, meditation can be fairly frustrating. Of course, I had this experience before I got sober, so maybe a sober person wouldn't feel that frustration so much. But I do know that there is a qualitative difference to the experience of the concentrated mind. Once we have broken that membrane it becomes easier to access concentration going forward. There will still be times when you can't get there because of the agitation in your heart/mind and body, but when the conditions are ripe again, you will slip into it like a familiar and comfortable old shirt.

One thing that makes concentration difficult is that it requires discipline, and this is a quality many people struggle with. People seem to associate discipline with negative images like abusive nuns with rulers or drill sergeants breathing down your neck. However, I've come to see it differently. The word *discipline* is related to the word *disciple,* someone who is devoted to a teacher or a practice. I like to think of myself as a disciple or a devotee of my meditation practice. I do it because I love and honor it. I show up out of respect and faith in the process. I also see it as a Third Step: Even when I don't feel like it, I know the value of practice, so I turn myself over to that process.

Concentration is probably the most powerful raw tool of the mind. While it can't permanently remove our shortcomings in the way that insight can, it's critical both in developing insight and in maintaining a peaceful heart and mind.

Love/Compassion

The cultivation of love and compassion is one of the practices that directly engage our negativity and help us to let go. While mindfulness has a neutral quality, just seeing things as they are and allowing that awareness to organically help us to let go, the practice of love and compassion is engaged in intentionally developing positive qualities.

So how do we do this? The simplest practice taught is to repeat phrases of lovingkindness like "May you be happy; may you be peaceful; may you be safe." As we repeat the phrases, we visualize different people, beginning with those closest to us, then moving to neutral people, those we encounter in our lives but who don't really have an impact on us, and finally to difficult people, the ones who have hurt us or whom we resent. The repetitive nature of this practice, as described fully in Sharon Salzberg's book *Lovingkindness,* has a calming effect, so the practice is used not just to develop love, but to develop concentration as well.

My first real engagement with this practice came on the last day of my first retreat. The meditation hall in the desert barely had room for the whole group, and the teacher asked us to face someone else, so I just turned around on my cushion. There was a slender young woman my age with short blond hair and prominent bones in her face. The teacher said that one person should close his or her eyes and the other one stare at the partner's face. While I was staring at this woman's face, I felt as though I could see her life's history etched out. The teacher reminded us that everyone suffers loss and pain; that each of us has moments of failure or humiliation; that we are all subject to the Truth of Suffering. As I gazed at this woman's face, my heart filled with compassion. I didn't even know her name, but I felt a sense of caring welling up unlike anything I'd ever experienced. After she had gazed at me, the teacher told everyone to open their eyes and stare together at each other. At this point, after five days of meditation and 20 minutes of gazing at each other's closed eyes, the moment was intense. A deep sense of connection came over me—and, I learned afterward, over my partner as well. Just letting ourselves stare into each other's eyes, something I'd never done before, felt so incredibly intimate and at the same time universal. Here was a person, just a person like any other, but the power of life, of consciousness, and of life's struggles was all there in front of me.

After the retreat, this woman whom I'd never met became a dear friend I still care for today. It seems that a bond was forged during those minutes of looking into each other's eyes that has lasted a lifetime.

Although I have done and taught this as a formal practice several times since then, it was when my mother lay dying that I did it with the most meaning. After a series of strokes, she had lost the ability to speak and was just lying in bed for a couple of months with her eyes open. When I visited her during that time, we just gazed at each other. The gentleness and love that I saw in her eyes during those minutes felt deeper than any connection I'd felt with her in my life. The relationship between a mother and son is complicated, and all the conflicts and confusion can make you question whether there is actually any love between you. But seeing her in silence like that made clear the deep bond we had and the love that she felt for me. The connection between mother-love and metta was apparent in those moments.

When I came home from that first retreat, I cried every day. At 30 years old, I hadn't really cried in years, and I certainly hadn't expected that result from the retreat. I was supposed to be a super-meditator now, not a quivering mass of sadness. I wrote a song that week, "Vipassana Blues," that had the line, "You're trying to open up your mind, and take a look at what's inside; but you better know, you might not like what you find." When we try to cultivate awareness and love, we first have to slog through the muck of ignorance, pain, and confusion that's built up over years of inattention, self-centeredness, and denial.

Our image of what "lovingkindness meditation" is might be quite different from what it feels like when we first engage it. Before we can get to the love, we first have to see the hate. This is why lovingkindness practice can also be an insight practice, as we start to see all the layers that cover over our innate loving hearts. As we touch those tender places, we see the suffering we've created in our lives; it's as if we were doing a "heart inventory," seeing where we have failed to love, to forgive, to open ourselves to the suffering of others. In this way, the lovingkindness practices are ideal for the amends of Steps Eight and Nine. Seeing this suffering, we are inspired to grow beyond those failures, to reveal the kind heart underneath those hardened layers.

Lovingkindness can be organically integrated into our days. While it can be difficult to get very concentrated in daily life, an intentional practice like metta can be done anytime. We can do metta for the birds or the police, for the person in the ambulance that flies by; we can do it for the person who is holding up the line at the grocery store or the person who cuts us off on the freeway. There are so many opportunities in our day. And don't forget to do it for yourself. In those tough times, moments of stress and worry, waiting for the job interview or sitting in the doctor's office, we can turn our attention to our hearts and wish ourselves happiness, peace, and safety. We know better than anyone else the struggles and difficulties we have experienced, so we, better than anyone else, can have compassion for ourselves.

As we try to let go of negative states in Step Seven, all the forms of the Brahma-Viharas can help us. When we notice some painful thought or emotion, we intentionally bring up a thought of love, compassion, appreciation, or equanimity. This is called "replacing with the opposite," and it is one of the skillful means the Buddha taught. It doesn't always work—sometimes the negativity is too strong to be countered so directly—and the best we might be able to muster is just to notice and feel the difficult thought or feeling. But as we become more committed to living with kindness and wisdom, it becomes easier to naturally incline the mind toward these states. And having a formal way to foster these qualities helps us to quickly reorient ourselves. As with all the meditation practices, the repetition of the practice deepens our tendency and ability to enter positive states.

Contemplation

When we learn meditation, we often get the idea that perfect meditation means not thinking at all. Perhaps there is a bias in this direction because Westerners place so much stock in thinking—Descartes's "I think, therefore I am" being the extreme version of this. While learning to drop thought or to see through thought is an important part of the process of developing meditative tools, learning how to think carefully and wisely is also important.

The word *contemplate* has to do with connecting heaven and earth. The design of temples was originally meant to correspond to the design of the home of the gods; in one definition, these structures "linked the geometries of heaven and earth." So, when we "con-template," we are trying to connect our thinking with this geometry, mimicking the thoughts of the gods.

Clearly the Buddha did a lot of thinking. Very good thinking. His formulation of the Four Noble Truths and everything that springs from that teaching required deep and careful thought. The Buddha doesn't say that after his enlightenment he stopped thinking, but rather that he is a "master of the courses of thought." He's not swept along by impulse and craving; rather, he stays on top of his thinking mind and directs it at will. We can infer from his teachings that the contemplation that guided him was "What is the cause of suffering, and how can I end it?" There's nothing esoteric or metaphysical about this question. It's quite straightforward and practical. So, while we should strive to overcome compulsive thought, we can benefit a great deal from directed, intentional, and conscious thought.

One of the ways contemplation is formally done is by taking some traditional spiritual question like "Who am I?" and asking it over and over, letting the answers penetrate deeper and deeper. This combines concentration with thought in an intentional way that can evoke a breakthrough in consciousness, a powerful new insight. The trick is to keep the mind on the question, and because we are so habituated to letting the mind wander, that's very difficult for a beginning meditator. That's probably why contemplation isn't emphasized when people teach beginning meditation.

A less formal kind of contemplation happens pretty naturally in practice. When our mind has settled a bit, sometimes some issue will come up, something that's been in the back of our minds that we haven't been addressing. If we look at such an issue carefully, without letting the mind just fall into digression (the free-associative drifting that characterizes much unconscious thought) or rumination (the self-destructive focus on our flaws), this can be very productive. But this practice has to be used sparingly and discreetly, or we'll never develop the mindfulness and concentration that allow for penetrating insight.

Our own study can also be a kind of contemplation. Some Twelve Step meetings are focused on the literature of the program, and this makes for a good way to reflect on those teachings. When we gather with others to discuss a text, our minds are focused on the topic, and hearing the opinions of others often helps to open up our own understanding.

When I go on self-retreat, I often take some of the traditional suttas along for study. These are not particularly entertaining, so I don't have to worry about becoming distracted as I might by a novel. I've found that my understanding of the suttas is much deeper when I am on retreat. Some centers and teachers are now offering trainings and retreats that bring in more of a contemplative study element. This is part of the maturing of the Dharma in the West, as we move beyond the limited idea of Buddhism as nothing more than silent meditation.

Focused, directed thought has other uses beyond study. Cognitive therapy, which is increasingly being merged with Buddhist mindfulness teachings, is another way to use thought intentionally, in this case as a healing. This work involves challenging subconscious, reactive thoughts with rational responses. In a way, this is another kind of contemplation, aligning our thinking with the "heaven" of our wise selves and dis-identifying with the "hell" of obsessive, fearful thought patterns.

In all of this we can see that contemplation is intertwined with mindfulness, especially mindfulness of thought, as well as with concentration, which is what allows us to think clearly and deeply. We see that these practices are not separate, but rather work together to support our growth. If we become too attached to one form, we lose the natural flow of practice. Wise practice involves asking ourselves, and our teachers, what would be a skillful way of working *with this moment.* This moment is unique. It must be addressed on its own terms. If we try to apply yesterday's solutions to today's problems, we'll always be a step behind. The challenge of mindfulness practice is to face each moment with attention and investigation, to try to find the best way of expressing love, compassion, and wisdom in each moment.

Insight takes different forms. The first insights people have are often personal and psychological. These come from seeing the habitual ways our minds work and what our thoughts create. But these are considered to be less important than the universal insights into suffering, impermanence, and corelessness that tend to be nonverbal and impersonal. These often don't require thought or contemplation, just very close and steady attention. If we focus only on the first kind of insight, then our practice can become like an extended form of psychotherapy, just problem-solving and processing emotions, thoughts, and memories. While this can serve a certain purpose, in terms of spiritual development it is limited. We need to have a balanced personal sense of self, some self-confidence and inner harmony, in order to grow on a spiritual path. But if we don't go beyond this to the transcendent aspect of practice, then we are abandoning the ultimate purpose of meditation: not just personal healing, but spiritual transformation.

LIVING THE PATH:
STEP ELEVEN

"Sought through prayer and meditation to improve our conscious contact with God, as we understood Him, *praying only for knowledge of His will for us and the power to carry that out."*

SEEKING GOD

Christina Grof, in her book *The Thirst for Wholeness,* says about addicts and alcoholics that our unfulfilled and misdirected spiritual longings are part of the reason we become addicted. The Twelve Step literature makes this connection when it talks about the two meanings of the word "spirit": the one that refers to our search for meaning and the one that refers to alcoholic "spirits." Obviously someone slamming back shots of tequila or snorting lines doesn't exactly look like someone on a spiritual quest, but the longing there, the desire to experience something beyond the limits of conventional life, is connected with that quest.

In the world of drugs, the spiritual search is sometimes explicit. Many of the experimenters of the '60s were motivated by a search for God or transcendence. People like Ram Dass and Timothy Leary were interested (at least at first) in more than just getting high. There are many native traditions that use drugs like peyote or ayahuasca to evoke spiritual experiences. While often said as a joke, expressions like "I saw God" or "I was out of my head" express something of the spiritual nature of some drug and alcohol experiences. Marijuana, too, can have a spiritual component.

Fall 1967, Bethlehem, Pennsylvania

I'm sitting on the daybed in the upstairs of my family's garage, gazing at the mess of hot-dog wrappers, empty soda bottles, and cigarette butts on the beat-up coffee table. This old garage, dating from the 19th century, was once a carriage house, and the upstairs rooms were where the hay was stored and the stable boys slept. Now it's the home of my band. The main room is filled with amps, guitars, drums, and an upright piano we hauled up with block and tackle through the wide hay door. The bedrooms are where we eat and drink and smoke and get high.

Today there's no rehearsal and I'm smoking pot alone, the weak October sun coming through dirt-smeared windows. My dealer said the pot is "Peruvian Gold," but who knows where it came from? Whatever it is, it works, and after half a joint I find myself spellbound by the objects in the room, the band refuse taking on the effect of a tableau, something laid out intentionally. It all looks perfect to me in this moment. Someone else—presumably someone who wasn't stoned—would just see a lot of junk that needed to be cleaned up, but I see—and feel—that things are just the way they are meant to be.

Looking back on that moment, which left a strong imprint on my mind, I see in my perception what in Zen is called "suchness," a kind of welcoming acceptance of what *is,* a full, mindful engagement with the magic contained in the mundane. Had I recognized the underlying spiritual nature of the experience, that moment could have been the springboard for my spiritual journey. If I had had some context in which to understand it beyond just being high, I might have been able to integrate that understanding into a new kind of engagement with my life. Instead, it just reinforced my growing addiction to marijuana. I liked the experience and wanted to repeat it.

I actually admire people who are able to see the spiritual nature of their drug experiences and move beyond the drugs. That takes some courage and wisdom. It's much easier to just depend on drugs to get your spiritual fix. But for someone on an authentic spiritual search, it's not about the high, it's about finding God. Truly evolved seekers may have completely different effects from drugs, as when Ram Dass gave LSD to his Indian guru. Ram Dass watched him for hours, and the guru showed no signs of being high. Finally he told Ram Dass that acid was like an imitation of a spiritual experience, not a real one. And that's the problem. A real spiritual experience takes devotion, discipline, commitment, and a willingness to go through the difficult as well as the pleasant.

If we see God as the Dharma, then seeking God is trying to understand, come into harmony with, and fulfill the Dharma. We may think of the spiritual seeker as someone living in an ashram in India or climbing the Himalayas in search of a wise master, but seeking God happens right here, right now. All we have to do is engage ourselves in our present-moment experience and right then we come into "conscious contact." Once we are present, we can ask ourselves, "What's a skillful way to respond to this moment?" If we understand the Five Precepts, we can ask if we are acting in harmony with the Law of Karma; if we understand the Eightfold Path, we can ask ourselves if there is some aspect of the path that we could encourage in ourselves in this moment—to make more effort to be mindful or concentrated, to speak or work more skillfully, to clarify our intention or view this moment through the lens of the Four Noble Truths; or we might see the need or opportunity to express more love, compassion, sympathetic joy, or equanimity. These are just some of the ways that, in this very moment, we can seek God, we can come into harmony with the power of the Dharma.

Using the practices I described in the last chapter mindfulness, concentration, lovingkindness, and contemplation—we can move ourselves closer to God, we can "improve our conscious contact." These practices give us the sensitivity and awareness to know both what is going on in our experience and how to respond to it. The powers of addiction and self-obsession are very difficult to counteract. Unless we train and continue to train our hearts and minds to return to the present moment and respond with love and wisdom, we will be swept away.

One of the risks on the spiritual path is that we start to overvalue certain aspects of the path while ignoring others. This is certainly what I did before I got sober, when all I was interested in was feeling good.

At that point I just tried to deepen concentration and the pleasant aspects of mindfulness. Strengthening these aspects through intensive practice can give us the sense of connecting with God or with a powerful spiritual experience, but if we don't take up the more mundane aspects of the path, the precepts, livelihood, relationships, then our spiritual growth will be very limited. This is actually a dangerous place to be. Many people have developed a kind of spiritual arrogance after touching some deep states and believe that they have evolved beyond the duality of right and wrong. If we are truly seeking God, we need to seek *the whole of God,* and in Buddhism this encompasses the three main aspects of the path: sila, the moral and ethical component, the way we live in the world; samadhi, the meditative component, the way we train our hearts and minds to be present, focused, and connected; and panna, the wisdom or discernment component, which uproots greed, hatred, and delusion.

THE WILL OF GOD

The idea that God has will presupposes that God is some entity who has preferences; He, She, or It wants certain things for us. This idea doesn't fit with the idea of a Dharma God, one that is impersonal, just a set of powers and energies. In order, then, to follow the will of a Dharma God, I have to come back to what the Buddha taught. But it seems odd to say there is will behind things like mindfulness, karma, and lovingkindness. What about natural laws like gravity? Could you say they have "will"? It doesn't make much sense. But you can certainly say that gravity has a very clear power and that trying to fight that power will only lead to problems—and probably some nasty bruises. So, let's just say that the will of gravity is for smaller objects to be drawn toward bigger objects. Seen in this light, the power of mindfulness is to wake us up, so the will of mindfulness is for us to move toward more awareness; the power of karma is to bring results for actions, so the will of karma is for our intentions and actions to be skillful; the power of lovingkindness is to connect people with each other and with the universe, so the will of lovingkindness is for us to open our hearts to this connection. Going against the will of God, then, is moving toward less awareness, becoming dulled and closing down—just what an addict does; acting unskillfully, breaking the precepts; fostering anger and resentment. The formula is pretty simple, perhaps simplistic, but in some essential way it works.

A couple of things are important about this interpretation of Buddhism and God. The first is that God in this sense is totally impersonal. There is no being here who wants or wills things. There are only forces, just like gravity, that function in their natural way. We, as conscious beings, can see these forces, understand them, and learn to interact with them skillfully. That's called "wisdom." A wise person sees the ways things work and learns how to get along with that. An unwise person, someone who goes against God's will, doesn't see the way things work and so is always stumbling and having problems that they don't understand; or they do see the way things work, but think they can beat the system—and therefore are always stumbling and having problems.

This means spiritual growth has two essential components: first, understanding how God works, and second, cooperating with that. Neither of these is so simple. Many aspects of human nature block us from understanding how God works. Our natural cravings put us in conflict with the Truth of the Cause of Suffering, with the Truth of Impermanence, with the Law of Karma, with the forces of love and compassion. These individual cravings are then expressed on a societal level in political, cultural, and economic systems. Instead of having a culture that is focused on harmony, caring for each other, and growing more wise, we have war, poverty, inadequate health care and education, rampant addiction, obesity, and promiscuity; we also have racism, sexism, and homophobia. These social forces resulting from individual greed, hatred, and delusion, once established, start to reinforce individual negativity, justifying our sordid impulses. People start to believe that war is inevitable, that hate and greed are human nature, that our animal instincts will always trump our intellect or compassion.

This runs counter to Buddhist teachings and the experience of meditation. What we discover in meditation, and what the Buddha taught, is that when we let go of the energies on the surface of our minds, the waves of disturbance that are embodied in the Five Hindrances, there is a calm, luminous, loving quality. The opposite of Original Sin, this is sometimes called our "Original Mind." When we see this Original Mind, even for a split second, our view of reality is transformed. Our understanding of who we are and of our potential is irrevocably altered.

Altering our instinctually and culturally imposed view of ourselves and our world doesn't take a great spiritual breakthrough. This understanding, which is essentially Right View, the first step on the Eightfold Path, is natural to us. As addicts, many of us sensed that our way of living wasn't working, but we were in denial. Denial is the active effort to suppress what we actually know, which means that we *did* know that we were going against God's will, or the moral forces of the universe, but we simply didn't want to face that fact. Addiction, because it becomes so powerfully conditioned in us, can block us from seeing the most obvious things—or at least to admitting to those things. Hitting bottom, whatever that is for us, and having a "moment of clarity" gives us the chance to see the truth and start to understand the "will of God."

The Eleventh Step, and indeed Buddhism, suggests that getting in touch with the will of God is enhanced by taking some actions, particularly practices of prayer and meditation. From a Buddhist perspective, when we pray, we are simply reminding ourselves of the fundamental truths of the Dharma, so that we will act in harmony with them. Our deep conditioning tends to pull us back over and over to acting out of selfishness, and prayer reminds us of the futility of those actions. We remind ourselves that the will of God is that we be unselfish, awake, and kind.

When we meditate, we watch the functioning of the Dharma. We see how a moment of wanting is painful and how a moment of letting go is freeing; we see the connection between our thoughts and feelings, our mind and body; we see the frail and fleeting quality of each moment, the impossibility of holding on to anything; we touch the mind that is beyond ego, the impersonal, universal quality of knowing that shows us our interconnection with all beings and all things; and we open our hearts to the universal love that is inside everyone of us. All of this loosens and undermines the conditioning that causes suffering, the ignorance and willfulness that keep tripping us up.

Once we understand the will of God, once we have "knowledge of His will for us" (pardon the gender), we're only halfway there. Then, according to the Step, which I think is quite right, we need to have the "power to carry that out." This is very much what we are saying when, in Step Three, we "turn our will and our lives over to the care of God." Carrying out God's will is living in harmony with the Dharma.

Acting on our beliefs is difficult. Many addicts have strong moral convictions and spiritual faith, but aren't able to fulfill them. When I was practicing meditation before I got sober, I felt committed to my path. I was inspired by my teachers' wise words and delighted by the states of calm and joy that arose on retreats. But somehow all of that didn't translate into living any differently. I still sought out the same pleasures and escapes that I always had, even though I'd heard, been moved by, and believed the teachings on non-attachment and loving-kindness. Years of conditioning weren't going to be altered through a few months of meditation and study. Real change takes time. When I look back over these 20-plus years of sobriety, I see a long journey toward awakening. Simply getting sober was hugely transforming. But that wasn't enough. I had to face all the issues around relationships and work just to get my life in order. I have also had to deal with the psychological demons of depression, anxiety, and self-doubt. I've very gradually learned to bring mindfulness into my life, and over time, layers of the "addictive personality" keep revealing themselves. Far from feeling that my work is complete, I am well of aware of many of my shortcomings and the ways that I don't fulfill the path of awakening.

In the Zen tradition they talk about "the long-enduring mind," the ability to stay with the practice over years and decades. The power to carry out the will of Dharma God grows slowly for most of us, and it's a power that seems to have no end. Connecting with this power is a lifelong task in which we wax and wane, sometimes connecting and living in harmony and other times getting lost, confused, despairing. This is why we have practices and a community, to bring us back to our central intention. Of course there is growth; we do progress. But the forces of ignorance and craving don't just disappear; we have to keep nurturing our awareness and non-clinging to counterbalance them. When Step Eleven says we "sought to improve," it's pointing to this fact: our work continues. Just like the Buddha, we will be attacked by Mara throughout our lives. It is only our awareness and commitment to truth that protect us. This is why we take Refuge in Buddha, Dharma, and Sangha every day, because these represent the archetypal elements of the path: wisdom, truth, and love.

DOES PRAYER WORK?

The focus of my teaching is on meditation and the ways that it can help us work the Steps and stay sober. But occasionally I'm asked about prayer. After all, in Step Eleven prayer is given just as important a place as meditation. People want to know if there is prayer in Buddhism and if I believe that prayer works.

My main concern about prayer is the expectations we bring to it. Do we think that by repeating certain words we're going to get what we want, that we or others are going to change? Are we expecting prayer to do the hard work of inner and outer transformation for us magically? Addicts have a tendency to get caught in fantasy—when we're under the influence, our minds spin out dreams of success, fame, and glory. Even in meditation, I find that addicts tend to go into bliss states or pleasant fantasies more frequently than others. In my teaching, I try to counterbalance these tendencies with a dose of reality, trying to help people to stay grounded in practical and logical perceptions of the world.

That being said, the question remains, "Does prayer work?" That is, can words we say silently in our hearts affect external things and other people? I don't know the answer to that, but I infer from one of the Buddhist teachings that this may be possible.

The Buddha said that one of the things that can't be measured, that is beyond comprehension, is the power of a concentrated mind. If that is the case, then perhaps the mind *can* affect the material world directly. That may give hope to those who want to change things with prayer. However, it's important to understand what is required to concentrate the mind to that level. First of all, concentration requires being free from the Five Hindrances. That means we need to be free of greed and ill will to get that concentrated. Following this logic, if we are free from greed, then our prayers can't be about acquiring anything for ourselves. If we are free from ill will, then our prayers can't be about hurting anyone or taking anything away from anyone. Essentially, this means that our prayers can't be selfish, which is exactly what Step Eleven says: "praying only for knowledge of [God's] will for us and the power to carry that out."

If you are still interested in using prayer to change the outer world, consider further what is required to attain that kind of concentration. The great concentration masters in the Buddhist tradition typically spend many years, either alone or in monastic settings, practicing silent meditation. This is a lifetime commitment, and I think, a worthy one. But most of us aren't willing to make it.

However, this isn't to say that prayer doesn't have its value for one whose meditation practice isn't so deep. The real purpose of prayer isn't to fix the outside world, but to reorient the inner world. This is what I'm trying to do when I make daily vows of Right Speech. The vow helps me to be more mindful of my tendencies. That leads to changes in the outside world, but it has to begin with an inner awakening. When I say, "Just for today, I will avoid teasing and sarcasm," it might not sound like a prayer to God, which might be "Please, God, stop me from being sarcastic." But I think it is accomplishing the same thing: it's reminding me each morning of my intention to change.

Other prayers have more to do with the heart. I do daily prayers of lovingkindness for myself and others, and these have the effect of taking me out of fear and resentment and reminding me of my core love. Breathing and softening my heart allows me, at least for those moments, to connect with what is really important and to drop the petty issues troubling my mind. I also do prayers for healing, again because it helps me to feel connected with people who I know are suffering. I suspend my doubts because I really don't know if these prayers have an effect. It's certainly possible.

The logical way of arriving at the possibility that prayer actually works in the material world is to consider our individual consciousness as connected to some universal consciousness. If we are all connected in this way, then my prayers are touching other consciousness. I'm not ready to completely buy into this idea, but I also know that there are limits to my knowledge. Rejecting ideas without proof just because they sound magical is just as bad as believing magical ideas because they make you feel good.

So, does prayer work? In some ways, I say, absolutely, in the ways it awakens and transforms my heart; in other ways, I say, "Don't know."

CONTINUING THE PATH
OF RECOVERY

People in Twelve Step programs sometimes debate whether they should say they are "recovered" or "recovering." Have they healed from their addiction now that they aren't actively drinking or using, or is there some aspect of their addiction that lives on in them? In the Big Book, the authors say they are recovered. And at the time that book was written, the most sobriety any of them had was four or five years. So why should someone like me who has decades of sobriety not make the same claim?

In terms of my addiction to alcohol and marijuana, I can certainly say that I have recovered. The main reason people say "recovering" is the understanding that even though you aren't active in your addiction, were you to pick up a drink or a drug today you could easily fall right back into those old habits—you have to continue to maintain your recovery. This is true for most of us. However, for me there's a more profound aspect of not claiming to have completed the process of recovery, and that relates to the teaching of the First Noble Truth, the Truth of Suffering. No matter how long it's been since I last drank or used, I am still susceptible to suffering. For me there is an aspect of woundedness in being human. The great writer Flannery O'Connor, when asked if someone had to have had special difficulties in life in order to be a good writer, said, "Anyone who has survived his child-hood has enough information about life to last him the rest of his days." Growing up is hard. The Buddha listed a litany of pains: birth, aging, sickness, death; not getting what you want; having what you don't want. A cynic would say, "Life is one insult after another," but that's an exaggeration. Life also has compliments. The thing is, everything is impermanent, and we are regularly going to face pain and difficulties. So, I think of recovery not as getting over some addiction or illness, but as learning to live with the Truth of Suffering. Buddhism and the Twelve Steps are two of the best tools I've found to do that.

Whether addicts or not, we are subject to greed, hatred, and delusion. If we don't watch out, we'll get hooked by them—and, in fact, even when we do watch out we can get hooked. The Buddhist practices help us to see what's happening. The Twelve Step practices help us to stay honest about what we see. Having the humility to see ourselves as imperfect is a great help—once we think we've arrived at perfection we stop growing. Having a community to rely on, to share with, and to guide us is another vital help. The lone seeker is a lovely, heroic image, but for most of us it's a dangerous way to live. Having a teacher, a mentor, or a sponsor is vital; being a teacher, a mentor, or a sponsor is also vital. Being able to accept help shows humility. Being able to give help shows generosity.

In his commentary on Step Eleven in the *Twelve and Twelve*, Bill Wilson says "Meditation is something which can always be further developed. It has no boundaries, either of width or height." Where does the path end? Does it end? I think that once we experience the joy and richness of a sober, spiritually motivated life, there's no need to answer those questions. We are grateful for that lack of boundaries, for the limitless possibilities of depth and breadth on the path. Certainly the challenges don't grow any easier, as the inevitability of aging, sickness, and death remind us. If we are, however, aiming to get the most out of life, it is the way of non-acquisition—of not *getting* anything— that is ultimately most fulfilling. Ever guided by Dharma God, focused on Its wisdom and power, we strive, not for some accomplishment or resolution, but just to live with as much clarity and kindness as we can in this very moment.

ACKNOWLEDGMENTS

I'm incredibly grateful to the three people who nurtured this book and me through the challenging process of putting it all together. Stephanie Tade has been with me since my first book, then as editor, now as agent, and has been much more to me than either of those titles suggests. Patty Gift took this project on with enthusiasm that has supported me through all the ups and down. Lisa Fugard's line editing was done with special care and devotion.

Ajahn Amaro continues to be a trusted reader, critic, and teacher. He went over much of this manuscript and gave vital guidance.

Guy Armstrong generously helped me sort out the Not-Self chapter.

Nancy Willoughby helped me find just the right words with a piece on relationship addiction.

Ernest Isaacs pointed me to Scott Peck's *The Different Drum*.

Thanks to all the Dharma centers and treatment centers that have supported my work, especially Spirit Rock Meditation Center. I'm deeply grateful to the devoted staff members of all these centers.

Thanks to Heather S. for sharing the teaching seat.

I am grateful to the many teachers and guides I have had on my path, and all my Twelve Step friends.

My wife Rosemary and daughter Graham are the greatest supports of all. Thank you for sharing my life with me.

RESOURCES

I've drawn on a variety of sources in this book. Perhaps the most important is the unpublished re-translation of *Christianity and Buddhism: Sinclaire Thompson Memorial Lecture,* by the Venerable Bhikkhu Buddhadasa Indapanno, translation and editing by Santikaro. Santikaro is a former Buddhist monk who has translated many of Buddhadasa's works. He has also given talks on the connection between Buddhism and the Steps which can be found (as of this writing) on the Website of his center: **www.liberationpark.org/**

Karen Armstrong's *A History of God* helped me to get a perspective on my topic.

What the Buddha Taught, by Walpola Rahula provides a traditional Theravada perspective.

The Different Drum, by M. Scott Peck has a chapter that talks about different levels of spiritual development that helped me in some of my thinking.

In the Buddha's Words, edited by Bhikkhu Bodhi, along with some of his other translations of the Pali canon, such as *The Middle Length Discourses of the Buddha*, provide me with most of my sutta references.

My other sutta source is Thanissaro Bhikkhu. His work is prominently featured on the Website www.accesstoinsight.org.

The Ayya Khema quotes mostly come from videos and recordings of her talks. Her books are wonderful: *Who Is My Self?*, *When the Iron Eagle Flies*, and *Being Nobody, Going Nowhere* are the best known.

Sandra Weinberg's quote is from Tricycle magazine's summer 2003 edition. The article was called "Eating and the Wheel of Life."

The quote from Wes Nisker comes from public talks I have attended. See www.wesnisker.com.

Several quotes from Ajahn Amaro come from Dharma talks I have heard or personal conversations. His talks can be downloaded from www.abhayagiri.org.

Sharon Salzberg's book *Lovingkindness: The Revolutionary Art of Happiness*, is an indispensable Dharma resource.

The Mindful Way Through Depression by Williams, Teasdale, Segal, and Kabat-Zinn is a terrific guide for working with this common ailment.

Of course, I drew on the A.A. books *Alcoholics Anonymous* and *Twelve Steps and Twelve Traditions*. I'm also inspired by the literature from other programs that I've read, such as the N.A. *Basic Text* and the S.L.A.A. literature.

The story from Ajahn Chah comes from Jack Kornfield, whose books are some of the best in the Western Dharma canon, especially *A Path with Heart*, *Living Dharma*, *After the Ecstasy, the Laundry* and *A Wise Heart*.

My discussion of Not-Self was informed by Guy Armstrong's talk entitled "Karma and the End of Karma" which can be found on the Dharma Seed Website, an incredible resource for Vipassana talks: www.dharmaseed.org.

The Flannery O'Connor quote comes from her classic book on writing called *Mystery and Manners*.

How We Choose to Be Happy by Foster and Hicks is an excellent guide for finding authentic joy.

The End of Faith by Sam Harris is a solid analysis of the problems with magical religious beliefs.

Byakuren Judith Ragir is Guiding Teacher at Clouds in Water Zen Center in St. Paul, MN. She has a great set of talks on Buddhism and the Twelve Steps on her Website: www.judithragir.org.

The Thirst for Wholeness by Christina Grof puts forth the theory that is in many ways the basis of the idea of a "burning desire."

Gil Fronsdal's translation of the *Dhammapada* is an excellent updating of this classic text.

Present Moment, Wonderful Moment by Thich Nhat Hanh is an amazing source for mindfulness exercises.

The Spirit Recovery organization and Lee McCormick, its founder, use Toltec wisdom in their recovery work. Although a different form than Buddhism, this approach shares many values with the Dharma. For information on their "journeys," see www.spiritrecovery.com.

The Buddhist Recovery Network is a resource for those interested in the confluence of Dharma and addiction treatment/recovery. www.buddhistrecovery.org.

ABOUT THE AUTHOR

Kevin Griffin is the author of the seminal 2004 book *One Breath at a Time: Buddhism and the Twelve Steps.* He has been practicing Buddhist meditation for three decades and has been in recovery since 1985. He's been a meditation teacher for almost 15 years. His teacher training was at Spirit Rock Meditation Center, where he currently leads Dharma and Recovery classes.

Kevin teaches nationally in Buddhist centers, treatment centers, professional conferences, and academic settings. He has worked as a consultant on NIH studies of mindfulness and taught meditation in prisons and homeless shelters. He specializes in helping people in recovery connect with meditation and a progressive understanding of the 12 Steps. His events range from evening classes, to daylong workshops and residential retreats.

Kevin grew up in Bethlehem, Pennsylvania, the youngest of five brothers. He dropped out of high school in the late '60s to pursue a career as a rock guitarist. In his 20s he lived in New England and played the club circuit until moving to LA in 1979 with an Afrobeat band called Zzebra. There Kevin found Buddhism and began to explore the spiritual life. After getting sober, he returned to school, earning his B.A. from U.C. Berkeley and M.F.A. in Creative Writing from U.C. Irvine. He is a published songwriter and unpublished novelist.

He now divides his time between writing, teaching, and family life with his wife and daughter. He still plays and writes music and is currently recording a CD of Dharma-related rock songs.

For more information, see: **www.kevingriffin.net**.

We hope you enjoyed this Hay House book.
If you'd like to receive our online catalog featuring
additional information onHay House books and products,
or if you'd like to find out more about the
Hay Foundation, please contact:

Hay House, Inc.
P.O. Box 5100
Carlsbad, CA 92018-5100

(760) 431-7695 or **(800) 654-5126**
(760) 431-6948 (fax) or **(800) 650-5115 (fax)**
www.hayhouse.com® • **www.hayfoundation.org**

Published and distributed in Australia by:
Hay House Australia Pty. Ltd., 18/36 Ralph St., Alexandria NSW 2015
Phone: 612-9669-4299 • *Fax:* 612-9669-4144 • www.hayhouse.com.au

Published and distributed in the United Kingdom by:
Hay House UK, Ltd., 292B Kensal Rd., London W10 5BE • *Phone:*
44-20-8962-1230 • *Fax:* 44-20-8962-1239 • www.hayhouse.co.uk

Published and distributed in the Republic of South Africa by:
Hay House SA (Pty), Ltd., P.O. Box 990, Witkoppen 2068 • *Phone/*
Fax: 27-11-467-8904 • info@hayhouse.co.za • www.hayhouse.co.za

Published in India by:
Hay House Publishers India, Muskaan Complex, Plot No. 3,
B-2, Vasant Kunj, New Delhi 110 070 • *Phone:* 91-11-4176-1620
Fax: 91-11-4176-1630 • www.hayhouse.co.in

Distributed in Canada by:
Raincoast, 9050 Shaughnessy St., Vancouver, B.C. V6P 6E5
Phone: (604) 323-7100 • *Fax:* (604) 323-2600 • www.raincoast.com

Take Your Soul on a Vacation

Visit **www.HealYourLife.com®** to regroup,
recharge, and reconnect with your own magnificence.
Featuring blogs, mind-body-spirit news, and life-
changing wisdom from Louise Hay and friends.

Visit **www.HealYourLife.com** today!